T0320065

Dynamic Networks and Evolutionary Variational Inequalities

NEW DIMENSIONS IN NETWORKS

Series Editor: Anna Nagurney, *John F. Smith Memorial Professor, Isenberg School of Management, University of Massachusetts at Amherst, USA*

Networks provide a unifying framework for conceptualizing and studying problems and applications. They range from transportation and telecommunication networks and logistic networks to economic, social and financial networks. This series is designed to publish original manuscripts and edited volumes that push the development of theory and applications of networks to new dimensions. It is interdisciplinary and international in its coverage, and aims to connect existing areas, unveil new applications and extend existing conceptual frameworks as well as methodologies. An outstanding editorial advisory board made up of scholars from many fields and many countries assures the high quality and originality of all of the volumes in the series.

Titles in the series include:

Supernetworks
Decision-Making for the Information Age
Anna Nagurney and June Dong

Innovations in Financial and Economic Networks
Edited by Anna Nagurney

Urban and Regional Transportation Modeling
Essays in Honor of David Boyce
Edited by Der-Horng Lee

The Network Organization
The Experience of Leading French Multinationals
Emmanuel Josserand

Dynamic Networks and Evolutionary Variational Inequalities
Patrizia Daniele

Dynamic Networks and Evolutionary Variational Inequalities

Patrizia Daniele

Associate Professor of Operational Research, Department of Mathematics and Computer Science, University of Catania, Italy

NEW DIMENSIONS IN NETWORKS

Edward Elgar
Cheltenham, UK • Northampton, MA, USA

Published by
Edward Elgar Publishing Limited
Glensanda House
Montpellier Parade
Cheltenham
Glos GL50 1UA
UK

Edward Elgar Publishing, Inc.
136 West Street
Suite 202
Northampton
Massachusetts 01060
USA

A catalogue record for this book
is available from the British Library

ISBN-13:   978 1 84376 929 3
ISBN-10:   1 84376 929 8

Printed and bound in Great Britain by MPG Books Ltd, Bodmin, Cornwall

Contents

List of Figures

List of Tables

Acknowledgments

This book is a collection of many results obtained in the theory of evolutionary variational inequalities and dynamic networks.

I am grateful to Professor Anna Nagurney of the University of Massachusetts for encouragement and supportive conversations and to Professor Monica Gabriela Cojocaru of the University of Guelph for the suggestions and the interesting scientific colloquia.

I am also obliged to the Rockefeller Foundation and to Dean Grosz of Harvard University for the opportunity to develop a part of the topics of this book, giving us the possibility of fascinating and productive meetings.

I am especially indebted to Professor Antonino Maugeri of the University of Catania for fruitful discussions and constant support. I would also like to thank my family for the continuous assistance.

A part of Section 4.1 of this book appeared in the volume **Variational Analysis and Applications**, NOIA 79, F. Giannessi and A. Maugeri (eds), published in 2005 by Springer in the chapter 'Variational Inequalities for General Evolutionary Financial Equilibrium', 279–99, written by myself, and it is reported here with kind permission of Springer Science and Business Media.

Further, a part of Section 4.2 of this book appeared in the volume **Innovations in Financial and Economic Networks**, A. Nagurney (ed), published in 2003 by Edward Elgar in the chapter 'Variational Inequalities for Evolutionary Financial Equilibrium', 84–109, written by myself, and it is reported here with kind permission of Edward Elgar Publishing.

Chapter 1

Introduction

This book is devoted to dynamic networks and evolutionary variational inequalities. The extraordinary impact of networks is self-evident today both in the fields of telecommunications, transportation, digital and electric power networks as well as in the fields of economic and financial equilibria. There is an important number of volumes being dedicated to the study of networks, which in themselves constitute a real scientific and social area of research interest (see, for instance, [39], [71], [73], [72], [108], [111], [134]). In contrast, an emerging new concept is that of dynamics of networks. This new concept arises from the observation that the physical structure of the networks can remain unchanged, but the phenomena which occur in these networks vary with time. The link with previous studies of static networks can be made in a natural way: a static configuration represents a snapshot at a fixed moment of time of an evolving real phenomenon. Therefore, studying the static case can be considered only a first approach to the understanding of the reality, which is useful and also essential for further developments. However, it is clear that the results obtained in the static case have a short range of validity and are only partially representative of the developing reality. The dynamic network setting arises when the constitutive elements of the economic or physical phenomena associated with the fixed geometry of the network, for example, the travel demands in the traffic models, the supplies, the demands, the supply prices, the demand prices and the shipments of commodities in the spatial price models, and the investments in assets and liabilities in the financial models, are considered, as they are

1

in reality, evolving with time. For the economic phenomena we deal with, we search the so-called **equilibrium solution** according to a suitable and reasonable definition, and the considered problem is obviously called an **equilibrium problem**.

It is not in the scope of this book to review the history and development of equilibrium problems. We would simply like to point out the impressive number of works dedicated to them over the years, first, using vector calculus and differential equations, then optimization and game theory methods. Later, starting in the 1970s, the theory of variational inequalities arose and the equilibrium problems are fully immersed in such a theory, and we refer the readers to the various published volumes and papers (see [2], [4], [39], [70], [71], [72], [73], [85], [87], [101], [103], [108], [111], [119], [127]).

We want to highlight the important fact that variational inequalities have provided a method of solving problems otherwise unsolvable. In fact, the complementarity conditions and the conservation laws expressing the equilibrium conditions of the various problems cannot be treated with the usual methods and, then, the result due to Smith [149] and Dafermos [25], who first proved that such problems fit very well with the variational inequality theory, already introduced by Stampacchia [151] and Fichera [60], has been a breakthrough scientific result.

In our dynamical formulation of equilibrium problems, the reader may encounter difficulties since equilibrium seems to exclude time; on the contrary, the scholar is invited to enlarge his point of view and understand that time is central in our world, in the physical-technological world as well as in the socio-economic one.

The central theme of the book is to deal with the strict connection between equilibrium problems in dynamic networks and the evolutionary variational inequalities, in the sense that the time-dependent equilibrium conditions of these problems are equivalently expressed in terms of evolutionary variational inequalities.

Even if it is known to the reader, it is worth remembering that there exist two different approaches for the study of equilibrium problems: the so-called *system optimization approach* and the so-called *user optimization approach*. In the first one, we consider an objective, like total cost, set by society or by some authority. In the second one, every user strives for the minimization of his individual cost function or, in other words, looks for an equilibrium distribution, which, once established, nobody has any interest in changing. As a consequence, the overall flow pattern is ruled by equilibrium conditions, which are essentially expressed in terms of a generalized complementarity problem leading to a variational inequality.

The two approaches are not at all equivalent or comparable: the first one produces an abstract evaluation of the cost of or the value of an economy, whereas the second one really represents the behavior of the users and suggests to the users the best choice. For this reason we absolutely focus on the study of this second approach, which, as seen above, establishes a connection between the dynamic networks and the evolutionary variational inequalities.

The evolutionary variational inequalities we meet are distinct from the usual variational inequalities of parabolic type well known in the theory of variational inequalities (see [9]). A very central feature we remark is the proof of the equivalence between time-dependent equilibrium conditions and evolutionary variational inequalities, which we set in the Lebesgue space $L^p([0, T], \mathbb{R}^q)$.

The first general result we obtain is that the equilibrium solution is a trajectory $u(t) \in L^p([0, T], \mathbb{R}^q)$, namely we are able to make precise, under minimal assumptions, that the dependence on time is of L^p-type and subsequently, under additional assumptions, that such a dependence can be of continuous-type. In addition, it is useful to remark that we are set into infinite-dimensional frameworks and, in order to give existence theorems, we must use delicate and recent results of functional analysis; for the reader's convenience, self-contained appendices allow one to become acquainted with all the topics, without further difficulties.

Moreover, in this book a relevant role is attributed to the Lagrangean variables that we have to search in the infinite-dimensional case and, as a consequence, we have also to provide an adjustment of the Lagrangean theory, which is quite distinct from the finite-dimensional one. On the other hand, the Lagrangean variables have an extraordinary meaning (for instance, in the spatial price equilibrium problems they provide the supply and demand excesses) and, hence, such an unexpected complication had to be solved.

For the sake of completeness, it is clear that we have also to propose efficient computational procedures for the calculus of solutions; we show that the direct method, although it has some limitations, is extremely efficient. We present also a global method, called the *subgradient method*, which theoretically runs very well, but it has the inconvenience of being very slow. Then, we provide a discretization method based on Mosco-convergence (see [76] and [140]), which, under suitable assumptions, reveals itself to be resourceful. Another calculation procedure we present comes from the projected dynamical systems theory, which takes up a chapter of the book. Such a theory was introduced first by Dupuis and Nagurney (see [56]) in the finite-dimensional case and was later extended to the infinite-dimensional case by Isac and Cojocaru ([83], [84]) and by Cojocaru [15], and to the evolutionary variational inequalities theory by Cojocaru, Daniele and Nagurney (see [16], [17], [18]). It is absolutely relevant that the solutions to evolutionary variational inequalities are the same as the critical points of a projected dynamical system. We present here an exceptional result: it is possible to associate with the same equilibrium problem two different timeframes and each one of them has an absolutely relevant significance. In any case the projected dynamical systems associated with the evolutionary variational inequalities allow us to provide another computational procedure, whenever the solution belongs to C^0.

Finally, since the equilibrium problems have a certain degree of instability, an analysis of the sensitivity is proposed and it allows us to establish the changes of the solution under small changes of the data.

All the problems we have considered till now can be grouped into a unified definition of the constraint set and it is very useful to obtain general properties which hold for all problems.

We conclude this introduction with a short compendium of the structure of this book. It consists of five chapters and appendices.

Chapter 2 focuses on the traffic network models, starting from the static case to the dynamic case and analyzing also models with additional constraints and models with retarded data. For each one of them a variational formulation, existence theorems, and computational procedures are studied together with some numerical examples.

Chapter 3 describes the evolutionary spatial price equilibrium using both the price formulation approach and the quantity formulation approach, as well as a sensitivity analysis of the equilibrium pattern. Moreover models in which demand markets of a commodity become supply markets of another commodity are also studied.

In Chapter 4 the evolutionary financial equilibrium problem is presented. In the first model a quadratic utility function is used, then a more general utility function and finally a model with policy intervention. Also in this case the variational inequality formulation and the existence results are examined. A short presentation of the quadratic case of utility function is also given in [36].

Chapter 5 addresses in detail the projected dynamical systems theory presented in a self-contained manner and highlights the strict connection between such a theory and that of the evolutionary variational inequalities, which developed in parallel. In particular, we introduce computational procedures originated by the projected dynamical systems theory.

Finally, the appendices contain some fundamental notions for the understanding of the treated topics, such as functions and multifunctions, cones, generalized derivatives, variational and quasi-variational inequalities, and infinite dimensional duality.

Chapter 2

The Traffic Equilibrium Problem

2.1 Static Case

The first author who studied transportation networks was Pigou in 1920 (see [135]). He had the idea of imposing some tolls on a network with only two paths in order to regulate the traffic congestion. But it was only during most recent decades that traffic network equilibrium problems have attracted the attention of several researchers. In 1952, Wardrop (see [157]) laid the foundations for the study of the traffic theory, stating two principles until now named after him. The rigorous mathematical formulation of Wardrop's principles was elaborated by Beckmann, McGuire and Winstein (see [6]) in 1956, when they showed the equivalence between the traffic equilibrium as stated by Wardrop and the Kuhn-Tucker conditions of a particular optimization problem under some symmetry assumptions.

Only later in 1979, Smith (see [149]) proved that the equilibrium solution can be expressed in terms of variational inequalities. This was a crucial step, because it allowed the application of the powerful tool of the variational inequalities to the study of traffic equilibrium problems in the most general framework.

Starting from that point, many authors (among them Dafermos [25]) dealt with the study of many features of the traffic equilibrium problem and a significant bibliography can be found in the volumes [39], [71], [73],

[101], [108] and [134]; see also [141].

For what we need in the sequel, we premise with a presentation of a general version of the traffic equilibrium problem in the static case, considering a model with capacity constraints on the flows. To this end, let us present a traffic network consisting of a set N of nodes and a set L of directed links between the nodes, a set $\mathcal{W}$ of origin–destination (O/D) pairs and a set $\mathcal{R}$ of routes. Each route $r \in \mathcal{R}$ links exactly one origin–destination pair $w \in \mathcal{W}$. The set of all $r \in \mathcal{R}$ connecting the same O/D pair $w \in \mathcal{W}$ is denoted by $\mathcal{R}(w)$. With each route $r \in \mathcal{R}$ we associate a flow F_r and denote by $F \in \mathbb{R}^{\mathcal{R}}$ the flow vectors. A feasible flow has to satisfy capacity restrictions $\lambda_r \leq F_r \leq \mu_r$ for all $r \in \mathcal{R}$, and a traffic conservation law $\displaystyle\sum_{r \in \mathcal{R}(w)} F_r = \rho_w$ for all $w \in \mathcal{W}$, where $\lambda \leq \mu$ are given in $\mathbb{R}^{\mathcal{R}}$, ρ_w is the travel demand related to the pair $w \in \mathcal{W}$ and $\rho \geq 0$ in $\mathbb{R}^{\mathcal{W}}$ denotes the travel demand vector. Introducing the pair-route incidence matrix $\Phi = (\Phi_{w,r})$ with $w \in \mathcal{W}$, $r \in \mathcal{R}$, namely

$$\Phi_{w,r} := \begin{cases} 1, & \text{if route } r \text{ connects the pair } w, \\ 0 & \text{else,} \end{cases}$$

the traffic conservation law can be written in matrix-vector notation as $\Phi F = \rho$. Thus the set of all feasible flows is given by

$$\mathbb{K} := \{ F \in \mathbb{R}^{\mathcal{R}} \,|\, \lambda \leq F \leq \mu, \ \Phi F = \rho \}. \tag{2.1}$$

Furthermore we are given a cost function $C \colon \mathbb{K} \to \mathbb{R}^{\mathcal{R}}$. Then to every feasible flow $F \in \mathbb{K}$ there corresponds a cost vector $C(F) \in \mathbb{R}^{\mathcal{R}}$; $C_r(F)$ gives the marginal cost of sending one additional unit of flow through route r, when the flow F is already present. We do not specify how $C(F)$ depends on F (for a more detailed physical model see [150], [58]).

Definition 2.1.1 *A flow $H \in \mathbb{R}^{\mathcal{R}}$ is called an equilibrium flow if and only if*

$$\forall\, w \in \mathcal{W} \text{ and } \forall\, q, s \in \mathcal{R}(w) \text{ there holds:}$$
$$C_q(H) < C_s(H) \Longrightarrow H_q = \mu_q \text{ or } H_s = \lambda_s.$$

Such a definition represents Wardrop's equilibrium condition in the generalized version introduced by [46]. In order to characterize it by means of a variational inequality formulation, we need the following result.

Lemma 2.1.1 *Let* $\mathbb{K}$ *be given by (2.1), let* $C \in \mathbb{R}^{\mathcal{R}}$ *and* $H \in \mathbb{K}$ *be arbitrary. Then the following conditions are equivalent:*

(i) $H \in \mathbb{K}$ *and* $\langle C(H), F - H \rangle \geq 0 \, \forall F \in \mathbb{K}$;

(ii) $\forall w \in \mathcal{W}$ *and* $\forall q, s \in \mathcal{R}(w)$ *there holds:*

$$C_q(H) < C_s(H) \Longrightarrow H_q = \mu_q \ or \ H_s = \lambda_s.$$

Proof: (a) Assume that (ii) does not hold. Select $w \in \mathcal{W}$ and $q, s \in \mathcal{R}(w)$ such that $C_q(H) < C_s(H)$, $H_q < \mu_q$, $H_s > \lambda_s$. Let

$$\delta := \min\{\mu_q - H_q, H_s - \lambda_s\},$$

and define a vector F whose components are $F_q := H_q + \delta$, $F_s := H_s - \delta$, $F_r := H_r$ for $r \neq q, s$. Then $F \in \mathbb{K}$ and

$$\langle C(H), F - H \rangle = \delta(C_q(H) - C_s(H)) < 0.$$

So (i) does not hold.

(b) Assume now that (ii) holds. Let $w \in \mathcal{W}$ and

$$A := \{q \in \mathcal{R}(w) \mid H_q < \mu_q\}, \quad B := \{s \in \mathcal{R}(w) \mid H_s > \lambda_s\}.$$

From (ii), $C_q(H) \geq C_s(H)$ for all $q \in A$, $s \in B$. So there exists $\gamma_w \in \mathbb{R}$ such that

$$\inf_{q \in A} C_q(H) \geq \gamma_w \geq \sup_{s \in B} C_s(H).$$

Let $F \in \mathbb{K}$ be arbitrary. Then, for every $r \in \mathcal{R}(w)$, $C_r(H) < \gamma_w$ implies $r \notin A$, hence $H_r = \mu_r$, hence $F_r - H_r \leq 0$, hence $(C_r(H) - \gamma_w)(F_r - H_r) \geq 0$. Likewise $C_r(H) > \gamma_w$ implies $(C_r(H) - \gamma_w)(F_r - H_r) \geq 0$. Thus

$$\sum_{r \in \mathcal{R}(w)} C_r(H)(F_r - H_r) \geq \gamma_w \sum_{r \in \mathcal{R}(w)} (F_r - H_r) = \gamma_w(\rho_w - \rho_w) = 0.$$

Hence
$$\langle C(H), F - H \rangle = \sum_{w \in \mathcal{W}} \sum_{r \in \mathcal{R}(w)} C_r(H)(F_r - H_r) \geq 0,$$

and (i) holds. $\qquad \square$

We observe that condition (ii) in Lemma 2.1.1 is equivalent to

(ii') for every $w \in \mathcal{W}$ there exists $\gamma_w \in \mathbb{R}$ such that, for all $r \in \mathcal{R}(w)$,

$$C_r(H) < \gamma_w \implies H_r = \mu_r, \quad C_r(H) > \gamma_w \implies H_r = \lambda_r.$$

In fact, the implication $(ii) \implies (ii')$ has been shown in the proof of Lemma 2.1.1, and the reverse implication is obvious.

If $\mu_r = +\infty$ for all $r \in \mathcal{R}$, then condition (ii) in Lemma 2.1.1 can be rewritten as follows:

$$\forall w \in \mathcal{W}, \text{ if } \gamma_w := \min_{r \in \mathcal{R}(w)} C_r(H), \text{ then}$$

$$(C_r(H) - \gamma_w)(H_r - \lambda_r) = 0 \; \forall r \in \mathcal{R}(w).$$

Such a condition perfectly agrees with the equilibrium definition given by Nagurney in [108], p. 140, where, adopting our notation, the author claims that

for every O/D pair w and for every path r connecting w it must hold

$$C_r \begin{cases} = \gamma_w, & \text{if } F_r > 0 \\ \geq \gamma_w, & \text{if } F_r = 0 \end{cases}$$

where γ_w is the equilibrium travel disutility associated with the O/D pair w.

2.2   Dynamic Case

We consider now the dynamic case. The traffic network, whose geometry remains fixed, is considered at all times $t \in \mathcal{T}$, where $\mathcal{T} := [0, T]$ (the discrete case where $\mathcal{T} := \{0, 1, \ldots, T\}$ will be trivially included in the following; see [150]).

For each time $t \in \mathcal{T}$ we have a route-flow vector $F(t) \in \mathbb{R}^{\mathcal{R}}$. The feasible flows have to satisfy the time-dependent capacity constraints and the traffic conservation law, namely that, almost everywhere on $\mathcal{T}$,

$$\lambda(t) \leq F(t) \leq \mu(t) \text{ and } \Phi F(t) = \rho(t),$$

where $\lambda(\cdot) \leq \mu(\cdot)$ as well as $\rho(\cdot)$ are given and Φ is again the pair-route incidence matrix. $F(\cdot) \colon \mathcal{T} \to \mathbb{R}^{\mathcal{R}}$ is the flow trajectory over time.

For technical reasons, we choose as the functional setting for the flow trajectories the reflexive Banach space $L^p(\mathcal{T}, \mathbb{R}^{\mathcal{R}})$ with $p > 1$. We abbreviate it by $\mathcal{L}$. The dual space $L^q(\mathcal{T}, \mathbb{R}^{\mathcal{R}})$, where $\frac{1}{p} + \frac{1}{q} = 1$, will be denoted by $\mathcal{L}^*$. On $\mathcal{L}^* \times \mathcal{L}$ we define the canonical bi-linear form by

$$\ll G, F \gg := \int_{\mathcal{T}} \langle G(t), F(t) \rangle dt, \quad G \in \mathcal{L}^*, \ F \in \mathcal{L}.$$

We define the set of feasible flows as

$$\mathbb{K} := \{ F \in \mathcal{L} \, | \, \lambda(t) \le F(t) \le \mu(t) \text{ a.e. on } \mathcal{T},$$
$$\Phi F(t) = \rho(t) \text{ a.e. on } \mathcal{T} \}. \tag{2.2}$$

We assume that λ, μ are in $\mathcal{L}$, $\lambda \le \mu$, and that, for all $w \in \mathcal{W}$, $\rho_w \ge 0$ is in $L^p(\mathcal{T}, \mathbb{R}^{\mathcal{W}})$. We assume also that

$$\Phi\lambda(t) \le \rho(t) \le \Phi\mu(t) \quad \text{a.e. on } \mathcal{T}. \tag{2.3}$$

We prove that (2.3) is enough to guarantee that $\mathbb{K} \neq \emptyset$, (see [77]). In fact, if $\mathbb{K} = \emptyset$, then ρ does not belong to the nonempty, convex, weakly compact set ΦG where

$$G = \{ F \in \mathcal{L} \, | \, \lambda(t) \le F(t) \le \mu(t) \text{ a.e. on } \mathcal{T} \}.$$

The separation theorem implies the existence of

$$\xi = (\xi_w)_{w \in \mathcal{W}} \in L^q \left([0, T], \mathbb{R}^{\mathcal{W}} \right), \ \frac{1}{p} + \frac{1}{q} = 1, \ \xi \neq 0,$$

and $\alpha \in \mathbb{R}$ such that

$$\langle \xi, \rho \rangle < \alpha \le \langle \xi, \Phi F \rangle, \ \forall F \in G. \tag{2.4}$$

Then choosing $\tilde{F} \in G$ a.e. on $\mathcal{T}$ by

$$\tilde{F}_r(t) = \begin{cases} \lambda_r(t) & \text{if } r \in \mathcal{R}(w) \text{ and } \xi_w(t) \ge 0 \\ \mu_r(t) & \text{if } r \in \mathcal{R}(w) \text{ and } \xi_w(t) < 0, \end{cases}$$

we obtain by (2.3)

$$\langle \xi, \Phi\tilde{F} \rangle = \sum_{w \in \mathcal{W}} \int_{\xi_w > 0} \xi_w(t)(\Phi\lambda)_w(t) \, dt + \int_{\xi_w < 0} \xi_w(t)(\Phi\mu)_w(t) \, dt \le \langle \xi, \rho \rangle,$$

which is in contradiction to (2.4). This proves that $\mathbb{K}$ is nonempty. It is easily seen that $\mathbb{K}$ is convex, closed, and bounded, hence weakly compact.

Furthermore, we are given a mapping $C\colon \mathbb{K} \to \mathcal{L}^*$, which assigns to each flow trajectory $F(\cdot) \in \mathbb{K}$ the cost trajectory $C(F(\cdot)) \in \mathcal{L}^*$.

Definition 2.2.1 *$H \in \mathcal{L}$ is an equilibrium flow if and only if*

$$\forall w \in \mathcal{W}, \forall q, s \in \mathcal{R}(w) \text{ and a.e. on } \mathcal{T},$$
$$C_q(H(t)) < C_s(H(t)) \Longrightarrow H_q(t) = \mu_q(t) \text{ or } H_s(t) = \lambda_s(t). \quad (2.5)$$

Also in this dynamic case we are able to characterize the equilibrium definition by means of an evolutionary variational inequality.

Theorem 2.2.1 *$H \in \mathbb{K}$ is an equilibrium flow in the sense of (2.5) if and only if*

$$H \in \mathbb{K} \text{ and } \ll C(H), F - H \gg \; \geq 0 \; \forall F \in \mathbb{K}. \quad (2.6)$$

Proof: (a) Assume that (2.5) holds. Let $F \in \mathbb{K}$. Since the union of finitely many nullsets is a nullset, it follows from Lemma 2.1.1 that $\langle C(H(t)), F(t) - H(t) \rangle \geq 0$ a.e. on $\mathcal{T}$. Hence $\ll C(H), F - H \gg \; \geq 0$, and H is an equilibrium.

(b) Assume that (2.5) does not hold. Then there exist $w \in \mathcal{W}$ and $q, s \in \mathcal{R}(w)$ together with a set $E \subseteq \mathcal{T}$ having positive measure such that

$$C_q(H(t)) < C_s(H(t)), \quad H_q(t) < \mu_q(t), \quad H_s(t) > \lambda_s(t) \quad \text{a.e. on } E.$$

For $t \in E$, let $\delta(t) := \min\{\mu_q(t) - H_q(t), H_s(t) - \lambda_s(t)\}$. Then $\delta(t) > 0$ a.e. on E and, as in the proof of Lemma 2.1.1, we can construct $F \in \mathbb{K}$ such that $F = H$ outside E, and

$$\ll C(H), F - H \gg \; = \int_E \delta(t) \left(C_q(H)(t) - C_s(H)(t) \right) dt < 0.$$

Thus H is not an equilibrium. $\qquad\qquad\qquad\qquad\qquad\qquad\qquad\square$

Condition (2.5) is Wardrop's condition for the time-dependent case. We observe that condition (2.5) is equivalent to the following: for every

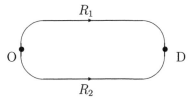

Figure 2.1: Network with travel demand $\rho(t) = t$

$w \in \mathcal{W}$ there exists a real-valued function $\gamma_w(\cdot)$ on $\mathcal{T}$ such that, for all $r \in \mathcal{R}(w)$ and a.e. on $\mathcal{T}$,

$$C_r(H)(t) < \gamma_w(t) \implies H_r(t) = \mu_r(t),$$
$$C_r(H)(t) > \gamma_w(t) \implies H_r(t) = \lambda_r(t).$$

Remark 2.2.1 It is worth noting that from part (a) of the proof of Theorem 2.2.1 it follows that the equilibrium condition (2.5) implies

$$\langle C(H(t)), F(t) - H(t) \rangle \geq 0 \quad \text{a.e. on } \mathcal{T}.$$

Vice versa, if (2.6) holds, then in part (b) of the proof of Theorem 2.2.1 we proved that (2.5) follows. Hence, using part (a), from (2.5) we obtain $\langle C(H(t)), F(t) - H(t) \rangle \geq 0$ a.e. on $\mathcal{T}$. Therefore we can conclude that the variational inequality (2.6) is equivalent to:

$$\langle C(H(t)), F(t) - H(t) \rangle \geq 0 \quad \forall F \in \mathbb{K}. \tag{2.7}$$

Moreover, this remark is interesting because we can apply to (2.7), among the others, the direct method (see [35], [44] and [95]) in order to find solutions to the variational inequality (2.6).

Example 2.2.1

In order to make clear the evolution of equilibrium trajectories in the dynamic case, we consider the network in Figure 2.1 consisting of a single origin–destination pair of nodes and two paths connecting these nodes of a single link each. The feasible set is given by

$$\mathbb{K} := \left\{ F \in L^2([0, 2], \mathbb{R}^2) \mid 0 \leq F_1(t) \leq t, \ 0 \leq F_2(t) \leq \frac{3}{2} t, \right.$$
$$\left. F_1(t) + F_2(t) = t, \ \text{a.e. on } [0, 2] \right\}, \tag{2.8}$$

where we choose $T = 2$, the travel demand $\rho(t) = t$ and $F(t)$ denotes the vector of path flows at t. The cost functions on the paths are defined as:

$$C_1(F) = 2F_1(t) - \frac{3}{2} \text{ and } C_2(F) = F_2(t) - 1.$$

Let us solve the problem by means of the direct method (see [35], [44] and [95]).

Taking into account Remark 2.2.1, the associated variational inequality is the following one:

$$C_1(H(t))(F_1(t) - H_1(t)) + C_2(H(t))(F_2(t) - H_2(t)) \geq 0$$
$$\forall F(t) \in \mathbb{K}. \tag{2.9}$$

From the traffic conservation law, we obtain $F_2(t) = t - F_1(t)$ a.e. in $[0, 2]$, therefore (2.9) becomes

$$\left[C_1(\tilde{H}(t)) - C_2(\tilde{H}(t)) \right] (F_1(t) - H_1(t)) \geq 0$$

$$\forall \tilde{F} \in \tilde{\mathbb{K}} = \left\{ F_1(t) \in L^2([0, 2], \mathbb{R}) \mid 0 \leq F_1(t) \leq t, \text{ a.e. on } [0, 2] \right\}.$$

In order to find the solution into the convex set $\tilde{\mathbb{K}}$, we have to solve the system

$$\begin{cases} \Gamma_1(\tilde{H}(t)) = C_1(\tilde{H}(t)) - C_2(\tilde{H}(t)) = 0 \\ \tilde{H}(t) \in \tilde{\mathbb{K}}, \end{cases}$$

whose solution is

$$\begin{cases} H_1(t) = \dfrac{2t + 1}{6} \\ H_2(t) = \dfrac{4t - 1}{6} \end{cases} \text{ if } \frac{1}{4} \leq t \leq 2.$$

Let $0 \leq t < \dfrac{1}{4}$ and examine the first face

$$\tilde{\mathbb{K}}^{(1)} = \{F_1(t) = 0\}.$$

The variational inequality becomes

$$\Gamma_1(\tilde{H}^{(1)}(t))(F_1(t) - H_1(t)) = \underbrace{\left(-t - \frac{1}{2} \right)}_{\leq 0} \cdot F_1(t) \geq 0$$

which is an absurdity.

Let us examine now the second face:

$$\tilde{\mathbb{K}}^{(2)} = \{F_1(t) = t\}.$$

The variational inequality becomes

$$\Gamma_1(\tilde{H}^{(2)}(t))(F_1(t) - H_1(t)) = \underbrace{\left(2t - \frac{1}{2}\right)}_{\leq 0} \cdot \underbrace{(F_1(t) - t)}_{\leq 0} \geq 0$$

which is satisfied.

Hence the solution of the problem is:

$$\begin{cases} H_1(t) = \begin{cases} t & \text{if } 0 \leq t \leq \dfrac{1}{4} \\ \dfrac{2t + 1}{6} & \text{if } \dfrac{1}{4} < t \leq 2 \end{cases} \\ \\ H_2(t) = \begin{cases} 0 & \text{if } 0 \leq t \leq \dfrac{1}{4} \\ \dfrac{4t - 1}{6} & \text{if } \dfrac{1}{4} < t \leq 2. \end{cases} \end{cases}$$

The total flow on the path r is given by $\displaystyle\int_0^T H_r(t)\, dt$.

2.3 Existence Theorems

There are two standard approaches to the existence of equilibria, namely with and without a monotonicity requirement (Stampacchia [151], Daniele *et al.* [46] and Maugeri [99]).

We recall here Theorems D.5 and D.6 of Appendix D in a unified structure (see also [133]).

Theorem 2.3.1 *Let E be a real topological vector space and $\mathbb{K} \subseteq E$ be convex and nonempty. Let $C : \mathbb{K} \to E^*$ be given such that*
(i) there exist $A \subseteq \mathbb{K}$ nonempty, compact, and $B \subseteq \mathbb{K}$ compact, convex such that, for every $x \in \mathbb{K} \setminus A$, there exists $y \in B$ with

$$\langle C(x), y - x \rangle < 0;$$

and either

(ii) C is hemicontinuous

or

(iii) C is pseudomonotone and hemicontinuous along line segments.

Then there exists $\overline{x} \in A$ such that $\langle C(\overline{x}), y - \overline{x} \rangle \geq 0$ for all $y \in \mathbb{K}$.

We may apply Theorem 2.3.1 choosing $E := \mathcal{L}$ and $\mathbb{K}$ given by (2.2). Being $\mathbb{K}$ a convex, closed, and bounded set, hence $\mathbb{K}$ is weakly compact. So if we endow $\mathcal{L}$ with the weak topology, then $\mathbb{K}$ is compact, and condition (i) in Theorem 2.3.1 is automatically satisfied by choosing $A := \mathbb{K}$ and $B := \emptyset$.

If we endow $\mathcal{L}$ with the strong topology, then $\mathbb{K}$ is no longer compact, and condition (i) must be used. In this case, since $\mathbb{K}$ is closed, the convexity of B in condition (i) is not needed. In fact, the convexity of B in the general case is only used to ensure that the convex hull of $B \cup G$ is compact for every finite subset $G \subseteq \mathbb{K}$. But we can work also with the closed convex hull of $B \cup G$ and, in a Banach space, the closed convex hull of any compact set is compact ([20], p. 180).

Of course, requirement (ii) is weakened, if we pass from the weak topology on $\mathcal{L}$ to the strong topology. For requirement (iii) it is not important which of the two topologies we use, since they coincide on line segments.

Altogether we obtain from Theorem 2.3.1 the following.

Corollary 2.3.1 *For $\mathbb{K} \subseteq \mathcal{L}$ given by (2.2) and $C : \mathbb{K} \to \mathcal{L}^*$ each of the following conditions is sufficient for the existence of a solution to (2.6):*

(i) C is hemicontinuous with respect to the strong topology on $\mathbb{K}$, and there exist $A \subseteq \mathbb{K}$ nonempty, compact, and $B \subseteq \mathbb{K}$ compact such that, for every $H \in \mathbb{K} \setminus A$, there exists $F \in B$ with

$$\ll C(H), F - H \gg < 0.$$

(ii) C is hemicontinuous with respect to the weak topology on $\mathbb{K}$.

(iii) C is pseudomonotone and hemicontinuous along line segments.

We shall employ the following result: under condition (iii) of Corollary 2.3.1, $H \in \mathcal{L}$ is a solution to (2.6) if and only if

$$H \in \mathbb{K} \text{ and } \ll C(F), H - F \gg \, \leq 0 \, \forall F \in \mathbb{K}. \qquad (2.10)$$

This is a slightly generalized form of a classical result of Minty. For the proof see [151], p. 116.

2.4 Additional Constraints

In order to get a more realistic model, we have to consider the possibility of introducing traffic controls such as traffic lights and one-way paths, or tolls on some links, or the addition of alternative routes.

We assume that these additional constraints can be described collectively by the requirement

$$F \in D,$$

where $D \subseteq \mathcal{L}$. We assume that D is a convex set such that

$$\mathbb{K} \cap \text{ int } D \neq \emptyset. \qquad (2.11)$$

$\mathbb{K}$ remains the same as in (2.2). The definition of an equilibrium flow has to be modified as follows:

$$H \in \mathbb{K} \cap D \text{ and } \ll C(H), F - H \gg \, \geq 0 \, \forall F \in \mathbb{K} \cap D. \qquad (2.12)$$

Then the following interesting characterization holds.

Theorem 2.4.1 $H \in \mathbb{K} \cap D$ *is a solution to (2.12) if and only if there exists $S \in \mathcal{L}^*$ such that*

$$\ll S, F - H \gg \, \leq 0 \quad \forall F \in D, \qquad (2.13)$$

$$\ll C(H) + S, F - H \gg \, \geq 0 \quad \forall F \in \mathbb{K}. \qquad (2.14)$$

Proof: If (2.13) and (2.14) are satisfied, then it is clear that

$$\ll C(H), F - H \gg \, \geq \, \ll C(H) + S, F - H \gg \, \geq 0 \quad \forall F \in \mathbb{K} \cap D,$$

and H is an equilibrium in the sense of (2.12).

Conversely, let H satisfy (2.12). We apply the separation theorem to the sets

$$A := \{(F, \gamma) \in D \times \mathbb{R} \mid \gamma < 0\},$$
$$B := \{(F, \gamma) \in \mathbb{K} \times \mathbb{R} \mid \ll C(H), F - H \gg \le \gamma\}.$$

Then A and B are nonempty and convex subsets of $\mathcal{L} \times \mathbb{R}$; moreover, they are disjoint because of (2.12) and A has nonempty interior, since D has nonempty interior. So, from the separation theorem for convex sets ([144], p. 58), there exist $(S, k) \in \mathcal{L}^* \times \mathbb{R}$, $(S, k) \ne (0, 0)$, and $\alpha \in \mathbb{R}$ such that

$$\ll S, F \gg + k\gamma \le \alpha \quad \forall (F, \gamma) \in A, \tag{2.15}$$

$$\ll S, F \gg + k\gamma \ge \alpha \quad \forall (F, \gamma) \in B. \tag{2.16}$$

It follows from (2.15) or (2.16) that $k \ge 0$. Let us prove that $k > 0$. Assume, for contradiction, that $k = 0$. Choose $F_0 \in \mathbb{K} \cap \operatorname{int} D$, which is possible because of (2.11). Then from (2.15) and (2.16) it follows $\ll S, F_0 \gg\, = \alpha$ and, since now $S \ne 0$, there exists $F \in \operatorname{int} D$ with $\ll S, F \gg\, > \alpha$, which contradicts (2.15). Thus $k > 0$, and we may normalize (S, k, α) such that $k = 1$, without affecting the validity of (2.15) and (2.16). Then we obtain, choosing γ arbitrarily close to zero in (2.15), that

$$\ll S, F \gg\, \le \alpha \quad \forall F \in D, \tag{2.17}$$

and, choosing $\gamma := \ll C(H), F - H \gg$ in (2.16), that

$$\ll S, F \gg + \ll C(H), F - H \gg\, \ge \alpha \quad \forall F \in \mathbb{K}. \tag{2.18}$$

In particular, setting $F := H$ in (2.17) and (2.18), we get

$$\ll S, H \gg\, = \alpha.$$

Substituting for α in (2.17) and (2.18) gives (2.13) and (2.14). $\square$

Roughly speaking, the additional constraints produce a worsening of the costs, which are shifted from $C(H)$ to $C(H) + S$.

From the proof of Theorem 2.2.1, replacing there $C(H)$ by
$$\overline{C} := C(H) + S,$$

it follows that (2.14) is equivalent to

$$\forall\, w \in \mathcal{W}, \ \forall\, q, s \in \mathcal{R}(w), \text{ and a.e. on } \mathcal{T},$$
$$\overline{C}_q(t) < \overline{C}_s(t) \Longrightarrow H_q(t) = \mu_q(t) \text{ or } H_s(t) = \lambda_s(t). \qquad (2.19)$$

Thus (2.14) and (2.19) for $\overline{C} := C(H) + S$ is the generalized Wardrop's condition corresponding to problem (2.12). It is necessary and sufficient for $H \in \mathbb{K} \cap D$ to be an equilibrium in the sense of (2.12).

As an example, the requirement $F \in D$ may express linear inequality constraints imposed upon the vector of link-flows (see [58], [89]). For each $t \in \mathcal{T}$, the vector of link-flows $f(t)$ depends on the vector of route-flows $F(t)$ by means of the estimate

$$f(t) = \Delta F(t),$$

where Δ is the link-route incidence matrix. The linear constraints on the link-flows may be written as

$$G(t)\, f(t) \leq g(t),$$

where the coefficient matrix G and the right-hand vector g vary with time. Then D takes the form

$$D := \{F \in \mathcal{L} \mid G(t)\Delta F(t) \leq g(t) \text{ a.e. on } \mathcal{T}\}.$$

If D is defined by convex inequalities, then every $S \in \mathcal{L}^*$ satisfying (2.13) admits an explicit representation in terms of Lagrange multipliers (for details about this and sensitivity analysis see [102], p. 190, and [58]).

In the remaining parts we shall return to the standard problem (2.6).

2.5 Calculation of the Solution

2.5.1 The Subgradient Method

First we recall the definition of a gap function, which will be used in the sequel. Given an abstract equilibrium problem of the form

$$H \in \mathbb{K}, \ \varphi(H, F) \geq 0 \ \forall\, F \in \mathbb{K}, \qquad (2.20)$$

where $\mathbb{K} \subseteq B$ and $\varphi : B \times B \to \mathbb{R}$, a gap function (see [3]) for problem (2.20) is a function $\Psi : B \to \mathbb{R} \cup \{+\infty\}$ such that, for all $H \in B$, $\Psi(H) \geq 0$, and moreover,

$$\Psi(H) = 0 \Longleftrightarrow H \text{ solves (2.20)}.$$

Then $H \in B$ solves (2.20) if and only if $\Psi(H) \leq 0$.

In connection with the equilibrium problem (2.6) we choose

$$B := \{F \in \mathcal{L} \mid \lambda(t) \leq F(t) \leq \mu(t) \text{ a.e. on } \mathcal{T}\},$$

since this set is easy to handle (for instance, projections onto B are readily available). Furthermore, we choose $\mathcal{L} = L^2(\mathcal{T}, \mathbb{R}^R) = \mathcal{L}^*$, a Hilbert space. Concerning the mapping $C : \mathbb{K} \to \mathcal{L}$ we make the following assumptions:

(C1) C is pseudomonotone;

(C2) C is hemicontinuous with respect to the weak topology on $\mathbb{K}$;

(C3) the set $\{C(F) \mid F \in \mathbb{K}\}$ is norm-bounded.

All other data are as introduced in Section 2.2. Recall that $\mathbb{K}$ is weakly compact. From (C1) and (C2) it follows that the solution set of (2.6) is nonempty and coincides with the solution set of (2.10). Let, for all $H \in B$,

$$\psi_1(H) := \max_{F \in \mathbb{K}} \ll C(F), H - F \gg, \quad \psi_2(H) := \int_{\mathcal{T}} \|\Phi H(t) - \rho(t)\|_2^2 \, dt.$$

Then the real-valued function $\Psi(H) := \max\{\psi_1(H), \psi_2(H)\}$ is easily seen to be a gap function for (2.10). The function $\psi_1(H)$, being the maximum of a family of continuous and affine functions, is convex and weakly lower semicontinuous. Then Ψ is convex and weakly lower semicontinuous too (in fact, the needed convexity of Ψ is the main reason for considering (2.10), instead of attacking (2.6) directly). Using (C2) we shall see below that the subdifferential

$$\partial \Psi(H) := \{\tau \in \mathcal{L} \mid \Psi(F) - \Psi(H) \geq \ll \tau, F - H \gg \quad \forall F \in B\}$$

is nonempty for all $H \in B$. Let

$$\Gamma := \{H \in B \mid \Psi(H) \leq 0\}.$$

Because of the equivalence between (2.6) and (2.10), $H \in \mathcal{L}$ is a solution of (2.6) if and only if $H \in \Gamma$. The subgradient method for finding an element of Γ runs as follows (see [132]).

Choose $H^0 \in B$ arbitrarily. Given $H^n \in B$, $H^n \notin \Gamma$, let

$$H^{n+1} := \operatorname{Proj}_B(H^n - \varrho_n \tau_n),$$

where $\tau_n \in \partial \Psi(H^n)$, $\varrho_n := \dfrac{\Psi(H^n)}{\|\tau_n\|^2}$ and Proj_B denotes the Euclidean projection onto B. We shall see below, using assumption (C3), that τ_n can be chosen in such a way that $\|\tau_n\|$ remains bounded. If $\|\tau_n\|$ remains bounded and $H^n \notin \Gamma$ for all n, then we have the following result.

Theorem 2.5.1 *There holds $\Psi(H^n) \to 0$. The sequence $\{H^n\}$ has weak cluster points, and every weak cluster point is in Γ. If the sequence $\{H^n\}$ has a strong cluster point $\overline{H}$, then $\overline{H}$ is unique and $\{H^n\}$ converges strongly to $\overline{H}$.*

Proof: For arbitrary $\gamma \in \Gamma$, using the nonexpansivity of the projection mapping and the support inequality

$$\ll \tau_n, \gamma - H^n \gg \, \le \Psi(\gamma) - \Psi(H^n) \le -\Psi(H^n),$$

we obtain

$$
\begin{aligned}
\|H^{n+1} - \gamma\|^2 \quad &\le \|H^n - \varrho_n \tau_n - \gamma\|^2 \\
&= \|H^n - \gamma\|^2 + 2\varrho_n \ll \tau_n, \gamma - H^n \gg + \varrho_n^2 \|\tau_n\|^2 \\
&\le \|H^n - \gamma\|^2 - 2\varrho_n \Psi(H^n) + \varrho_n^2 \|\tau_n\|^2 \\
&= \|H^n - \gamma\|^2 - \frac{\Psi(H^n)^2}{\|\tau_n\|^2}.
\end{aligned}
\tag{2.21}
$$

Since the sequence $\{\|H^n - \gamma\|^2\}$ is decreasing and bounded from below, and since $\|\tau_n\|$ are bounded from above, it follows that $\Psi(H^n) \to 0$.

In particular, $\|H^n - \gamma\| \le \|H^0 - \gamma\|$ for all n. This shows that $\{H^n\}$ is bounded and therefore has a weak cluster point. Since $\Psi(H^n) \to 0$, and since Ψ is weakly lower semicontinuous, it follows, if $\overline{H}$ is a weak cluster point, that $\Psi(\overline{H}) \le 0$, hence $\overline{H} \in \Gamma$.

Now let $\overline{H}$ be a strong cluster point of $\{H^n\}$. Choosing $\gamma := \overline{H}$ in (2.21), we obtain

$$\|H^{n+1} - \overline{H}\| \le \|H^n - \overline{H}\| \; \forall n,$$

and since $\|H^{n(j)} - \overline{H}\| \to 0$ for some sub-sequence $\{H^{n(j)}\}$, we obtain $\|H^n - \overline{H}\| \to 0$ for the entire sequence $\{H^n\}$.   □

If $\mathcal{L}$ is finite-dimensional (the case $\mathcal{T} := \{0, 1, \dots, T\}$), then weak and strong cluster points coincide. Hence in this situation the entire sequence $\{H^n\}$ converges to some $\overline{H} \in \Gamma$.

It remains to discuss the choice of $\tau \in \partial\Psi(H)$. For given $H \in B$, define $\tau^1 \in \mathcal{L}$ by

$$\tau^1(t) := C(\overline{F}(t)), \quad t \in \mathcal{T},$$

where $\overline{F}$ is a solution of $\max\{\ll C(F), H - F \gg \,|\, F \in \mathbb{K}\}$. Such an $\overline{F}$ exists because of assumption (C2). Then $\tau^1 \in \partial\psi_1(H)$. Define $\tau^2 \in \mathcal{L}$ by

$$\tau^2(t) := 2\Phi^T(\Phi H(t) - \rho(t)), \quad t \in \mathcal{T}.$$

Then $\tau^2 \in \partial\psi_2(H)$. Now define $\tau := \tau^1$, if $\Psi(H) = \psi_1(H) > \psi_2(H)$, and $\tau := \tau^2$, if $\Psi(H) = \psi_2(H)$. Then $\tau \in \partial\Psi(H)$, and these τ remain bounded, if H varies in B, because of assumption (C3). In particular, if we select $\tau_n \in \partial\Psi(H^n)$ according to this rule, then $\|\tau_n\|$ remains bounded, as stipulated for Theorem 2.5.1.

In order to illustrate how this method runs, we present an example of calculation (see [138]).

Example 2.5.1

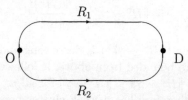

Figure 2.2: Network with general travel demand $\rho(t)$

We report here the example due to Raciti [138]. We consider the network in Figure 2.2 consisting of a single origin–destination pair of nodes and two paths connecting these nodes of a single link each. The feasible set is given by

$$\mathbb{K} := \left\{ F \in L^2([0,1], \mathbb{R}^2) : F(t) \geq 0,\ F_1(t) + F_2(t) = \rho(t),\ \text{a.e. on } [0,1] \right\}.$$

We assign now the cost operator:

$$\begin{cases} C_1[F(t)] = b_1\, F_1(t) \\ C_2[F(t)] = b_2\, F_2(t) \end{cases} \quad \forall\, t \in [0,1].$$

It is easy to prove that the exact equilibrium solution is reached in:

$$\begin{cases} H_1(t) = \rho(t)\, \dfrac{b_2}{b_1 + b_2} \\[2mm] H_2(t) = \rho(t)\, \dfrac{b_1}{b_1 + b_2} \end{cases} \quad \forall\, t \in [0,1].$$

We apply now the subgradient method.

In order to find elements of $\partial \psi_1(H)$ we have, first of all, to solve $\forall H \in B$ the problem:

$$\max_{F \in \mathbb{K}} \ll C(F), H - F \gg$$

$$= \max_{F \in \mathbb{K}} \int_0^1 \left\{ b_1\, F_1(t)\, (H_1(t) - F_1(t)) + b_2\, F_2(t)\, (H_2(t) - F_2(t)) \right\} dt$$

$$= \max_{0 \leq F_2(t) \leq \rho(t)} \int_0^1 \left\{ b_1\, (\rho(t) - F_2(t))\, (H_1(t) - \rho(t) + F_2(t)) \right.$$

$$\left. + b_2\, F_2(t)\, (H_2(t) - F_2(t)) \right\} dt$$

$$= \max_{0 \leq F_2(t) \leq \rho(t)} \int_0^1 \left\{ b_1\, H_1(t)\, \rho(t) - b_1\, \rho^2(t) + b_1\, \rho(t)\, F_2(t) - b_1\, H_1(t) F_2(t) \right.$$

$$\left. + b_1 \rho(t) F_2(t) - b_1\, F_2^2(t) + b_2\, H_2(t)\, F_2(t) - b_2\, F_2^2(t) \right\} dt$$

$$= \max_{0 \leq F_2(t) \leq \rho(t)} \int_0^1 \left\{ -(b_1 + b_2)\, F_2^2(t) + (2b_1\, \rho(t) - b_1\, H_1(t) + b_2\, H_2(t))\, F_2(t) \right.$$

$$\left. + b_1\, H_1(t)\, \rho(t) - b_1\, \rho^2(t) \right\} dt = \max_{0 \leq F_2(t) \leq \rho(t)} \int_0^1 I[F_2(t)]\, dt,$$

where

$$I[F_2(t)] = -(b_1 + b_2)\, F_2^2(t) + (2b_1\, \rho(t) - b_1\, H_1(t) + b_2\, H_2(t))\, F_2(t)$$
$$+b_1\, H_1(t)\, \rho(t) - b_1\, \rho^2(t).$$

The maximal solution is

$$\overline{F}_2(t) = \frac{2b_1\, \rho(t) - b_1\, H_1(t) + b_2\, H_2(t)}{2(b_1 + b_2)}.$$

As a consequence, $\forall\, t \in [0, 1]$, the solution is

$$\begin{cases} \begin{cases} \overline{F}_2(t) = \dfrac{2b_1\, \rho(t) - b_1\, H_1(t) + b_2\, H_2(t)}{2(b_1 + b_2)} & \text{if } 0 < \overline{F}_2(t) < \rho(t) \\ \overline{F}_1(t) = \rho(t) - \overline{F}_2(t) \end{cases} \\ \begin{cases} \overline{F}_2(t) = \rho(t) \\ \overline{F}_1(t) = 0 \end{cases} & \text{if } \overline{F}_2(t) = \rho(t) \\ \begin{cases} \overline{F}_2(t) = 0 \\ \overline{F}_1(t) = \rho(t) \end{cases} & \text{if } \overline{F}_2(t) = 0. \end{cases}$$

Thus

$$C(\overline{F}_1(t), \overline{F}_2(t)) \in \partial \psi_1(H(t))$$

and replacing $(\overline{F}_1(t), \overline{F}_2(t))$ in $\psi_1(H(t))$, we have:

$$\psi_1(H(t)) = \int_0^1 \left[(b_1 + b_2)\overline{F}_2^2(t) + b_1\, H_1(t)\, \rho(t) - b_1\, \rho^2(t) \right]\, dt.$$

Moreover, $\psi_2(H(t)) = \displaystyle\int_0^1 (H_1(t) + H_2(t) - \rho(t))^2\, dt$. The calculation of elements of $\partial \psi_2(H(t))$ is straightforward because an explicit formula is known:

$$\tau^2(t) = 2\Phi^T \left(\Phi\, H(t) - \rho(t) \right) = 2 \begin{bmatrix} 1 \\ 1 \end{bmatrix} (H_1(t) + H_2(t) - \rho(t))$$

$$= 2\, (H_1(t) + H_2(t) - \rho(t),\, H_1(t) + H_2(t) - \rho(t)) \in \partial \psi_2(H(t)).$$

If we choose now $b_1 = 1$, $b_2 = \dfrac{1}{2}$ and $\rho(t) = t\ \forall\, t \in [0, 1]$, then the exact equilibrium solution is:

$$\begin{cases} H_1(t) = t/3 \\ H_2(t) = 2t/3. \end{cases}$$

For the calculation of elements of $\partial\psi_2(H(t))$, let us observe that:

$$I[F_2(t)] = -\frac{3}{2}F_2^2(t) + \left(2t - H_1(t) + \frac{1}{2}H_2(t)\right)F_2(t) + H_1(t)t - t^2,$$

which yields

$$\overline{F}_2(t) = \begin{cases} \dfrac{2t - H_1(t) + \frac{1}{2}H_2(t)}{3} & \text{if } 0 < \overline{F}_2(t) < t \\ 0 & \text{if } \overline{F}_2(t) = 0 \\ t & \text{if } \overline{F}_2(t) = t. \end{cases}$$

Then

$$C(\overline{F}(t)) = \left(\overline{F}_1(t), \frac{\overline{F}_2(t)}{2}\right)$$

$$= \begin{cases} \left(\dfrac{t + H_1(t) - H_2(t)/2}{3}, \dfrac{t - H_1(t)/2 + H_2(t)/4}{3}\right) & \text{if } 0 < \overline{F}_2(t) < t \\ (t, 0) & \text{if } \overline{F}_2(t) = 0 \\ (0, t) & \text{if } \overline{F}_2(t) = t. \end{cases}$$

The other quantities we need before starting the algorithm are:

$$\psi_1(H(t)) = \int_0^1 \left(\frac{3}{2}\overline{F}_2^2(t) + H_1(t)\,t - t^2\right)dt,$$

$$\psi_2(H(t)) = \int_0^1 (H_1(t) + H_2(t) - t)^2\,dt,$$

$$\|\tau^1\|^2 = \|C(\overline{F}(t))\|^2$$

$$= \frac{1}{9}\left[\left(t + H_1(t) - \frac{H_2(t)}{2}\right)^2 + \left(t - \frac{H_1(t)}{2} + \frac{H_2(t)}{4}\right)^2\right],$$

$$\|\tau^2\|^2 = 8\,(H_1(t) + H_2(t) - \rho(t))^2.$$

Let us choose now, for example, $H^0 = (0, t) \in B \setminus \Gamma$ and define the usual error:

$$E^{(n)} = \|H - H^{(n)}\|_{L^2}.$$

With simple calculations, it is possible to see that after 10 iterations, we get $E^{(n)} = 0.2112$, after 100 iterations, we get $E^{(n)} = 0.1180$, and after 1.000 iterations, we get $E^{(n)} = 0.0436$. So we can deduce that the convergence is very slow.

If we choose now as coercivity constant $b_2 = \dfrac{1}{200}$, then the cost operator is given by:

$$\begin{cases} C_1[F(t)] = F_1(t) \\ C_2[F(t)] = \dfrac{1}{200} F_2(t) \end{cases} \quad \forall\, t \in [0,1].$$

In this case the exact equilibrium solution is:

$$\begin{cases} H_1(t) = t/201 \\ H_2(t) = 200\, t/201. \end{cases}$$

Solving the problem by means of the subgradient method, we find out that after 10 iterations $E^{(n)} = 0.1599$ and after 100 iterations $E^{(n)} = 0.0073$. So we have a faster convergence and we can conclude that to a decreasing of the coercivity constant corresponds an increasing of the velocity of convergence.

2.5.2   A Discretization Procedure

In this section we apply a general discretization procedure, which does not require any regularity of the solution. It is applied to a significant model with an affine operator (see also [140]). Such a method is useful to find the approximation of the solutions to the evolutionary variational inequality which expresses the equilibrium problem. We start by considering a convex set where the upper and lower bounds as well as the travel demand do not depend on time, and we construct piecewise constant approximations to solutions to the variational inequality. Further, we turn back to the general case of dynamic convex set and we construct, also in this case, piecewise constant approximations to the solution. An example of this discretization technique is presented by Raciti in [140], but it is confined to the case of a convex set with upper and lower bounds and without any conservation law.

We consider a sequence $\{\pi_n\}$ of partitions of $[0, T]$, such that:

$$\pi_n = (t_n^0, t_n^1, \ldots, t_n^{N_n}), \ 0 = t_n^0 < t_n^1 < \ldots < t_n^{N_n} = T$$

and

$$\delta_n := \max \left\{ t_n^j - t_n^{j-1} : j = 1, \ldots, N_n \right\}$$

with $\lim_{n \to \infty} \delta_n = 0$.

We introduce the space of $\mathbb{R}^m$-value piecewise constant functions induced by π_n:

$$P_n \left([0, T], \mathbb{R}^m\right) := \left\{ v \in L^\infty \left([0, T], \mathbb{R}^m\right) : v_{(t_n^{j-1}, t_n^j]} = v_j \in \mathbb{R}^m, \right.$$

$$\left. j = 1, \ldots, N_n \right\} \tag{2.22}$$

where v_j denotes the constant value of v on $(t_n^{j-1}, t_n^j]$.

The mean value operators $\mu_n : L^1 \left([0, T], \mathbb{R}^m\right) \to P_n \left([0, T], \mathbb{R}^m\right)$ are then denoted by:

$$\mu_n v_{(t_n^{j-1}, t_n^j]} := \frac{1}{t_n^j - t_n^{j-1}} \int_{t_n^{j-1}}^{t_n^j} v(s) \, ds. \tag{2.23}$$

We need to recall the following Lemma (see [12]).

Lemma 2.5.1 *Let $1 \le p < \infty$. Then, the linear operators*

$$\mu_n : L^p \left([0, T], \mathbb{R}^m\right) \to L^p \left([0, T], \mathbb{R}^m\right)$$

are uniformly bounded and:

$$\mu_n v \to v \text{ in } L^p \left([0, T], \mathbb{R}^m\right)$$

as $n \to \infty$, $\forall v \in L^p \left([0, T], \mathbb{R}^m\right)$.

We consider first the following closed and convex set:

$$\mathbb{K} := \left\{ F(t) \in L^2 \left([0, T], \mathbb{R}^m\right) : \lambda \le F(t) \le \nu, \text{ a.e. in } [0, T], \right.$$

$$\left. \Phi F(t) = \rho, \ \lambda, \ \nu \ge 0, \right\} \tag{2.24}$$

where the upper and lower bounds and the demand are constant (that is, not time-dependent) functions, and an affine mapping

$$C : [0, T] \times \mathbb{K} \to L^2 \left([0, T], \mathbb{R}^m\right) :$$

$$C[t, F(t)] = A(t) F(t) + B(t),$$

$$A(t) \in L^\infty\left([0,T],\mathbb{R}^{m^2}\right), \quad B(t) \in L^2\left([0,T],\mathbb{R}^m\right).$$

Thus we are led to solve the problem of finding $H(t) \in \mathbb{K}$:

$$\int_0^T \langle A(t)\,H(t) + B(t), F(t) - H(t)\rangle\,dt \geq 0, \quad \forall F(t) \in \mathbb{K}. \qquad (2.25)$$

In correspondence to each partition we can write:

$$\int_0^T \langle A(t)\,H(t) + B(t), F(t) - H(t)\rangle\,dt$$

$$= \sum_{j=1}^{N_n} \int_{t_n^{j-1}}^{t_n^j} \langle A(t)\,H(t) + B(t), F(t) - H(t)\rangle\,dt. \qquad (2.26)$$

Hence, in each interval $[t_n^{j-1}, t_n^j]$ we can consider the problem of finding $H_j^n(t) \in \mathbb{K}$:

$$\int_{t_n^{j-1}}^{t_n^j} \langle A(t)\,H_j^n(t) + B(t), F_j^n(t) - H_j^n(t)\rangle\,dt \geq 0, \quad \forall F_j^n(t) \in \mathbb{K}. \quad (2.27)$$

We solve now the finite-dimensional problem of finding $H_j^n \in \mathbb{K}_m \subset \mathbb{R}^m$:

$$\langle A_j^n\,H_j^n + B_j^n, F_j^n - H_j^n\rangle \geq 0, \quad \forall F_j^n \in \mathbb{K}_m \qquad (2.28)$$

where

$$A_j^n = \frac{1}{t_n^j - t_n^{j-1}} \int_{t_n^{j-1}}^{t_n^j} A(t)\,dt; \quad B_j^n = \frac{1}{t_n^j - t_n^{j-1}} \int_{t_n^{j-1}}^{t_n^j} B(t)\,dt \qquad (2.29)$$

and consider H_j^n as constant approximations of the solutions $H_j^n(t)$ to (2.27). The set $\mathbb{K}_m$ is the convex subset of $\mathbb{R}^m$ with the same lower and upper bounds and the same demand as $\mathbb{K}$.

Our aim is to prove that the functions:

$$H_n(t) = \sum_{j=1}^{N_n} \chi(t_n^{j-1}, t_n^j)\,H_j^n \qquad (2.30)$$

are, in a suitable sense, piecewise constant approximations to solutions to the original problem (2.25). We can then prove the following theorem.

Theorem 2.5.2 *Let $\mathbb{K}$ be as in (2.24) and in addition let $A(t)$ be positive definite a.e. in $[0, T]$. Then, the set $U = \{H_n\}_{n \in \mathbb{N}}$ is (weakly) compact and its cluster points are feasible. Moreover, if $\bar{H}$ is a weak cluster point for U, then $\bar{H}$ solves (2.25).*

Proof: The set $U := \{H_n\}_{n \in \mathbb{N}}$ is norm bounded because, by construction, its elements belong to $\mathbb{K}$. In fact:

$$\|H_n(t)\|_{L^2}^2 = \int_0^T \sum_{i,j=1}^{N_n} \chi_{(t_n^{j-1}, t_n^j)} \, \chi_{(t_n^{i-1}, t_n^i)} \, H_j^n \, H_i^n \, dt$$

$$\leq \sum_{i,j=1}^{N_n} \int_0^T H_j^n \, H_i^n \, dt = \sum_{i,j=1}^{N_n} H_j^n \, H_i^n \int_0^T dt = T \sum_{i,j=1}^{N_n} H_j^n \, H_i^n.$$

Thus, $\{H_n\}_{n \in \mathbb{N}}$ is weakly compact. Let us note that this compactness argument still holds if the upper and lower bounds and the demand which define $\mathbb{K}$ are time-dependent L^2 functions. Let $\bar{H}$ be a weak cluster point for U. Since $\mathbb{K}$ is strongly closed (as follows from the properties of L^2 convergence) and convex, then it is also weakly closed, hence $\bar{H} \in \mathbb{K}$. Let $n \in \mathbb{N}$ and consider the piecewise constant approximations H_n to a solution and F_n to a generic element $F(t)$ of $\mathbb{K}$ obtained using the mean value operator. Thus, we have, by construction, that:

$$\langle A_j^n \, H_j^n + B_j^n, F_j^n \rangle \geq \langle A_j^n \, H_j^n + B_j^n, H_j^n \rangle \quad \forall F_j^n \in \mathbb{K}_m, \tag{2.31}$$

which implies

$$\left\langle \left(\frac{1}{t_n^j - t_n^{j-1}} \int_{t_n^{j-1}}^{t_n^j} A(t) \, dt \right) H_j^n + \left(\frac{1}{t_n^j - t_n^{j-1}} \int_{t_n^{j-1}}^{t_n^j} B(t) \, dt \right), F_j^n \right\rangle \geq$$

$$\left\langle \left(\frac{1}{t_n^j - t_n^{j-1}} \int_{t_n^{j-1}}^{t_n^j} A(t) \, dt \right) H_j^n + \left(\frac{1}{t_n^j - t_n^{j-1}} \int_{t_n^{j-1}}^{t_n^j} B(t) \, dt \right), H_j^n \right\rangle$$

$$\forall F_j^n \in \mathbb{K}_m,$$

hence:

$$\int_{t_n^{j-1}}^{t_n^j} \langle A(t) \, H_j^n + B(t), F_j^n \rangle \, dt \geq \int_{t_n^{j-1}}^{t_n^j} \langle A(t) \, H_j^n + B(t), H_j^n \rangle \, dt.$$

As a consequence, summing all the intervals yields:

$$\int_0^T \langle C[t, H_n(t)], F_n(t)\rangle\, dt \geq \int_0^T \langle C[t, H_n(t)], H_n(t)\rangle\, dt, \forall n \in \mathbb{N}. \quad (2.32)$$

Now, $C[t, H_n(t)]$ converges to $C[t, \bar{H}]$ (weakly), because C is affine. Moreover, $F_n(t)$ converges to $F(t)$ (strongly) because of Lemma 2.5.1. Thus, from well-known properties of weak topology, we get:

$$\int_0^T \langle C[t, H_n(t)], F_n(t)\rangle\, dt \to \int_0^T \langle C[t, \bar{H}(t)], F(t)\rangle\, dt.$$

Since A is a positive definite matrix, we get that

$$\int_0^T \langle C[t, F(t)], F(t)\rangle\, dt$$

is weakly lower semicontinuous. We can then conclude that:

$$\limsup_n \int_0^T \langle C[t, H_n(t)], F_n(t)\rangle\, dt = \lim_n \int_0^T \langle C[t, H_n(t)], F_n(t)\rangle\, dt$$

$$= \int_0^T \langle C[t, \bar{H}(t)], F(t)\rangle\, dt \geq \limsup_n \int_0^T \langle C[t, H_n(t)], H_n(t)\rangle\, dt$$

$$\geq \liminf_n \int_0^T \langle C[t, H_n(t)], H_n(t)\rangle\, dt = \int_0^T \langle C[t, \bar{H}(t)], \bar{H}(t)\rangle\, dt$$

and the theorem is proved. $\square$

In Theorem 2.5.2 we have considered the constant convex set (2.24). Now we turn back to the case of a time-dependent convex set:

$$\mathbb{K} := \big\{ F(t) \in L^2\left([0, T], \mathbb{R}^m\right) : \; \lambda(t) \leq F(t) \leq \nu(t), \text{ a.e. in } [0, T],$$
$$\lambda(t),\; \nu(t) \geq 0,\; \Phi F(t) = \rho(t) \text{ a.e. in } [0, T]\big\} \quad (2.33)$$

and consider piecewise constant approximations for it. We need to recall some basic definitions of set convergence.

Definition 2.5.1 *Let S be a metric space and $\{\mathbb{K}_n\}$ a sequence of sets of S. We say that $\mathbb{K}_n$ is Kuratowsky-convergent to $\mathbb{K}$ if and only if:*

$$\liminf_n \mathbb{K}_n = \limsup_n \mathbb{K}_n = \mathbb{K},$$

where

$$\limsup_n \mathbb{K}_n := \left\{ y \in S : \exists n_1 < n_2 < \ldots, \ with \ y_{n_i} \in \mathbb{K}_n, \ y = \lim_i y_{n_i} \right\}$$

$$\liminf_n \mathbb{K}_n := \left\{ y \in S : \exists n_0 \in \mathbb{N} : \forall n > n_0 \ \exists y_n \in \mathbb{K}_n, \ and \ \lim_n y_n = y \right\}.$$

Definition 2.5.2 *Let S be a normed space and $\{\mathbb{K}_n\}$ a sequence of closed and convex subsets of S. We say that $\mathbb{K}_n$ is Mosco-convergent to $\mathbb{K}$ (see [106] and [107]) if and only if:*

$$w - \limsup_n \mathbb{K}_n \subset \mathbb{K} \subset s - \liminf \mathbb{K}_n \tag{2.34}$$

where w and s mean weak and strong topology, respectively.

Let us turn now to the set $\mathbb{K}$ defined in (2.33) and, in correspondence to each partition π_n of $[0, T]$, we consider the sets:

$$\mathbb{K}_j^n := \big\{ F_j \in \mathbb{R}^m : \bar{\lambda}_{j,n} \le F_j \le \bar{\nu}_{j,n}, \ \text{a.e. in } (t_{j-1}, t_j),$$
$$\Phi \, F_j = \bar{\rho}_{j,n}, \ \text{a.e. in } (t_{j-1}, t_j) \big\}, \tag{2.35}$$

where $\bar{\lambda}_{j,n} = \mu_{j,n} \lambda(t)$, $\bar{\nu}_{j,n} = \mu_{j,n} \nu(t)$ and $\bar{\rho}_{j,n} = \mu_{j,n} \rho(t)$ are the mean values of $\lambda(t)$, $\nu(t)$ and $\rho(t)$ on (t_{j-1}, t_j). Thus, we can consider the set $\mathbb{K}_n = \bigcap_j \mathbb{K}_j^n$ which, $\forall n \in \mathbb{N}$, has piecewise constant lower and upper bounds and demand which we denote by $\bar{\lambda}_n$, $\bar{\nu}_n$ and $\bar{\rho}_n$, respectively.

Lemma 2.5.2 *The sequence of sets $\mathbb{K}_n$ converges to $\mathbb{K}$ (in the Mosco sense).*

Proof: We have to prove that, if we set

$$\liminf_n \mathbb{K}_n = \bigg\{ F \in L^2([0, T], \mathbb{R}^m) : \exists \nu : \forall n > \nu$$

$$\exists F_n \in \mathbb{K}^n \text{ such that } \lim_n F_n \overset{L^2}{=} F \Big\}$$

and

$$\limsup_n \mathbb{K}_n = \Big\{ F \in L^2([0,T], \mathbb{R}^m) : \exists n_1 < n_2 < \ldots < n_i < \ldots$$

$$\text{such that } F_{n_i} \in \mathbb{K}^{n_i} \text{ and } \lim_i F_{n_i} = F \Big\},$$

then $\mathbb{K}_n \to \mathbb{K}$ in the Mosco sense if and only if

$$w - \limsup_n \mathbb{K}_n \subset \mathbb{K} \subset s - \liminf_n \mathbb{K}_n.$$

1. We show first that $\mathbb{K} \subset s - \liminf\limits_n \mathbb{K}_n$. Let $F(t) \in \mathbb{K}$ and consider the piecewise constant function $F_n(t) = \mu_n F(t)$. Since

$$\lambda(t) \le F(t) \le \nu(t),$$

then it follows:

$$\mu_n \lambda(t) \le \mu_n F(t) \le \mu_n \nu(t), \quad \forall n \in \mathbb{N}.$$

Moreover, since $\Phi F(t) = \rho(t)$, it is easy to see that $\Phi \mu_{j,n} F(t) = \mu_{j,n} \rho(t)$. In fact, from the estimate $\sum\limits_{j=1}^m \varphi_{jl} F_j(t) = \rho(t)$, integrating in $[t_{j-1}, t_j]$ and dividing by $t_j - t_{j-1}$, we get:

$$\frac{\sum\limits_j \varphi_{jl} \int_{t_{j-1}}^{t_j} F_j(t)\, dt}{t_j - t_{j-1}} = \frac{\int_{t_{j-1}}^{t_j} \rho(t)\, dt}{t_j - t_{j-1}},$$

that is $\Phi \mu_{j,n} F_j(t) = \mu_{j,n} \rho(t)$ and $\Phi \mu_n F(t) = \mu_n \rho(t)$. As a consequence $\mu_n F(t) \in \mathbb{K}^n$, $\forall n \in \mathbb{N}$. Moreover, by virtue of Lemma 2.5.1, we have:

$$\lim_n \mu_n F(t) = F(t), \quad \text{in } L^2([0,T], \mathbb{R}^m)$$

and

$$\lim_n \mu_n \rho(t) = \rho(t), \quad \text{in } L^2([0,T], \mathbb{R}^m).$$

Therefore $F(t)$ is the strong limit of a sequence whose elements belong to $\mathbb{K}_n$, which means that $F(t) \in s - \liminf \mathbb{K}_n$.

2. We show now that $w - \limsup_n \mathbb{K}_n \subset \mathbb{K}$. Let $\mathbb{K} = X \cap Y \cap Z$ where

$$X := \left\{ F(t) \in L^2\left([0,T], \mathbb{R}^m\right) : \lambda(t) \leq F(t) \text{ a.e. in } [0,T], \ \lambda(t) \geq 0 \right\},$$
$$Y := \left\{ F(t) \in L^2\left([0,T], \mathbb{R}^m\right) : F(t) \leq \nu(t) \text{ a.e. in } [0,T], \ \nu(t) \geq 0 \right\},$$

and

$$Z := \left\{ F(t) \in L^2\left([0,T], \mathbb{R}^m\right) : \Phi F(t) = \rho(t) \text{ a.e. in } [0,T], \ \rho(t) \geq 0 \right\}.$$

Let us prove first that:

$$w - \limsup_n H_n \subset X$$

where the sets H_n are constructed like $\mathbb{K}_n$, but taking into account only the lower bounds $\bar{\lambda}_n(t) = \mu_n \lambda(t)$. We want to show that if $F_{n_i}(t) \in H_{n_i}$ is such that

$$w - \lim_i F_{n_i}(t) = F(t),$$

then $F(t) \geq \lambda(t)$ a.e. in $[0,T]$. Let us choose an arbitrary

$$\xi(t) \in C^- = \left\{ \xi(t) \in L^2\left([0,T], \mathbb{R}^m\right) : \xi(t) \leq 0, \text{ a.e. in } [0,T] \right\}$$

and define $\xi_{n_i}(t) = \mu_{n_i} \xi(t)$. Obviously we have:

$$F_{n_i}(t) \geq \bar{\lambda}_{n_i}(t) \implies F_{n_i}(t) - \bar{\lambda}_{n_i}(t) \geq 0 \text{ and } \lim_i \mu_{n_i} \xi(t) \overset{s}{=} \xi(t).$$

Therefore

$$\underbrace{\langle F_{n_i}(t) - \bar{\lambda}_{n_i}(t)}_{\geq 0}, \underbrace{\xi_{n_i}(t) \rangle}_{\leq 0} \leq 0 \quad \forall i \in \mathbb{N}, \quad \forall \xi_{n_i} \leq 0. \tag{2.36}$$

When i diverges to $+\infty$, then we get:

$$0 \geq \langle F_{n_i}(t) - \bar{\lambda}_{n_i}(t), \xi_{n_i}(t) - \xi(t) + \xi(t) \rangle$$
$$= \langle F_{n_i}(t) - \bar{\lambda}_{n_i}(t), \xi(t) \rangle + \langle F_{n_i}(t) - \bar{\lambda}_{n_i}(t), \xi_{n_i}(t) - \xi(t) \rangle$$

which converges to

$$\langle F(t) - \bar{\lambda}(t), \xi(t) \rangle, \quad \forall \xi(t) \leq 0.$$

Hence $F(t) - \bar{\lambda}(t)$ is greater than or equal to 0. In fact, if there exists a subset E of $[0,T]$ with positive measure where $F(t) - \bar{\lambda}(t) < 0$, when we choose
$$\xi(t) = \begin{cases} F(t) - \bar{\lambda}(t) & \text{in } E \\ 0 & \text{otherwise,} \end{cases}$$
we get $\langle F(t) - \bar{\lambda}(t), F(t) - \bar{\lambda}(t) \rangle > 0$, which is an absurdity.

Analogously we can prove that $w - \limsup\limits_n G_n \subset Y$. It remains to prove that
$$w - \limsup_i F_{n_i} \subset Z,$$
where $F_{n_i} = \bigcap\limits_j F_j^n$ and

$$F_j^n = \left\{ F(t) \in L^2([0,T], \mathbb{R}^m) : \text{ piecewise constant:} \right.$$
$$\left. \Phi F(t) = \mu_{j,n_i} \rho(t) \right\}.$$
So we have to prove that, if $F_{n_i}(t) \in F_{n_i}$ and $w - \lim\limits_i F_{n_i}(t) = F(t)$, then $\Phi F(t) = \rho(t)$ a.e. in $L^2([0,T], \mathbb{R}^m)$.

Since $\Phi F_{n_i} = \mu_{n_i} \rho(t)$, then we have:
$$\langle \Phi F_{n_i}, \xi(t) \rangle = \langle \mu_{n_i} \rho(t), \xi(t) \rangle \quad \forall i, \ \forall \xi(t) \in L^2([0,T], \mathbb{R}^m).$$

Moreover, since F_{n_i} weakly converges to F and $\mu_{n_i} \rho(t)$ converges to $\rho(t)$ (also strongly), by Lemma 2.5.1, it follows
$$\langle \Phi F(t), \xi(t) \rangle = \langle \rho(t), \xi(t) \rangle \quad \forall \xi \in L^2([0,T], \mathbb{R}^m),$$
that is
$$\langle \Phi F(t) - \rho(t), \xi(t) \rangle = 0.$$
Finally, if we choose $\xi(t) = \Phi F(t) - \rho(t)$, it follows
$$\Phi F(t) - \rho(t) = 0$$
and the assertion is proved.   □

Let us come back now to our problem of finding $H(t) \in \mathbb{K}(t)$:

$$\int_0^T \langle C[t, H(t)], F(t) - H(t) \rangle \, dt \geq 0, \quad \forall F(t) \in \mathbb{K}(t) \qquad (2.37)$$

and, $\forall F(t) \in \mathbb{K}(t)$, consider $F_n(t) \in \mathbb{K}_n$ such that $F_n(t) \to F(t)$ (strongly). Such an $F_n(t)$ exists because of the first part of the proof of Lemma 2.5.2. $\forall n \in \mathbb{N}$ let us consider a solution $H_n(t)$ to the variational inequality (2.32).

We are now able to prove the final result.

Theorem 2.5.3 *Let $A(t)$ be positive definite a.e. in $[0,T]$. Then the sequence $H_n(t)$ defined in (2.30) admits weak cluster points. Each cluster point is feasible and solves the original variational inequality.*

Proof: From the proof of Theorem 2.5.2, the set $H_n(t)$ is norm bounded, hence weakly compact. If $\bar{H}(t)$ is a cluster point for $H_n(t)$, then it is an element of $\mathbb{K}$ because of the second part of the proof of Lemma 2.5.2. Then, using the same inequalities chain as in Theorem 2.5.2, we get that $\bar{H}(t)$ solves the original variational inequality (2.37). □

In order to highlight the discretization method we have just illustrated, we examine now the following example.

Example 2.5.2

Assume we have a traffic network consisting of one O/D pair and two paths connecting the two nodes. Define the following matrix and vectors:

$$A(t) = \begin{bmatrix} 2+t & 0 \\ 0 & 1 \end{bmatrix}, \quad F(t) = \begin{bmatrix} F_1(t) \\ F_2(t) \end{bmatrix}, \quad B(t) = \begin{bmatrix} -\dfrac{3}{2} \\ -1 \end{bmatrix}$$

and the set of feasible flows:

$$\mathbb{K} = \left\{ F \in L^2([0,2], \mathbb{R}^2) : \ 0 \le F_1(t) \le t; \ 0 \le F_2(t) \le 3; \right.$$
$$\left. F_1(t) + F_2(t) = t \ \text{a.e. in } [0,2] \right\}.$$

Let us consider a partition of the time interval $[0,2]$ by means of the points:

$$0 < \frac{2}{n} < \frac{4}{n} < \ldots < (j-1)\frac{2}{n} < j\frac{2}{n} < \ldots < (n-1)\frac{2}{n} < 2$$

such that $t_j^n - t_{j-1}^n = \dfrac{2}{n}$, $\forall j = 1, \ldots, n$. Let us consider the variational inequality (2.27):

$$\langle A_j^n H_j^n + B_j^n, F_j^n - H_j^n \rangle \ge 0 \quad \forall F_j^n \in \mathbb{K}_j^n$$

where

$$\mathbb{K}_j^n = \left\{ F_j^n \in \mathbb{R}^2 : 0 \le F_{j1}^n \le \frac{n}{2} \int_{(j-1)\frac{2}{n}}^{j\frac{2}{n}} t \, dt; \right.$$

$$\left. 0 \le F_{j2}^n \le \frac{n}{2} \int_{(j-1)\frac{2}{n}}^{j\frac{2}{n}} 3 \, dt; \quad F_{j1}^n + F_{j2}^n = \frac{n}{2} \int_{(j-1)\frac{2}{n}}^{j\frac{2}{n}} t \, dt \right\}$$

$$= \left\{ F_j^n \in \mathbb{R}^2 : \ 0 \le F_{j1}^n \le \frac{2j-1}{n}; \ 0 \le F_{j2}^n \le 3; \ F_{j1}^n + F_{j2}^n = \frac{2j-1}{n} \right\},$$

and $\mathbb{K}_n = \bigcap_j \mathbb{K}_j^n$. So we have:

$$\frac{n}{2} \int_{(j-1)\frac{2}{n}}^{j\frac{2}{n}} \left\{ \left[(2+t) H_{j1}^n - \frac{3}{2} \right] \cdot \left(F_{j1}^n - H_{j1}^n \right) \right.$$

$$\left. + \left(H_{j2}^n - 1 \right) \cdot \left(F_{j2}^n - H_{j2}^n \right) \right\} dt$$

$$= \left[\left(2 + \frac{2j-1}{n} \right) H_{j1}^n - \frac{3}{2} \right] \left(F_{j1}^n - H_{j1}^n \right) + \left(H_{j2}^n - 1 \right) \left(F_{j2}^n - H_{j2}^n \right) \ge 0$$

$$\forall F_j^n \in \mathbb{K}_j^n. \tag{2.38}$$

We are now able to solve (2.38) by means of the direct method. If we substitute $F_{j2}^n = \dfrac{2j-1}{n} - F_{j1}^n$ in the variational inequality, then we obtain:

$$\left[\left(2 + \frac{2j-1}{n} \right) H_{j1}^n - \frac{3}{2} - \frac{2j-1}{n} + H_{j1}^n + 1 \right] \left(F_{j1}^n - H_{j1}^n \right) \ge 0,$$

from which:

$$\left(3 + \frac{2j-1}{n} \right) H_{j1}^n - \frac{2j-1}{n} - \frac{1}{2} = 0 \implies H_{j1}^n = \frac{4j-2+n}{2(3n+2j-1)}.$$

Condition $H_{j1}^n \le \dfrac{(2j-1)}{n}$ is satisfied if and only if

$$n^2 - 4(2j-1)n - 2(2j-1)^2 \le 0 \iff 1 \le n \le (2+\sqrt{6})(2j-1).$$

Hence, the solution is given by:

$$H_{j1}^n = \begin{cases} \dfrac{2j-1}{n} & \text{if } 1 \le j < \dfrac{1}{2}\left(1 + \dfrac{n}{2+\sqrt{6}}\right), \\[3mm] \dfrac{4j-2+n}{2(3n+2j-1)} & \text{if } j > \dfrac{1}{2}\left(1 + \dfrac{n}{2+\sqrt{6}}\right), \end{cases}$$

$$\text{(2.39)}$$

$$H_{j2}^n = \begin{cases} 0 & \text{if } 1 \le j < \dfrac{1}{2}\left(1 + \dfrac{n}{2+\sqrt{6}}\right), \\[3mm] \dfrac{-n^2 + 4(2j-1)n + 2(2j-1)^2}{2n(3n+2j-1)} & \text{if } j > \dfrac{1}{2}\left(1 + \dfrac{n}{2+\sqrt{6}}\right). \end{cases}$$

Finally, the approximation to the solution is:

$$H_n(t) = \sum_{j=1}^n \chi_{[(j-1)\frac{2}{n}, j\frac{2}{n}]} H_j^n$$

where H_j^n is given by (2.39).

If we solve the initial problem by means of the direct method, then taking into account Remark 2.2.1, the variational inequality we have to solve is the following:

$$\left[(2+t)\,H_1(t) - \frac{3}{2}\right][F_1(t) - H_1(t)] + [H_2(t) - 1]\,[F_2(t) - H_2(t)] \ge 0$$

$$\forall F(t) \in \mathbb{K} = \{F \in L^2([0,2], \mathbb{R}^2) : \ 0 \le F_1(t) \le t;$$
$$0 \le F_2(t) \le 3; \ F_1(t) + F_2(t) = t, \text{ a.e. in } [0,2]\}.$$

So, if we substitute $F_2(t) = t - F_1(t)$, then the set of feasible flows becomes:

$$\tilde{\mathbb{K}} = \{F_1(t) \in L^2([0,2], \mathbb{R}) : \ 0 \le F_1(t) \le t\}$$

and the variational inequality becomes:

$$\left[(2+t)\,H_1(t) - \frac{3}{2} - t + H_1(t) + 1\right][F_1(t) - H_1(t)] \ge 0 \quad \forall F_1(t) \in \tilde{\mathbb{K}}.$$

Solving the system

$$\begin{cases} \Gamma[H_1(t)] = 3(2+t)H_1(t) - t - \dfrac{1}{2} = 0 \\ H_1(t) \in \tilde{\mathbb{K}}, \end{cases}$$

we obtain the exact solution:

$$
\begin{cases}
H_1(t) = \begin{cases}
t & \text{if} \quad 0 \leq t \leq \dfrac{\sqrt{6}}{2} - 1, \\[2mm]
\dfrac{2t+1}{2t+6} & \text{if} \quad \dfrac{\sqrt{6}}{2} - 1 < t \leq 2,
\end{cases} \\[6mm]
H_2(t) = \begin{cases}
0 & \text{if} \quad 0 \leq t \leq \dfrac{\sqrt{6}}{2} - 1, \\[2mm]
\dfrac{2t^2 + 4t - 1}{2t+6} & \text{if} \quad \dfrac{\sqrt{6}}{2} - 1 < t \leq 2.
\end{cases}
\end{cases}
$$

Then the theory ensures that the sequence $(H_1^n(t), H_2^n(t))$ weakly converges to $(H_1(t), H_2(t))$.

2.6   Delay and Elastic Model

In the papers [61], [137], [146] the authors have recently introduced delay effects in traffic network models, developing them within the variational framework. Since the information through the network travels at finite speed, then the users take a certain time before adjusting their path choices and reaching an equilibrium state. As a consequence, it is reasonable to think that demand requirements at time t are satisfied only at time $t + h$, namely after a delay $h > 0$. In reality, the delay should depend on the variable t, but, for the sake of simplicity, it is assumed that it has a constant positive value.

The following definition (see [137]) represents Wardrop's user principle in a constrained and time-dependent setting.

Definition 2.6.1 *A flow $H \in L^2([0,T], \mathbb{R}^m_+)$ is said to be a retarded equilibrium if and only if $\forall w_j \in \mathcal{W}, \forall q, s \in \mathcal{R}_j$ and a.e. in $[0,T]$:*

$$
C_q(t, H(t+h)) < C_s(t, H(t+h)) \Rightarrow
$$
$$
H_q(t+h) = \mu_q(t+h) \text{ or } H_s(t+h) = \lambda_s(t+h). \tag{2.40}
$$

Definition 2.6.1 has the following meaning: when users realize that path q is more convenient than path s, they are led to change their path choices and the resulting distribution of flows will be either maximum on q, or minimum on s. Nevertheless, since the shift to the less costly path occurs only after a finite time, there is a gap, that is a delay h, between the recognition of the preferable path and the adjustment of the choices. Moreover, the equilibrium definition perfectly agrees with Definition 3 in [61], which introduces the concept of simultaneous path-departure equilibrium.

In order to describe and analyze the departure rates in the model, the following condition is assumed to hold:

$$\lim_{|h| \to 0} \int_0^T |F(t+h) - F(t)|^2 \, dt = 0, \tag{2.41}$$

uniformly in F, namely $\forall \varepsilon > 0 \; \exists \delta > 0$ such that $\forall h \in \mathbb{R}$, $|h| < \delta$ and $\forall F$

$$\int_0^T |F(t+h) - F(t)|^2 \, dt < \varepsilon,$$

provided that $F(t) = 0$ if $t \notin [0, T]$.

The regularity condition (2.41) may be interpreted as the uniform integral continuity of flow rates, which must be maintained through all the paths and ensures a real control on departure rates.

As in [61] and [147], let $v(t)$ denote the flow rate, namely the derivative of the path flow which enters the first link of the path at time t:

$$\frac{d}{dt} F_r(t+h) = v_r(t) \text{ a.e. in } [0, T], \; r = 1, \ldots, m.$$

As a consequence, condition (2.41) is obviously satisfied if, for instance,

$$\exists \eta \in \mathbb{R}_+ : \|v(t)\|_{L^2} \leq \eta \; \forall v(t) = (v_1(t), \ldots, v_m(t))^T$$

or if the flows verify an integral Hölder condition:

$$\int_0^T |F(t+h) - F(t)|^2 \, dt \leq L|h|^\alpha, \; 0 < \alpha \leq 1, \; L \in \mathbb{R}_+.$$

Until now we have dealt with traffic equilibrium models with fixed travel demands, but this kind of approach corresponds to studying only a first approximation of the problem. In fact it is clear that travel demands are influenced by the evaluation of the amount of traffic flows on the paths, namely by the forecasted equilibrium solutions. For this reason some authors (see, for instance, [49], [50], [130]), by means of different approaches, have been interested in the so-called elastic models, in which the demands depend on the equilibrium solution. Here we present an approach in which the demand requirements are given on average with respect to the time, namely $\rho = \dfrac{1}{T} \displaystyle\int_0^T \rho(t, H(\tau))\, dt$ (see [44] and [147]). In fact, travel demands are supposed to depend on the user's evaluation of the flows. So one can expect that travelers evaluate the network practicability not instant by instant, but by an average with respect to the whole time interval.

Under this perspective, the set of feasible flows becomes as follows. Let

$$E = \Big\{ F(t + h) \in L^2\left([0, T], \mathbb{R}^m_+\right) :$$

$$\lambda_r(t + h) \le F_r(t + h) \le \mu_r(t + h) \text{ a.e. in } [0, T], r = 1, \dots, m;$$

$$\lim_{|h| \to 0} \int_0^T |F(t + h) - F(t)|^2\, dt = 0 \text{ uniformly in } F,$$

$$F(t) = 0 \text{ if } t \notin [0, T] \Big\},$$

hence the set of feasible flows is given by:

$$\mathbb{K}_h(H) = \Big\{ F(t + h) \in E : \sum_{r=1}^m \varphi_{jr} F_r(t + h) = \frac{1}{T} \int_0^T \rho_j(t, H(\tau))\, d\tau$$

$$\text{a.e. in } [0, T], \ j = 1, \dots, l \Big\}.$$

The following theorem (see also [137] and [146]) establishes a complete characterization of the retarded equilibrium flow by means of the variational formulation.

Theorem 2.6.1 *A feasible flow is a retarded equilibrium flow if and only if it solves the following retarded quasi-variational inequality (RQVI):*

$$H \in \mathbb{K}_h(H), \ \int_0^T \langle C(t, H(t + h)), F(t + h) - H(t + h) \rangle\, dt \ge 0,$$

$$\forall F \in \mathbb{K}_h(H).$$

It is worth remarking that in this case we have obtained a quasi-variational inequality, for which we can provide an existence theorem.

In order to obtain an existence theorem for the solutions to the retarded equilibrium problem with capacity constraints, we have to recall first the L^2-version of Ascoli's theorem, due to Riesz, Fréchet and Kolmogorov (see [10]), adapted to our case.

Theorem 2.6.2 *Let $\mathcal{F}$ be a bounded set in $L^2(0,T)$. Suppose that*

$$\lim_{|h|\to 0} \|F(t+h) - F(t)\|_{L^2} = 0 \quad uniformly\ in\ F \in \mathcal{F},$$

provided that $F(t) = 0$ if $t \notin [0,T]$. Then $\mathcal{F}$ has compact closure in $L^2(0,T)$.

Now, we get the following result (see [146]).

Theorem 2.6.3 *Let*

$$C : [0,T] \times \mathbb{R}_+^m \to \mathbb{R}_+^m \ and \ \rho : [0,T] \times \mathbb{R}_+^m \to \mathbb{R}_+^l$$

satisfy the following conditions:

(a) $C(t,v)$ is measurable in t $\forall v \in \mathbb{R}_+^m$, continuous in v for t a.e. in $[0,T]$, $\exists \gamma \in L^2(0,T) : |C(t,v)| \leq \gamma(t) + |v|$;

(b) $\rho(t,v)$ is measurable in t $\forall v \in \mathbb{R}_+^m$, continuous in v for t a.e. in $[0,T]$, $\exists \psi \in L^1(0,T) : |\rho(t,v)| \leq \psi(t) + |v|^2$;

(c) $\exists \nu(t) \geq 0$ a.e. in $[0,T]$, $\nu \in L^2(0,T)$: $\forall v_1, v_2 \in \mathbb{R}_+^m$, $|\rho(t,v_1) - \rho(t,v_2)| \leq \nu(t)|v_1 - v_2|$.

Then the RQVI admits a solution.

Sketch of the proof: A detailed proof can be found in [49] and [146]. We report here only the main steps. At first, we observe that under the hypotheses *(a)* and *(b)* and if $H(t+h) \in L^2(0,T;\mathbb{R}_+^m)$, it results that

$$C(t, H(t+h)) \in L^2(0,T;\mathbb{R}_+^m) \ and \ \rho(t, H(t)) \in L^1(0,T;\mathbb{R}_+^l).$$

Moreover, by *(a)* and *(b)* it follows that C and ρ belong to the class of Nemytskii operators.

Therefore if $\{H^n\} \xrightarrow{L^2} H$, then

$$\|C(t, H^n(t + h)) - C(t, H(t + h))\|_{L^2} \to 0,$$

$$\|\rho(t, H^n(t)) - \rho(t, H(t))\|_{L^1} \to 0,$$

and the functions C and ρ are L^2- and L^1-continuous respectively.

Now, in order to prove that $\mathbb{K}_h(H)$ is a closed multifunction, the following condition is shown:

$$\forall\{H^n\} \xrightarrow{L^2} H, \ \forall\{F^n\} \xrightarrow{L^2} F \text{ with } F^n \in \mathbb{K}_h(H^n) \ \forall n \in \mathbb{N},$$

then $F \in \mathbb{K}_h(H)$.

Let $\{H^n\}$, $\{F^n\}$ be two arbitrary convergent sequences in $L^2([0, T])$. Since $F^n \in \mathbb{K}_h(H^n)$, it results that:

$$\lambda_r(t + h) \leq F_r^n(t + h) \leq \mu_r(t + h) \text{ a.e. in } [0, T], \ r = 1, 2, \ldots, m,$$

and the convergence of the sequence $\{F^n\}$ in L^2 implies that even F satisfies capacity constraints. It can be easily proved that F verifies (2.41), since F^n satisfies the above assumption and L^2-converges to F.

Moreover, the following relationship holds:

$$\sum_{r=1}^{m} \varphi_{jr} F_r^n(t + h) = \frac{1}{T} \int_0^T \rho_j(t, H^n(\tau)) d\tau \text{ a.e. in } [0, T], \ j = 1, 2, \ldots, l.$$

The left-hand side converges almost everywhere to $\displaystyle\sum_{r=1}^{m} \varphi_{jr} F_r(t + h)$; the right-hand side, meanwhile, results in:

$$\left| \int_0^T \rho_j(t, H^n(\tau)) d\tau - \int_0^T \rho_j(t, H(\tau)) d\tau \right|$$

$$\leq \int_0^T |\rho_j(t, H^n(\tau)) - \rho_j(t, H(\tau))| d\tau$$

$$\leq \nu(t) \int_0^T |H^n(\tau) - H(\tau)| d\tau.$$

By applying condition (c) and considering that the convergence of $\{H^n\}$ in L^2 implies convergence even in L^1, the assertion is achieved.

In order to show the lower semi-continuity of $\mathbb{K}_h(H)$, it is sufficient to prove that $\forall \{H^n\} \xrightarrow{L^2} H$, $\forall F \in \mathbb{K}_h(H)$ there exists $\{F^n\}$ such that:

$$\{F^n\} \xrightarrow{L^2} F \text{ with } F^n \in \mathbb{K}_h(H^n) \ \forall n \in \mathbb{N}$$

and we refer to [49] and [146] for this result. $\square$

In 1993 Friesz *et al.* (see [61]) studied a dynamic traffic model, found an equilibrium condition consistent with Wardrop's user equilibrium principle and also established that the users are allowed to choose their own paths as well as the departure times. If we apply the first-in-first-out (FIFO) queue discipline to our model with delay, we have to require that, on average, the traffic which enters the first link of a path will exit first, or equivalently that vehicles do not pass each other. In [61] the authors have shown that the FIFO type behavior is ensured by the invertibility of exit time functions. Moreover, it is proved that for any linear traversal time function the resulting exit time function is strictly increasing and hence invertible. Let $D_r(t) = \alpha_r\, t + \beta_r\, h$, $\alpha, \beta \in \mathbb{R}_+^m$ denote the traversal time for path r, assuming that the departure time from the origin is $t = 0$. Let also $\tau_r(t) = t + D_r(t)$ be the exit time function for path r. Since $D_r(t) = \alpha_r\, t + \beta_r\, h$, it follows that the invertibility of exit time functions is ensured and FIFO requirements are satisfied.

Throughout this section a formulation with path-flow variables is adopted, nevertheless path traversal functions can be expressed in terms of link traversal functions. In fact, it is easy to see that, if $\theta_a(t)$ is the exit time function on link a, then $D_r(t) = \displaystyle\sum_{a=1}^{n} \delta_{ar}\, [\theta_a(t) - \theta_{a-1}(t)]$.

In addition, it is worth observing that congestion effects are also expressed by means of some additional constraints on link flows. For this aim, consider the following relationship

$$G(t)f(t) \leq g(t) \text{ or } G(t)\Delta F(t) \leq g(t), \tag{2.42}$$

where G is an opportune matrix and g is a vector, both depending on time. Let us define the set:

$$D = \{F \in L^2([0,T]; \mathbb{R}_+^m) : G(t)\Delta F(t) \leq g(t) \text{ a.e. in } [0,T]\},$$

then the constraints (2.42) on link flows are described in terms of path flows and each feasible flow satisfies the requirement $F \in \mathbb{K}_h \cap D$. Such a new problem may then be solved by means of the Lagrangean functional, whose multipliers represent the queue delays on the paths; see [46], [58], [89], [100].

Example 2.6.1

Consider the network as in Figure 2.3, where $N = \{P_1, P_2, P_3, P_4\}$ is the set of nodes and $L = \{(P_1, P_2), (P_1, P_3), (P_2, P_4), (P_4, P_3)\}$ is the set of links.

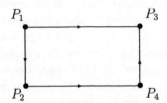

Figure 2.3: Rectangular network

The origin–destination pair is represented by (P_1, P_3), so that the paths are the following ones:

$$R_1 = (P_1, P_3) \quad \text{and} \quad R_2 = (P_1, P_2) \cup (P_2, P_4) \cup (P_4, P_3).$$

The path costs are:

$$C_1(F(t)) = \beta F_1(t) + \alpha \quad \text{and} \quad C_2(F(t)) = 2\beta F_2(t) + \alpha,$$

where $\alpha, \beta \geq 0$.

The set of feasible flows is given by:

$$\mathbb{K}(H) = \left\{ F(t) = (F_1(t), F_2(t)) \in L^2([0,T]; \mathbb{R}^2_+) : \right.$$

$$\frac{\gamma t}{4} + \frac{\delta \gamma T}{8(3 - 2\delta)} \leq F_1(t) \leq 3\gamma t + \frac{7\delta \gamma T}{3 - 2\delta} \quad \text{a.e. in } [0, T];$$

$$\frac{\gamma t}{4} + \frac{\delta \gamma T}{8(3 - 2\delta)} \leq F_2(t) \leq \gamma t + \frac{\delta \gamma T}{3 - 2\delta} \quad \text{a.e. in } [0, T];$$

$$\left. F_1(t) + F_2(t) = \frac{1}{T} \int_0^T (\gamma t + \delta H_1(\tau)) \, d\tau \text{ a.e. in } [0, T] \right\},$$

where $\gamma \geq 0$, and $0 \leq \delta < \dfrac{3}{2}$. The equilibrium flow is the solution to the quasi-variational inequality:

$$H \in \mathbb{K}(H) : \quad \int_0^T \sum_{r=1}^{2} C_r(H(t))(F_r(t) - H_r(t)) \, dt \geq 0, \quad \forall F \in \mathbb{K}(H).$$

Following the procedure shown in [50] and [95], one has:

$$F_2(t) = \frac{1}{T} \int_0^T (\gamma t + \delta H_1(\tau)) \, d\tau - F_1(t),$$

the set of feasible flows becomes:

$$\tilde{\mathbb{K}}(H) = \left\{ \tilde{F}(t) \in L^2([0,T], \mathbb{R}_+) : \right.$$

$$\frac{\gamma t}{4} + \frac{\delta \gamma T}{8(2 - \delta)} \leq F_1(t) \leq 3\gamma t + \frac{3\delta \gamma T}{2 - \delta} \quad \text{a.e. in } [0,T];$$

$$\frac{1}{T} \int_0^T (\gamma t + \delta H_1(\tau)) \, d\tau - \left(\gamma t + \frac{\delta \gamma T}{3 - 2\delta} \right) \leq F_1(t)$$

$$\leq \frac{1}{T} \int_0^T (\gamma t + \delta H_1(\tau)) \, d\tau - \left(\frac{\gamma t}{4} + \frac{\delta \gamma T}{8(3 - 2\delta)} \right) \quad \text{a.e. in } [0,T] \left. \right\},$$

and

$$\begin{aligned}
\Gamma(\tilde{H}(t)) &= C_1(\tilde{H}(t)) - C_2(\tilde{H}(t)) \\
&= 3\beta H_1(t) - \frac{2\beta}{T} \int_0^T (\gamma t + \delta H_1(\tau)) \, d\tau.
\end{aligned}$$

Thus, the problem is written as:

$$\tilde{H} \in \tilde{\mathbb{K}}(\tilde{H}) : \quad \int_0^T \Gamma(\tilde{H}(t))(\tilde{F}(t) - \tilde{H}(t)) \, dt \geq 0, \quad \forall \tilde{F} \in \tilde{\mathbb{K}}(\tilde{H}). \quad (2.43)$$

It is necessary to show that we have to solve the system

$$\begin{cases} \Gamma(\tilde{H}) = 3\beta H_1(t) - \dfrac{2\beta}{T} \displaystyle\int_0^T (\gamma t + \delta H_1(\tau)) \, d\tau = 0 \\ \tilde{H} \in \tilde{\mathbb{K}}(\tilde{H}), \end{cases} \quad (2.44)$$

in order to find the solution $\tilde{H}(t)$ to the quasi-variational inequality (2.43). Solving the system (2.44), we get:

$$3H_1(t) = \frac{2}{T} \int_0^T (\gamma t + \delta H_1(\tau)) \, d\tau$$

and hence:

$$3H_1(t) = 2\gamma t + \frac{2\delta}{T} \int_0^T H_1(\tau) \, d\tau. \qquad (2.45)$$

By integrating with respect to t in $[0, T]$, we have:

$$3 \int_0^T H_1(t) \, dt = 2\gamma \left[\frac{t^2}{2}\right]_0^T + 2\delta \int_0^T H_1(\tau) \, d\tau$$

and therefore:

$$\int_0^T H_1(\tau) \, d\tau = \frac{\gamma T^2}{3 - 2\delta}.$$

So, from (2.45) it results:

$$H_1(t) = \frac{2\gamma t}{3} + \frac{2\delta\gamma T}{3(3 - 2\delta)} \quad \text{and} \quad H_2(t) = \frac{1}{2}H_1(t) = \frac{\gamma t}{3} + \frac{\delta\gamma T}{3(3 - 2\delta)},$$

under the constraints

$$\frac{\gamma t}{2} + \frac{\delta\gamma T}{4(3 - 2\delta)} \leq H_1(t) \leq 2\gamma t + \frac{2\delta\gamma T}{3 - 2\delta}.$$

Now, after introducing a delay $h \in \left[0, \frac{T}{4}\right]$, the new set of feasible flows is given by:

$$\mathbb{K}_h(H) = \left\{ F(t+h) = (F_1(t+h), F_2(t+h)) \in L^2([0,T]; \mathbb{R}_+^2) : \right.$$

$$\frac{\gamma t}{4} + \frac{\delta \gamma (T-2h)}{8(3-2\delta)} \leq F_1(t+h) \leq 3\gamma t + \frac{7\delta \gamma (T-2h)}{3-2\delta} \quad \text{a.e. in } [0,T],$$

$$\frac{\gamma t}{4} + \frac{\delta \gamma (T-2h)}{8(3-2\delta)} \leq F_2(t+h) \leq \gamma t + \frac{\delta \gamma (T-2h)}{3-2\delta} \quad \text{a.e. in } [0,T],$$

$$F_1(t+h) + F_2(t+h) = \frac{1}{T} \int_0^T (\gamma t + \delta H_1(\tau)) \, d\tau \text{ a.e. in } [0,T];$$

$$\lim_{|h| \to 0} \int_0^T |F(t+h) - F(t)|^2 \, dt = 0 \text{ uniformly in } F,$$

$$\left. F(t) = 0, \text{ if } t \notin [0,T] \right\}.$$

The equilibrium flow is the solution to the quasi-variational inequality:

$$\int_0^T \sum_{r=1}^2 C_r(H(t+h))(F_r(t+h) - H_r(t+h)) \, dt \geq 0 \quad \forall F \in \mathbb{K}_h(H). \quad (2.46)$$

Let:

$$F_2(t+h) = \frac{1}{T} \int_0^T (\gamma t + \delta H_1(\tau)) \, d\tau - F_1(t+h),$$

then the set of feasible flows becomes:

$$\tilde{\mathbb{K}}_h(H) = \left\{ \tilde{F}(t+h) \in L^2([0,T], \mathbb{R}_+) : \right.$$

$$\frac{\gamma t}{4} + \frac{\delta \gamma (T-2h)}{8(3-2\delta)} \leq F_1(t+h) \leq 3\gamma t + \frac{7\delta \gamma (T-2h)}{3-2\delta} \quad \text{a.e. in } [0,T];$$

$$\frac{1}{T} \int_0^T (\gamma t + \delta H_1(\tau)) \, d\tau - \left(\gamma t + \frac{\delta \gamma (T-2h)}{3-2\delta} \right) \leq F_1(t)$$

$$\leq \frac{1}{T} \int_0^T (\gamma t + \delta H_1(\tau)) \, d\tau - \left(\frac{\gamma t}{4} + \frac{\delta \gamma (T-2h)}{8(3-2\delta)} \right) \quad \text{a.e. in } [0,T];$$

$$\lim_{|h| \to 0} \int_0^T |F_1(t+h) - F_1(t)|^2 \, dt = 0 \text{ uniformly in } F,$$

$$\left. F(t) = 0, \text{ if } t \notin [0,T] \right\},$$

and the problem is written as:

$$\tilde{H} \in \tilde{\mathbb{K}}_h(\tilde{H}) : \quad \int_0^T \Gamma(\tilde{H}(t+h))(\tilde{F}(t+h) - \tilde{H}(t+h))\, dt \geq 0$$

$$\forall \tilde{F} \in \tilde{\mathbb{K}}_h(\tilde{H}), \tag{2.47}$$

where

$$\begin{aligned}
\Gamma(\tilde{H}(t+h)) &= C_1(\tilde{H}(t+h)) - C_2(\tilde{H}(t+h)) \\
&= 3\,\beta\, H_1(t+h) - \frac{2\beta}{T} \int_0^T (\gamma t + \delta\, H_1(\tau))\, d\tau.
\end{aligned}$$

If $\tilde{H}(t+h)$ satisfies the system:

$$\begin{cases} \Gamma(\tilde{H}) = 3\,\beta\, H_1(t+h) - \dfrac{2\beta}{T} \displaystyle\int_0^T (\gamma t + \delta\, H_1(\tau))\, d\tau = 0 \\[2mm] \tilde{H} \in \tilde{\mathbb{K}}_h(\tilde{H}), \end{cases} \tag{2.48}$$

then it solves the retarded variational inequality (2.47). Solving the system (2.48), we get:

$$3\, H_1(t+h) = \frac{2}{T} \int_0^T (\gamma t + \delta\, H_1(\tau))\, d\tau$$

and hence:

$$3\, H_1(t+h) = 2\gamma t + \frac{2\delta}{T} \int_0^T H_1(\tau)\, d\tau. \tag{2.49}$$

By integrating with respect to t in $[-h, T-h]$, we have:

$$3 \int_{-h}^{T-h} H_1(t+h)\, dt = 2\gamma \int_{-h}^{T-h} t\, dt + \frac{2\delta}{T} \int_0^T H_1(\tau)\, d\tau \int_{-h}^{T-h} dt.$$

If we set $t + h = \tau$, then the previous integral becomes:

$$3 \int_0^T H_1(\tau)\, d\tau = 2\gamma \left[\frac{(\tau - h)^2}{2} \right]_0^T + 2\delta \int_0^T H_1(\tau)\, d\tau,$$

from which:

$$\int_0^T H_1(\tau)\, d\tau = \frac{\gamma\,(T^2 - 2\,h\,T)}{3 - 2\,\delta}.$$

So, from (2.49) it results:

$$
\begin{cases}
H_1(t+h) &= \dfrac{2\gamma t}{3} + \dfrac{2\delta\gamma\,(T-2h)}{3(3-2\delta)} \\[4mm]
H_2(t+h) &= \dfrac{1}{2}H_1(t+h) = \dfrac{\gamma t}{3} + \dfrac{\delta\gamma\,(T-2h)}{3(3-2\delta)},
\end{cases}
$$

under the constraints:

$$
\frac{\gamma t}{2} + \frac{\delta\gamma\,(T-2h)}{4(3-2\delta)} \leq H_1(t+h) \leq 2\gamma t + \frac{2\delta\gamma\,(T-2h)}{3-2\delta}.
$$

It is worth highlighting that the retarded equilibrium depends explicitly on the delay h and the flow rate is finite, since it results that:

$$
\frac{d}{dt}H_1(t+h) = \frac{2}{3}\gamma, \quad \text{and} \quad \frac{d}{dt}H_2(t+h) = \frac{1}{3}\gamma.
$$

2.7 Sources and Remarks

In the literature the time-dependent variational inequalities have been introduced first in a pioneering paper by Lions and Stampacchia [91], in the study of equilibrium problems such as the obstacle problem, Signorini problem, etc., for parabolic partial differential equations. The theory and the results presented in this chapter originated in the papers by Daniele *et al.* (see [45], [46]), by Maugeri (see [97]) and in the following papers by Raciti (see [138], [139], [140]). These papers have laid the foundations of the theory of time-dependent variational inequalities for the traffic equilibrium network problems and for the calculation of solutions using different methods appropriate for the evolutionary problems. We have also to mention the paper by Friesz *et al.* (see [61]), who, using different approaches and proofs, have reached the same variational inequality in the functional space L^2. Moreover, they perform an analysis of the FIFO queue discipline, under suitable regularity conditions (see also [147]).

Following the approach of [61], Bliemer and Bovy propose in [7] a calculus of the solution for a time-dependent variational inequality using a discretization procedure and a finite quasi-variational inequality.

Another more general paper on the same topic is [147] where Scrimali considers the more realistic case of presence of delay effects. Then the author proposes a variational approach (see also [69], [96], [98] and [148]) to the corresponding traffic equilibrium problem and shows an equivalence between the variational inequality formulation and the retarded equilibrium condition. Moreover, Scrimali analyzes the elastic case, namely the one where the demand depends on the solution (as a kind of 'intelligent departures'), and she proves that this model is equivalent to a quasi-variational inequality for which existence results are proved (see also [23], [24] and [31] for general existence results).

Other papers devoted to traffic equilibrium networks are [42] and [59], where the authors deal with a continuum model and a framework with capacity constraints respectively.

In [77] Gwinner provides a survey of several classes of time-dependent variational inequalities that model various constrained evolution problems and time-dependent variational inequalities with memory terms (see also [152]).

The time-dependent traffic equilibrium problem will be treated again in Chapter 5, which introduces the Projected Dynamical System theory. There we shall see that such a problem can be inserted into a more general framework and we also develop another method for the calculation of the solution.

Chapter 3

Evolutionary Spatial Price Equilibrium

3.1 The Price Formulation

3.1.1 The Static Model

In this section we present the static model of the spatial price equilibrium problem in order to provide some important features useful for understanding the time-dependent case. We consider first the spatial price equilibrium problem in the case of the so-called price formulation in the presence of supply and demand excesses (see also [131]). In Section 3.2 we shall deal with another approach to the same problem, that is the quantity formulation.

The equilibrium conditions that describe this 'disequilibrium' model (we use the term 'disequilibrium' to highlight the presence of the supply and demand excesses) in the case of price formulation are expressed in terms of variational inequalities, for which the existence of solutions is provided by means of general existence results. In addition, a calculation of the solution is performed using different methods.

This more general and realistic model, which generalizes the classical spatial price equilibrium problems formulated by Cournot in [22], Pigou in [135], Enke in [57], Samuelson in [143], Takayama and Judge in [153], Nagurney in [108], Nagurney and Zhao in [130], and Gwinner in [76], adopts, unchanged, the concept of equilibrium, namely that the demand price is equal to the supply price plus the cost of transportation, if there is trade between the pair of supply and demand markets.

It is worth remarking that this classical equilibrium principle follows the user-optimized approach instead of the system-optimized one and that these different approaches have been first noted by Pigou in [135].

Moreover, Enke in [57] established the connection between spatial price equilibrium problems and electronic circuit networks, and Takayama and Judge in [153] presented many potential applications, for example, to study problems in agriculture, in finance, in mineral economics, etc.

In this section we also deal with the Lagrangean theory of the model and, as an interesting consequence, we obtain that Lagrangean variables provide the excesses of supply and of demand, which represent important features of the economic problem. Moreover, we provide a dual formulation of the equilibrium conditions (see also [13], [29] and [63]) where among the dual variables there are the supply and demand excesses. These results have a remarkable importance since the price model can never be symmetric (see [26]), and hence can never be cast into an equivalent convex minimization problem in the usual sense, namely without an appeal to some kind of Gap function or to the Lagrangean theory.

We consider a single commodity that is produced at n supply markets and consumed at m demand markets. There is a total supply g_i in each supply market i, where $i = 1, 2, \ldots, n$ and a total demand f_j in each demand market j, where $j = 1, 2, \ldots, m$. Since the markets are spatially separated, x_{ij} units of commodity are transported from i to j.

If we consider the supply excess s_i, $i = 1, \ldots, n$ and the demand excess d_j, $j = 1, \ldots, m$, we must have

$$g_i = \sum_{j=1}^{m} x_{ij} + s_i \qquad i = 1, \ldots, n \tag{3.1}$$

$$f_j = \sum_{i=1}^{n} x_{ij} + d_j \qquad j = 1, \ldots, m. \tag{3.2}$$

Note that $s_i \geq 0$, $\forall i = 1, \ldots, n$ and $d_j \geq 0$, $\forall j = 1, \ldots, m$.

With each supply market i we associate a supply price p_i, and with each demand market j a demand price q_j. A fixed minimal supply price $\underline{p}_i \geq 0$ (price floor) for each supply market i and a fixed maximum demand price $\bar{q}_j > 0$ (price ceiling) for each demand market j are given. Moreover, the transportation from i to j gives rise to unit costs c_{ij}. Finally, upper bounds $\bar{x}_{ij} > 0$ for the transportation flows are included.

Grouping the introduced quantities into vectors, we have the total supply vector $g \in \mathbb{R}^n$, the total supply price vector $p \in \mathbb{R}^n$, the total demand vector $f \in \mathbb{R}^m$, the total demand price vector $q \in \mathbb{R}^m$, the flow vector $x \in \mathbb{R}^{nm}$, and the unit flow cost vector $c \in \mathbb{R}^{nm}$. Then the feasible set for the vectors $u = (p, q, x)$ is given by the product set

$$\mathbb{K} = \prod_{i=1}^{n} [\underline{p}_i, \infty[\times \prod_{j=1}^{m} [0, \bar{q}_j] \times \prod_{i=1}^{n} \prod_{j=1}^{m} [0, \bar{x}_{ij}] = \mathbb{K}_1 \times \mathbb{K}_2 \times \mathbb{K}_3.$$

As in unconstrained market equilibria (see [26], [30]), we assume that we are given the functions

$$g : \mathbb{K}_1 \to \mathbb{R}^n, \quad f : \mathbb{K}_2 \to \mathbb{R}^m, \quad c : \mathbb{K}_3 \to \mathbb{R}^{nm}$$

which express:

- the dependence of the total supply g on the price p;

- the dependence of the total demand f on the price q;

- the dependence of trasportation unit cost c on the flow vector x.

According to perfect equilibrium, the economic market conditions governing the 'disequilibrium' model take the following form (see [26], [34], [108], [130]).

Definition 3.1.1 *A vector* $u = (p, q, x) \in \mathbb{K}$ *is a market equilibrium if and only if the following conditions are satisfied:*

$$\text{if } s_i > 0, \text{ then } p_i = \underline{p}_i; \quad \text{if } p_i > \underline{p}_i, \text{ then } s_i = 0, \quad i = 1, \ldots, n; \quad (3.3)$$

$$\text{if } d_j > 0, \text{ then } q_j = \bar{q}_j; \quad \text{if } q_j < \bar{q}_j, \text{ then } d_j = 0, \ j = 1, \ldots, m; \quad (3.4)$$

$$p_i + c_{ij} \begin{cases} \geq q_j & if \ x_{ij} = 0 \\ = q_j & if \ 0 < x_{ij} < \bar{x}_{ij}, \ i = 1, \ldots, n, \ j = 1, \ldots, m. \ (3.5) \\ \leq q_j & if \ x_{ij} = \bar{x}_{ij} \end{cases}$$

As is proved in [43] and in [76], such equilibrium conditions are equivalent to a variational inequality. In fact the following result holds (see [34], [43], [76]).

Theorem 3.1.1 *Suppose that for each $i = 1, 2, \ldots, n$ and $j = 1, 2, \ldots, m$ there holds*

$$q_j = 0 \Rightarrow f_j(q) \geq 0 \quad and \quad x_{ij} > 0 \Rightarrow c_{ij}(x) > 0. \tag{3.6}$$

Then $u^* = (p^*, q^*, x^*) \in \mathbb{K}$ satisfies the market equilibrium conditions (3.3)–(3.5) if and only if u^* is a solution to the variational inequality

$$\langle v(u^*), u - u^* \rangle$$

$$= \sum_{i=1}^{n} \left(g_i(p^*) - \sum_{j=1}^{m} x_{ij}^* \right) (p_i - p_i^*) - \sum_{j=1}^{m} \left(f_j(q^*) - \sum_{i=1}^{n} x_{ij}^* \right) (q_j - q_j^*)$$

$$+ \sum_{i=1}^{n} \sum_{j=1}^{m} \left(p_i^* + c_{ij}(x^*) - q_j^* \right) (x_{ij} - x_{ij}^*) \geq 0$$

$$\forall u = (p, q, x) \in \mathbb{K}. \tag{3.7}$$

In the previous inequality $v(u)$ is the operator $v : \mathbb{K} \to \mathbb{R}^{n+m+nm}$ defined by setting

$$v(u) = \left(\left(g_i(p) - \sum_{j=1}^{m} x_{ij} \right)_{i=1,\ldots,n}, -\left(f_j(q) - \sum_{i=1}^{n} x_{ij} \right)_{j=1,\ldots,m}, \right.$$

$$\left. (p_i + c_{ij}(x) - q_{ij})_{\substack{i=1,\ldots,n \\ j=1,\ldots,m}} \right).$$

Also in [76] and [43] existence results for the variational inequality (3.7) can be found, under suitable assumptions of pseudomonotonicity and hemicontinuity.

We are now concerned with the Lagrangean theory (see also [33]) associated with the variational inequality (3.7), using the following Lagrangean functional

$$\mathcal{L}(u, \alpha, \beta, \gamma) = \ll v(u^*), u - u^* \gg - \sum_{i=1}^{n} \alpha_i(p_i - \underline{p}_i) - \sum_{j=1}^{m} \beta_j(\overline{q}_j - q_j)$$

$$- \sum_{i=1}^{n} \sum_{j=1}^{m} \gamma_{ij}(\overline{x}_{ij} - x_{ij}),$$

where $u^* \in \mathbb{K}$.

In particular, we are able to prove the following theorem (see [34]).

Theorem 3.1.2 $u^* = (p^*, q^*, x^*) \in \mathbb{K}$ *is a solution to (3.7) if and only if there exist* $\bar{\alpha} \in \mathbb{R}^n$, $\bar{\beta} \in \mathbb{R}^m$, $\bar{\gamma} \in \mathbb{R}^{nm}$ *such that:*

$$g_i(p^*) - \sum_{j=1}^{m} x_{ij}^* - \bar{\alpha}_i = 0, \quad -f_j(q^*) + \sum_{i=1}^{n} x_{ij}^* + \bar{\beta}_j = 0,$$

$$p_i^* + c_{ij}(x^*) - q_j^* + \bar{\gamma}_{ij} = 0 \tag{3.8}$$

$$\bar{\alpha}_i(\underline{p}_i - p_i^*) = 0, \quad \bar{\beta}_j(q_j^* - \bar{q}_j) = 0, \quad \bar{\gamma}_{ij}(x_{ij}^* - \bar{x}_{ij}) = 0 \tag{3.9}$$

$$\bar{\alpha}_i, \quad \bar{\beta}_j, \quad \bar{\gamma}_{ij} \geq 0 \quad \forall i = 1, 2, \dots, n, \quad \forall j = 1, 2, \dots, m \tag{3.10}$$

$$\underline{p}_i - p_i^* \leq 0, \quad q_j^* - \bar{q}_j \leq 0, \quad x_{ij}^* - \bar{x}_{ij} \leq 0$$

$$\forall i = 1, 2, \dots, n, \quad \forall j = 1, 2, \dots, m. \tag{3.11}$$

Proof: In order to obtain such a result, we take into account Theorem 4.2 in [66], which can be applied to problem (3.7) written in the form

$$\min_{u \in \mathbb{K}} \langle v(u^*), u - u^* \rangle = 0 \tag{3.12}$$

and to the Lagrangean functional

$$\mathcal{L}(u, \alpha, \beta, \gamma) = \langle v(u^*), u - u^* \rangle - \sum_{i=1}^{n} \alpha_i(p_i - \underline{p}_i) - \sum_{j=1}^{m} \beta_j(\bar{q}_j - q_j)$$

$$- \sum_{i=1}^{n} \sum_{j=1}^{m} \gamma_{ij}(\bar{x}_{ij} - x_{ij}).$$

Moreover, the Slater condition on the constraints is obviously satisfied and, then, by virtue of such a theorem, $u^* = (p^*, q^*, x^*) \in \mathbb{K}$ is a solution to the problem (3.12) and hence to problem (3.7), if and only if

$$g_i(p^*) - \sum_{j=1}^{m} x_{ij}^* - \bar{\alpha}_i = 0, \quad -f_j(q^*) + \sum_{i=1}^{n} x_{ij}^* + \bar{\beta}_j = 0,$$

$$p_i^* + c_{ij}(x^*) - q_j^* + \bar{\gamma}_{ij} = 0; \tag{3.13}$$

$$\sum_{i=1}^{n} \bar{\alpha}_i(p_i^* - \underline{p}_i) = 0, \quad \sum_{j=1}^{m} \bar{\beta}_j(\bar{q}_j - q_j^*) = 0,$$

$$\sum_{i=1}^{n} \sum_{j=1}^{m} \bar{\gamma}_{ij}(\bar{x}_{ij} - x_{ij}^*) = 0; \tag{3.14}$$

$$\overline{\alpha}_i, \quad \overline{\beta}_j, \quad \overline{\gamma}_{ij} \geq 0 \quad \forall i = 1, 2, \ldots, n, \quad \forall j = 1, 2, \ldots, m; \qquad (3.15)$$

$$\underline{p}_i - p_i^* \leq 0, \quad q_j^* - \overline{q}_j \leq 0, \quad x_{ij}^* - \overline{x}_{ij} \leq 0$$
$$\forall i = 1, 2, \ldots, n, \quad \forall j = 1, 2, \ldots, m. \qquad (3.16)$$

Since $\overline{\alpha}_i \geq 0$, $\underline{p}_i - p_i^* \leq 0$ and the first part of (3.14) holds, it must be that

$$\overline{\alpha}_i(\underline{p}_i - p_i^*) = 0, \quad \forall i = 1, \ldots, n.$$

Analogously, since $\overline{\beta}_j \geq 0$, $q_j^* - \overline{q}_j \leq 0$ and the second part of (3.14) holds, it will be that

$$\overline{\beta}_j(q_j^* - \overline{q}_j) = 0, \quad \forall j = 1, \ldots, m.$$

Finally, since $\overline{\gamma}_{ij} \geq 0$, $x_{ij}^* - \overline{x}_{ij} \leq 0$ and the third part of (3.14) holds, then we have

$$\overline{\gamma}_{ij}(x_{ij}^* - \overline{x}_{ij}) = 0, \quad \forall i = 1, \ldots, n, \quad \forall j = 1, \ldots, m.$$

Hence the assertion of Theorem 3.1.2 is achieved. $\qquad\qquad\qquad\square$

Remark 3.1.1 The Lagrangean variables $\overline{\alpha}_i$, $\overline{\beta}_j$ play a very important role in the theory of the spatially distributed economic markets. In fact the supply excess s_i and the demand excess d_j satisfy the same estimates

$$s_i(\underline{p}_i - p_i^*) = 0 \quad \text{and} \quad d_j(q_j - \overline{q}_j^*) = 0.$$

Moreover, from the first part of (3.13), that is $g_i(p^*) - \sum_{j=1}^{m} x_{ij}^* = \overline{\alpha}_i$ and equality (3.1), and from the second part of (3.13), that is $-f_j(q^*) + \sum_{i=1}^{n} x_{ij}^* = \overline{\beta}_j$, it follows that $\overline{\alpha}_i$, and $\overline{\beta}_j$ coincide with s_i and d_j respectively. Therefore the Lagrangean theory provides directly these important features of the market.

Further, we can characterize the solution to the variational inequality as a saddle point of $\mathcal{L}$ and we can prove the following theorem (see [34]).

Theorem 3.1.3 $u^* = (p^*, q^*, x^*) \in \mathbb{K}$ *is a solution to (3.7) if and only if* $(u^*, \overline{\alpha}, \overline{\beta}, \overline{\gamma}) \in \mathbb{R}^{n+m+nm} \times \mathbb{R}^n \times \mathbb{R}^m \times \mathbb{R}^{nm}$ *is a saddle point of the Lagrangean functional*

$$\mathcal{L}(u, \alpha, \beta, \gamma) = \langle v(u^*), u - u^* \rangle - \sum_{i=1}^{n} \alpha_i(p_i - \underline{p}_i) - \sum_{j=1}^{m} \beta_j(\overline{q}_j - q_j)$$

$$- \sum_{i=1}^{n} \sum_{j=1}^{m} \gamma_{ij}(\overline{x}_{ij} - x_{ij}).$$

Proof: Let us prove the sufficient condition and so let $(u^*, \overline{\alpha}, \overline{\beta}, \overline{\gamma}) \in \mathbb{R}^{n+m+nm} \times \mathbb{R}^n \times \mathbb{R}^m \times \mathbb{R}^{nm}$ be a saddle point of the Lagrangean functional. It means:

$$\mathcal{L}(u^*, \alpha, \beta, \gamma) \leq \mathcal{L}(u^*, \overline{\alpha}, \overline{\beta}, \overline{\gamma}) \leq \mathcal{L}(u, \overline{\alpha}, \overline{\beta}, \overline{\gamma})$$
$$\forall u \in \mathbb{R}^{n+m+nm}, \quad \forall \alpha \in \mathbb{R}^n_+, \quad \forall \beta \in \mathbb{R}^m_+, \quad \forall \gamma \in \mathbb{R}^{nm}_+, \qquad (3.17)$$

that is, taking into account that $\mathcal{L}(u^*, \overline{\alpha}, \overline{\beta}, \overline{\gamma}) = 0$:

$$- \sum_{i=1}^{n} \alpha_i(p_i^* - \underline{p}_i) - \sum_{j=1}^{m} \beta_j(\overline{q}_j - q_j^*) - \sum_{i=1}^{n} \sum_{j=1}^{m} \gamma_{ij}(\overline{x}_{ij} - x_{ij}^*)$$

$$\leq - \sum_{i=1}^{n} \overline{\alpha}_i(p_i^* - \underline{p}_i) - \sum_{j=1}^{m} \overline{\beta}_j(\overline{q}_j - q_j^*) - \sum_{i=1}^{n} \sum_{j=1}^{m} \overline{\gamma}_{ij}(\overline{x}_{ij} - x_{ij})$$

$$\leq \langle v(u^*), u - u^* \rangle - \sum_{i=1}^{n} \overline{\alpha}_i(p_i - \underline{p}_i)$$

$$- \sum_{j=1}^{m} \overline{\beta}_j(\overline{q}_j - q_j) - \sum_{i=1}^{n} \sum_{j=1}^{m} \overline{\gamma}_{ij}(\overline{x}_{ij} - x_{ij}). \qquad (3.18)$$

In the left-hand side of (3.18) let us choose $\beta_j = \overline{\beta}_j$ and $\gamma_{ij} = \overline{\gamma}_{ij}$ and let α_i be running in $\mathbb{R}^n$. Then we obtain:

$$- \sum_{i=1}^{n} \alpha_i(p_i^* - \underline{p}_i) \leq - \sum_{i=1}^{n} \overline{\alpha}_i(p_i^* - \underline{p}_i),$$

namely

$$\sum_{i=1}^{n} \alpha_i(p_i^* - \underline{p}_i) \geq \sum_{i=1}^{n} \overline{\alpha}_i(\underline{p}_i - p_i^*) \qquad (3.19)$$

and, if we choose $\alpha_i = 0$, then we have:

$$\sum_{i=1}^{n} \overline{\alpha}_i(p_i^* - \underline{p}_i) \leq 0. \tag{3.20}$$

Since $\alpha_i \geq 0$, there cannot exist $\overline{i}$ such that $p_{\overline{i}}^* - \underline{p}_{\overline{i}} < 0$, because in this case the left-hand side of (3.19) would diverge to $-\infty$ when α_i diverges to ∞, and then it must be $p_i^* - \underline{p}_i \geq 0 \quad \forall i = 1, 2, \ldots, n$. As a consequence, (3.20) becomes:

$$\sum_{i=1}^{n} \overline{\alpha}_i(\underline{p}_i - p_i^*) = 0, \quad \overline{\alpha}_i \geq 0, \quad p_i^* - \underline{p}_i \geq 0 \tag{3.21}$$

and, therefore,

$$\overline{\alpha}_i(\underline{p}_i - p_i^*) = 0, \quad \forall i = 1, 2, \ldots, n.$$

If we now set $\alpha_i = \overline{\alpha}_i$ and $\beta_j = \overline{\beta}_j$ in the left-hand side of (3.18), we obtain:

$$-\sum_{i=1}^{n}\sum_{j=1}^{m} \gamma_{ij}(\overline{x}_{ij} - x_{ij}^*) \leq -\sum_{i=1}^{n}\sum_{j=1}^{m} \overline{\gamma}_{ij}(\overline{x}_{ij} - x_{ij}^*),$$

that is

$$\sum_{i=1}^{n}\sum_{j=1}^{m} \gamma_{ij}(\overline{x}_{ij} - x_{ij}^*) \geq \sum_{i=1}^{n}\sum_{j=1}^{m} \overline{\gamma}_{ij}(\overline{x}_{ij} - x_{ij}^*). \tag{3.22}$$

If we choose $\gamma_{ij} = 0$, we have:

$$\sum_{i=1}^{n}\sum_{j=1}^{m} \overline{\gamma}_{ij}(\overline{x}_{ij} - x_{ij}^*) \leq 0. \tag{3.23}$$

Let us remark that there cannot be any pair $\overline{i}$, $\overline{j}$ such that $\overline{x}_{\overline{i}\overline{j}} - x_{\overline{i}\overline{j}}^* < 0$ since in such a case the left-hand side of (3.22) would diverge to $-\infty$ and, then, it must be $\overline{x}_{ij} - x_{ij}^* \geq 0$. As a consequence, (3.23) becomes

$$\sum_{i=1}^{n}\sum_{j=1}^{m} \overline{\gamma}_{ij}(\overline{x}_{ij} - x_{ij}^*) = 0, \; \overline{\gamma}_{ij} \geq 0, \; \overline{x}_{ij} - x_{ij}^* \geq 0,$$

$$\forall i = 1, 2, \ldots, n, \quad \forall j = 1, 2, \ldots, m \tag{3.24}$$

and, therefore,

$$\overline{\gamma}_{ij}(\overline{x}_{ij} - x_{ij}^*) = 0 \quad \forall i = 1, 2, \dots, n, \quad \forall j = 1, 2, \dots, m. \tag{3.25}$$

Finally, if we set $\alpha_i = \overline{\alpha}_i$ and $\gamma_{ij} = \overline{\gamma}_{ij}$ in the left-hand side of (3.18), we obtain:

$$-\sum_{j=1}^{m} \beta_j(\overline{q}_j - q_j^*) \leq -\sum_{j=1}^{m} \overline{\beta}_j(\overline{q}_j - q_j^*),$$

that is

$$\sum_{j=1}^{m} \beta_j(\overline{q}_j - q_j^*) \geq \sum_{j=1}^{m} \overline{\beta}_j(\overline{q}_j - q_j^*). \tag{3.26}$$

If we choose $\beta_j = 0$, (3.26) becomes:

$$\sum_{j=1}^{m} \overline{\beta}_j(\overline{q}_j - q_j^*) \leq 0. \tag{3.27}$$

Since $\beta \geq 0$, there cannot be $\overline{j}$ such that $\overline{q}_{\overline{j}} - q_{\overline{j}}^* < 0$, because in such a case the left-hand side of (3.26) would diverge to $-\infty$ and, then, it must be $\overline{q}_{\overline{j}} - q_{\overline{j}}^* \geq 0 \quad \forall j = 1, 2, \dots, m$. As a consequence, (3.27) becomes:

$$\sum_{j=1}^{m} \overline{\beta}_j(\overline{q}_j - q_j^*) = 0, \ \overline{\beta}_j \geq 0, \ \overline{q}_j - q_j^* \geq 0, \ \forall j = 1, 2, \dots, m \tag{3.28}$$

and, therefore,

$$\overline{\beta}_j(\overline{q}_j - q_j^*) = 0, \quad \forall j = 1, 2, \dots, m.$$

From the right-hand side of (3.18), taking into account (3.21), (3.24) and (3.28), we obtain:

$$\mathcal{L}(u, \overline{\alpha}, \overline{\beta}, \overline{\gamma}) \geq 0 = \mathcal{L}(u^*, \overline{\alpha}, \overline{\beta}, \overline{\gamma}) \quad \forall u \in \mathbb{K}.$$

Since the convex and differentiable function $\mathcal{L}(u, \overline{\alpha}, \overline{\beta}, \overline{\gamma})$ assumes its minimum value at u^*, then it must be:

$$\frac{\partial \mathcal{L}}{\partial p_i} = g_i(p^*) - \sum_{j=1}^{m} x_{ij}^* - \overline{\alpha}_i = 0, \quad \frac{\partial \mathcal{L}}{\partial q_j} = -f_j(q^*) + \sum_{i=1}^{n} x_{ij}^* + \overline{\beta}_j = 0,$$

$$\frac{\partial \mathcal{L}}{\partial x_{ij}} = p_i^* + c_{ij}(x^*) - q_j^* + \overline{\gamma}_{ij} = 0.$$

Hence all the conditions of Theorem 3.1.2 are satisfied, and then $u^* = (p^*, q^*, x^*) \in \mathbb{K}$ is a solution to (3.7).

Vice versa, let us assume that $u^* = (p^*, q^*, x^*) \in \mathbb{K}$ is solution to the variational inequality (3.7) and then $(u^*, \overline{\alpha}, \overline{\beta}, \overline{\gamma})$ satisfies (3.8)–(3.11). Let us prove that $(u^*, \overline{\alpha}, \overline{\beta}, \overline{\gamma})$ is a saddle point of the Lagrangean functional, that is

$$\mathcal{L}(u^*, \alpha, \beta, \gamma) \leq \mathcal{L}(u^*, \overline{\alpha}, \overline{\beta}, \overline{\gamma}) \leq \mathcal{L}(u, \overline{\alpha}, \overline{\beta}, \overline{\gamma}).$$

Taking into account (3.8)–(3.11), we get:

$$\mathcal{L}(u^*, \overline{\alpha}, \overline{\beta}, \overline{\gamma}) = 0.$$

So, we have to prove that $\mathcal{L}(u^*, \alpha, \beta, \gamma) \leq 0$ and that $\mathcal{L}(u, \overline{\alpha}, \overline{\beta}, \overline{\gamma}) \geq 0$.

Let us prove that $\mathcal{L}(u^*, \alpha, \beta, \gamma) \leq 0$. Since

$$\mathcal{L}(u^*, \alpha, \beta, \gamma)$$

$$= -\sum_{i=1}^{n} \alpha_i(\underline{p}_i - p_i^*) - \sum_{j=1}^{m} \beta_j(q_j^* - \overline{q}_j) - \sum_{i=1}^{n} \sum_{j=1}^{m} \gamma_{ij}(x_{ij}^* - \overline{x}_{ij}),$$

our request is verified by assumption.

Let us now prove that $\mathcal{L}(u, \overline{\alpha}, \overline{\beta}, \overline{\gamma}) \geq \mathcal{L}(u^*, \overline{\alpha}, \overline{\beta}, \overline{\gamma}) = 0$, where

$$\mathcal{L}(u, \overline{\alpha}, \overline{\beta}, \overline{\gamma}) = \langle v(u^*), u - u^* \rangle - \sum_{i=1}^{n} \overline{\alpha}_i(p_i - \underline{p}_i) - \sum_{j=1}^{m} \overline{\beta}_j(\overline{q}_j - q_j)$$

$$- \sum_{i=1}^{n} \sum_{j=1}^{m} \overline{\gamma}_{ij}(\overline{x}_{ij} - x_{ij}).$$

The function $\mathcal{L}(u, \overline{\alpha}, \overline{\beta}, \overline{\gamma})$ is convex with respect to u and, then, the conditions (3.8) are sufficient to ensure that $\mathcal{L}(u, \overline{\alpha}, \overline{\beta}, \overline{\gamma})$ assumes its minimum value at $u = u^*$.   □

The results above allow us to obtain a dual formulation of the variational inequality (3.7). In fact, if we set

$$\mathbb{K}^* = \{(u, \alpha, \beta, \gamma) \in \mathbb{R}^{n+m+nm} \times \mathbb{R}^n \times \mathbb{R}^m \times \mathbb{R}^{nm} :$$

$$\alpha_i = \sum_{i=1}^{n} x_{ij} - g_i(p), \quad \beta_j = \sum_{i=1}^{n} x_{ij} - f_j(q), \quad \gamma_{ij} = q_j - p_i - c_{ij}(x),$$

$$\underline{p}_i - p_i \leq 0, \quad q_j - \overline{q}_j \leq 0, \quad x_{ij} - \overline{x}_{ij} \leq 0\},$$

then we call *dual variational inequality* the problem:

$$\text{find } (u^*, \overline{\alpha}, \overline{\beta}, \overline{\gamma}) \in \mathbb{K}^* :$$

$$\sum_{i=1}^{n} (\alpha_i - \overline{\alpha}_i)(\underline{p}_i - p_i) + \sum_{j=1}^{m} (\beta_j - \overline{\beta}_j)(q_j - \overline{q}_j)$$

$$+ \sum_{i=1}^{n} \sum_{j=1}^{m} (\gamma_{ij} - \overline{\gamma}_{ij})(x_{ij} - \overline{x}_{ij}) \geq 0$$

$$\forall (u, \alpha, \beta, \gamma) \in \mathbb{K}^*.$$

It is interesting to solve the dual variational inequality in view of a market evaluation, since it provides the supply and demand excesses and allows one to organize a better management and control of the market.

3.1.2 The Dynamic Model

We now consider the dynamic case. The supply markets $P_1, P_2, \ldots, P_n$ and the demand markets $Q_1, Q_2, \ldots, Q_m$ of the commodity m_1 are considered at all time $t \in [0, T] = \mathcal{T}$. For each time $t \in \mathcal{T}$ we have: the total supply vector $g(t) \in \mathbb{R}^n$, the supply price vector $p(t) \in \mathbb{R}^n$, the total demand vector $f(t) \in \mathbb{R}^m$, the demand price vector $q(t) \in \mathbb{R}^m$, the flow vector $x(t) \in \mathbb{R}^{nm}$, the unit cost vector $c(t) \in \mathbb{R}^{nm}$.

Moreover, another important aspect that is inserted in this section (see also [43] and [35]) is the ability to add upper bounds to the supply price vector, lower bounds to the demand price vector and lower bounds to the transported quantities. In such a way, the model deals with realistic phenomena, such as the control of the markets by authority which, for social and political reasons, could require that the prices don't exceed a ceiling price or that a minimum quantity of a commodity must be bought or transported. As a consequence, the feasible vectors $u(t) = (p(t), q(t), x(t))$ have to satisfy the time-dependent constraints on prices and transportation flows, namely:

$$u(t) \in \prod_{i=1}^{n} [\underline{p}_i(t), \overline{p}_i(t)] \times \prod_{j=1}^{m} [\underline{q}_j(t), \overline{q}_j(t)] \times \prod_{i=1}^{n} \prod_{j=1}^{m} [\underline{x}_{ij}(t), \overline{x}_{ij}(t)]$$

where $\underline{p}_i(t), \overline{p}_i(t), \underline{q}_j(t), \overline{q}_j(t), \underline{x}_{ij}(t), \overline{x}_{ij}(t)$ are given.

For technical reasons, the functional setting for the trajectories $u(t)$ is the Hilbert space:

$$L = L^2([0,T], \mathbb{R}^n) \times L^2([0,T], \mathbb{R}^m) \times L^2([0,T], \mathbb{R}^{nm}).$$

The set of feasible vectors $u(t) = (p(t), q(t), x(t))$ is given by

$$\mathbb{K} = \mathbb{K}_1 \times \mathbb{K}_2 \times \mathbb{K}_3$$
$$= \{p \in L^2([0,T], \mathbb{R}^n) : \underline{p}(t) \leq p(t) \leq \overline{p}(t) \text{ a.e. on } [0,T]\}$$
$$\times \{q \in L^2([0,T], \mathbb{R}^m) : \underline{q}(t) \leq q(t) \leq \overline{q}(t) \text{ a.e. on } [0,T]\}$$
$$\times \{x \in L^2([0,T], \mathbb{R}^{nm}) : \underline{x}(t) \leq x(t) \leq \overline{x}(t) \text{ a.e. on } [0,T]\},$$

where it is assumed that

$$\underline{p}(t),\ \overline{p}(t) \in L^2([0,T], \mathbb{R}^n),\ \underline{q}(t),\ \overline{q}(t) \in L^2([0,T], \mathbb{R}^m),$$
$$\underline{x}(t), \overline{x}(t) \in L^2([0,T], \mathbb{R}^{nm}).$$

It is easy to note that $\mathbb{K}$ is a convex, closed, and bounded set. Furthermore, we are giving the mappings:

$$g = g(p(t)) : \mathbb{K}_1 \rightarrow L^2([0,T], \mathbb{R}^n),$$

$$f = f(q(t)) : \mathbb{K}_2 \rightarrow L^2([0,T], \mathbb{R}^m),$$
$$c = c(x(t)) : \mathbb{K}_3 \rightarrow L^2([0,T], \mathbb{R}^{nm}),$$

which assign to each price trajectory $p \in \mathbb{K}_1$ and $q \in \mathbb{K}_2$ the supply $g \in L^2([0,T], \mathbb{R}^n)$ and the demand $f \in L^2([0,T], \mathbb{R}^m)$ respectively and to the flow trajectory $x \in \mathbb{K}_3$ the cost $c \in L^2([0,T], \mathbb{R}^{nm})$.

By introducing the supply excesses $s_i(t)$ and the demand excesses $d_j(t)$, we must have:

$$g_i(p(t)) = \sum_{j=1}^{m} x_{ij}(t) + s_i(t) \quad i = 1, 2, \ldots, n \tag{3.29}$$

$$f_j(q(t)) = \sum_{i=1}^{n} x_{ij}(t) + d_j(t) \quad j = 1, 2, \ldots, m. \tag{3.30}$$

Obviously $s(t) \in L^2([0,T], \mathbb{R}^n)$ and $d(t) \in L^2([0,T], \mathbb{R}^m)$. The 'dynamic' market equilibrium takes the following form.

Definition 3.1.2 $u(t) = (p(t), q(t), x(t)) \in L$ *is a dynamic market equilibrium if and only if for each $i = 1, 2, \ldots, n$ and $j = 1, 2, \ldots, m$ and a.e. on T there hold:*

$$\begin{cases} if \ s_i(t) > 0, \ then \ p_i(t) = \underline{p}_i(t); \\ if \ \underline{p}_i(t) < p_i(t) \le \overline{p}_i(t), \ then \ s_i(t) = 0; \end{cases} \tag{3.31}$$

$$\begin{cases} if \ d_j(t) > 0, \ then \ q_j(t) = \overline{q}_j(t); \\ if \ \underline{q}_j(t) \le q_j(t) < \overline{q}_j(t), \ then \ d_j(t) = 0; \end{cases} \tag{3.32}$$

$$p_i(t) + c_{ij}(t) \begin{cases} > q_j(t) & if \quad x_{ij}(t) = \underline{x}_{ij}(t) \\ = q_j(t) & if \quad \underline{x}_{ij}(t) \le x_{ij}(t) \le \overline{x}_{ij}(t) \\ < q_j(t) & if \quad x_{ij}(t) = \overline{x}_{ij}(t). \end{cases} \tag{3.33}$$

Let $v : \mathbb{K} \to L$ be the operator defined by setting

$$\begin{aligned} v &= v(u(t)) = v(p(t), q(t), x(t)) \\ &= \left(\left(g_i(p(t)) - \sum_{j=1}^{m} x_{ij}(t) \right)_{i=1,\ldots,n}, - \left(f_j(q(t)) - \sum_{i=1}^{n} x_{ij}(t) \right)_{j=1,\ldots,m}, \right. \\ &\quad \left. (p_i(t) + c_{ij}(x(t)) - q_j(t))_{\substack{i=1,\ldots,n \\ j=1,\ldots,m}} \right). \end{aligned}$$

The following characterization holds.

Theorem 3.1.4 *Suppose that for each $i = 1, \ldots, n$ and $j = 1, \ldots, m$ there hold*

1. $q_j(t) = \underline{q}_j(t)$ *on a set $E \subseteq T$ having positive measure implies*

$$f_j(q(t)) \ge 0 \quad in \ E;$$

2. $x_{ij}(t) > \underline{x}_{ij}(t)$ *on a set $E \subseteq T$ having positive measure implies*

$$c_{ij}(x(t)) > 0 \quad in \ E.$$

Then $u(t) = (p(t), q(t), x(t)) \in \mathbb{K}$ is a dynamic market equilibrium if and only if $u(t)$ is a solution to

$$\ll v(u), \tilde{u} - u \gg = \int_0^T \langle v(u(t), \tilde{u}(t) - u(t)) \rangle \, dt$$

$$= \int_0^T \left\{ \sum_{i=1}^n \left(g_i(p(t)) - \sum_{j=1}^m x_{ij}(t) \right) (\tilde{p}_i(t) - p_i(t)) \right.$$

$$- \sum_{j=1}^m \left(f_j(q(t)) - \sum_{i=1}^n x_{ij}(t) \right) (\tilde{q}_j(t) - q_j(t))$$

$$\left. + \sum_{i=1}^n \sum_{j=1}^m \left(p_i(t) + c_{ij}(x(t)) - q_j(t) \right) (\tilde{x}_{ij}(t) - x_{ij}(t)) \right\} \, dt \geq 0$$

$$\forall \tilde{u} = (\tilde{p}, \tilde{q}, \tilde{x}) \in \mathbb{K}. \qquad (3.34)$$

Proof: Assume that (3.29)–(3.33) hold. Let $\tilde{u} \in \mathbb{K}$. It follows:

$$\sum_{i=1}^n \left(g_i(p(t)) - \sum_{j=1}^m x_{ij}(t) \right) (\tilde{p}_i(t) - p_i(t))$$

$$- \sum_{j=1}^m \left(f_j(q(t)) - \sum_{i=1}^n x_{ij}(t) \right) (\tilde{q}_j(t) - q_j(t))$$

$$+ \sum_{i=1}^n \sum_{j=1}^m \left(p_i(t) + c_{ij}(x(t)) - q_j(t) \right) (\tilde{x}_{ij}(t) - x_{ij}(t)) \geq 0$$

a.e. on $[0, T]$.

Hence (3.34) follows.

Vice versa, let us assume that (3.34) holds. As a consequence we obtain, assuming in turns $\tilde{q} = q$ and $\tilde{x} = x$, $\tilde{p} = p$ and $\tilde{x} = x$, $\tilde{p} = p$ and $\tilde{q} = q$:

$$\int_0^T \sum_{i=1}^n \left(g_i(p(t)) - \sum_{j=1}^m x_{ij}(t) \right) (\tilde{p}_i(t) - p_i(t)) \, dt \geq 0 \quad \forall p \in \mathbb{K}_1,$$

$$\int_0^T \sum_{j=1}^m \left(f_j(q(t)) - \sum_{i=1}^n x_{ij}(t) \right) (\tilde{q}_j(t) - q_j(t)) \, dt \geq 0 \quad \forall q \in \mathbb{K}_2,$$

$$\int_0^T \sum_{i=1}^n \sum_{j=1}^m \Big(p_i(t) + c_{ij}(x(t)) - q_j(t) \Big) \big(\tilde{x}_{ij}(t) - x_{ij}(t) \big) \, dt \geq 0 \quad \forall x \in \mathbb{K}_3$$

from which (3.29) and (3.31), (3.30) and (3.32), and (3.33) follow respectively.

In fact, let us assume that (3.29) does not hold. Then there exists an index i^* together with a set $E \subseteq \mathcal{T}$ having positive measure such that

$$s_{i^*}(t) = g_{i^*}(t) - \sum_{j=1}^m x_{i^* j}(t) < 0 \quad \text{on } E.$$

Then the choice

$$\tilde{p}_i(t) = p_i(t) \quad \text{for} \quad i \neq i^*$$

$$\tilde{p}_{i^*}(t) \begin{cases} = p_i(t) & \text{on} \quad [0, T] - E \\ > p_i(t) & \text{on} \quad E \end{cases}$$

leads to a contradiction:

$$\int_0^T \sum_{i=1}^n \Big(g_i(p(t)) - \sum_{j=1}^m x_{ij}(t) \Big) \big(\tilde{p}_i(t) - p_i(t) \big) \, dt$$

$$= \int_E \Big(g_{i^*}(p(t)) - \sum_{j=1}^m x_{i^* j}(t) \Big) \big(\tilde{p}_{i^*}(t) - p_i(t) \big) \, dt < 0.$$

Suppose now that (3.31) is not verified. Then there exists an index i^* together with a set $E \subset \mathcal{T}$ having positive measure such that either $s_{i^*}(t) > 0$ and $p_{i^*}(t) > \underline{p}_{i^*}(t)$ or $p_{i^*}(t) > \underline{p}_{i^*}(t)$ and $s_{i^*}(t) > 0$ on E.

In both cases the choice

$$\tilde{p}_i(t) = p_i(t) \quad \text{for} \quad i \neq i^*$$

$$\tilde{p}_{i^*}(t) = \begin{cases} p_{i^*}(t) & \text{on} \quad [0, T] - E \\ \underline{p}_{i^*}(t) & \text{on} \quad E \end{cases}$$

leads to a contradiction. Similarly, one can proceed in other cases and the equivalence is achieved. $\qquad \square$

Remark 3.1.2 With analogous comments to those in Remark 2.2.1, we have that the variational inequality (3.34) is equivalent to:

$$\langle v(u(t)), \tilde{u}(t) - u(t) \rangle \geq 0 \quad \forall \tilde{u} \in \mathbb{K}, \text{ a.e. in } [0, T]. \tag{3.35}$$

Moreover, this remark is interesting because we can apply to (3.35), among the others, the direct method in order to find solutions to the variational inequality (3.34).

About the existence of the solution to the variational inequality associated with the spatially distributed market problem, we may provide some existence theorems under general assumptions.

Adapting Theorem 2.3.1 to our case, we have the following.

Theorem 3.1.5 *Each of the following conditions is sufficient for the existence of a solution to the variational inequality:*

1. *$v(u)$ is hemicontinuous with respect to the strong topology and there exist $A_1 \subseteq \mathbb{K}_1$, $A_2 \subseteq \mathbb{K}_2$, $A_3 \subseteq \mathbb{K}_3$ compact and $B_1 \subseteq \mathbb{K}_1$, $B_2 \subseteq \mathbb{K}_2$, $B_3 \subseteq \mathbb{K}_3$ convex and compact such that*

$$\forall u_1 = (p_1, q_1, x_1) \in (\mathbb{K}_1 \setminus A_1) \times (\mathbb{K}_2 \setminus A_2) \times (\mathbb{K}_3 \setminus A_3),$$

$$\exists u_2 = (p_2, q_2, x_2) \in B_1 \times B_2 \times B_3 : \ll v(u_1), u_2 - u_1 \gg < 0;$$

2. *$v(u)$ is pseudomonotone and hemicontinuous along line segments;*

3. *$v(u)$ is hemicontinuous with respect to the weak topology on $\mathbb{K}$.*

3.1.3 Computational Procedure

We suppose, for sake of simplicity, that the monotonicity condition holds in order to ensure the uniqueness of the solution. We may use the direct method of [95]. This method consists of the following steps.

1. Check if the system

$$\begin{cases} v(u(t)) = 0 \\ u \in \mathbb{K} \end{cases}$$

admits a solution. If this system has no solutions, the solution to the variational inequality lies on the boundary of the polyhedron $\mathbb{K}$, and it is represented by faces.

2. Let us fix an index $i \in \{1, 2, \ldots, n\}$ and consider the face

$$\mathbb{K} \cap \{p_i(t) = \underline{p}_i(t)\} = \mathbb{K}_i$$

and the system

$$
\begin{cases}
g_l(p(t)) - \displaystyle\sum_{j=1}^{m} x_{lj}(t) = 0 & l = 1, \ldots, n \quad l \neq i \\[2mm]
f_j(q(t)) - \displaystyle\sum_{l=1}^{n} x_{lj}(t) = 0 & j = 1, \ldots, m \\[2mm]
p_l(t) + c_{lj}(x(t)) - q_j(t) = 0 & \begin{aligned} l &= 1, \ldots, n \\ j &= 1, \ldots, m \end{aligned} \\[2mm]
u(t) \in \mathbb{K}_i.
\end{cases}
\qquad (3.36)
$$

If this system admits a solution $(p(t), q(t), x(t)) \in \mathbb{K}_i$, it is the solution to the variational inequality if and only if

$$g_i(p(t)) - \sum_{j=1}^{m} x_{ij}(t) > 0. \qquad (3.37)$$

Analogously, if we fix an index $j \in \{1, 2, \ldots, m\}$ and consider the face $\mathbb{K} \cap \{q_j(t) = 0\} = \mathbb{K}^j$, we must examine the system

$$
\begin{cases}
g_i(p(t)) - \displaystyle\sum_{k=1}^{m} x_{ik}(t) = 0 & i = 1, \ldots, n \\[2mm]
f_k(q(t)) - \displaystyle\sum_{i=1}^{n} x_{ik}(t) = 0 & k = 1, \ldots, m \quad k \neq j \\[2mm]
p_i(t) + c_{ik}(x(t)) - q_k(t) = 0 & \begin{aligned} i &= 1, \ldots, n \\ k &= 1, \ldots, m \end{aligned} \\[2mm]
u(t) \in \mathbb{K}^j
\end{cases}
\qquad (3.38)
$$

and the eventual solution to this system is the solution to the variational inequality if and only if

$$f_j(q(t)) - \sum_{i=1}^{n} x_{ij}(t) > 0. \qquad (3.39)$$

If we consider the face $\mathbb{K} \cap \{q_j(t) = \bar{q}_j(t)\} = \tilde{\mathbb{K}}^j$ and check if the system

$$
\begin{cases}
g_i(p(t)) - \displaystyle\sum_{k=1}^{m} x_{ik}(t) = 0 & i = 1, \ldots, n \\[2mm]
f_k(q(t)) - \displaystyle\sum_{i=1}^{n} x_{ik}(t) = 0 & k = 1, \ldots, m, \quad k \neq j \\[2mm]
p_i(t) + c_{ik}(x(t)) - q_k(t) = 0 & \begin{aligned} i &= 1, \ldots, n \\ k &= 1, \ldots, m \end{aligned} \\[2mm]
u(t) \in \tilde{\mathbb{K}}^j
\end{cases}
\tag{3.40}
$$

admits solution, this eventual solution is the solution of the variational inequality if and only if

$$
f_j(q(t)) - \sum_{i=1}^{n} x_{ij}(t) < 0.
\tag{3.41}
$$

Finally, if we fix two indexes $i \in \{1, \ldots, n\}$ and $j \in \{1, \ldots, m\}$ and consider the face $\mathbb{K} \cap \{x_{ij}(t) = 0\} = \mathbb{K}_{ij}$ and the system

$$
\begin{cases}
g_i(p(t)) - \displaystyle\sum_{j=1}^{m} x_{ij}(t) = 0 & i = 1, \ldots, n \\[2mm]
f_j(q(t)) - \displaystyle\sum_{i=1}^{n} x_{ij}(t) = 0 & j = 1, \ldots, m \\[2mm]
p_l(t) + c_{lk}(x(t)) - q_k(t) = 0 & \begin{aligned} l &= 1, \ldots, n, \quad l \neq i \\ k &= 1, \ldots, m \quad k \neq j \end{aligned} \\[2mm]
u(t) \in \mathbb{K}_{ij},
\end{cases}
\tag{3.42}
$$

the eventual solution to this system is the solution to the variational inequality if and only if

$$
p_i(t) + c_{ij}(x(t)) - q_j(t) > 0.
\tag{3.43}
$$

On the contrary, if we consider the face $\mathbb{K} \cap \{x_{ij}(t) = \bar{x}_{ij}(t)\} = \tilde{\mathbb{K}}_{ij}$ and the system

$$
\begin{cases}
g_i(p(t)) - \sum_{j=1}^{m} x_{ij}(t) = 0 & i = 1, \ldots, n \\
f_j(q(t)) - \sum_{i=1}^{n} x_{ij}(t) = 0 & j = 1, \ldots, m \\
p_l(t) + c_{lk}(x(t)) - q_k(t) = 0 & l = 1, \ldots, n, \quad l \neq i, \\
& k = 1, 2, \ldots, m \quad k \neq j \\
u(t) \in \tilde{\mathbb{K}}_{ij},
\end{cases}
\tag{3.44}
$$

the eventual solution is the solution to the variational inequality if and only if

$$
p_i(t) + c_{ij}(x(t)) - q_j(t) < 0.
\tag{3.45}
$$

3. If the conditions (3.37), (3.39), (3.41), (3.43), (3.45) are not fulfilled, the variational inequality cannot have solutions in the interior of the sets $\mathbb{K}_i$, $\mathbb{K}^j$, $\tilde{\mathbb{K}}^j$, $\mathbb{K}_{ij}$, $\tilde{\mathbb{K}}_{ij}$, whereas if the systems (3.36), (3.38), (3.40), (3.42), (3.44) admit no solutions, the solution of the variational inequality has to lie on the boundary of some of these faces. In any case, if (3.37), (3.39), (3.41), (3.43), (3.45) are not verified or the systems (3.36), (3.38), (3.40), (3.42), (3.44) admit no solutions, the solution to the variational inequality must be searched on the boundary of the faces, that is on faces whose dimension is reduced by 1 unit. We obtain such faces by fixing two indexes $i_1, i_2 \in \{1, 2, \ldots, n\}$ or $j_1, j_2 \in \{1, 2, \ldots, m\}$ or $(i_1, j_1), (i_2, j_2) \in \{1, 2, \ldots, n\} \times \{1, 2, \ldots, m\}$ or a mixture of them. For these new faces we can repeat procedure 2 with the same criteria on the sign and we may obtain the solution or iterate the method.

An evaluation of the 'effectiveness' of this direct method is given in [95] which also provides a comparison with other methods.

Example 3.1.1 (The direct method)

Let us consider the network in Figure 3.1 consisting of two supply markets and two demand markets. The supply functions and the demand functions depend on two non-negative parameters h and k, by means of which it is possible to control the production and the demand. The supply and demand functions are given as follows:

$$
\begin{array}{ll}
g_1(p_1(t), p_2(t)) = p_1(t) + h, & g_2(p_1(t), p_2(t)) = p_2(t) + k; \\
f_1(q_1(t), q_2(t)) = q_1(t), & f_2(q_1(t), q_2(t)) = q_1(t) - q_2(t) + h.
\end{array}
$$

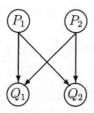

Figure 3.1: Network with two supply and two demand markets

The transportation cost functions are:

$$c_{11}(x(t)) = x_{11}(t) + 1, \qquad c_{12}(x(t)) = x_{12}(t) + 1,$$
$$c_{21}(x(t)) = x_{21}(t), \qquad c_{22}(x(t)) = x_{22}(t) + 1.$$

Let us choose as functional setting the set $\mathbb{K}$ defined as follows:

$$\mathbb{K} = \{u(t) = (p(t), q(t), x(t)) \in$$
$$L^2\left([0,1], \mathbb{R}^2\right) \times L^2\left([0,1], \mathbb{R}^2\right) \times L^2\left([0,1], \mathbb{R}^4\right) :$$
$$p(t) \geq 0, \ q(t) \geq 0, \ x(t) \geq 0\}.$$

The operator $v(u(t))$ has the following components:

$$
\begin{aligned}
g_1(p(t)) - x_{11}(t) - x_{12}(t) &= p_1(t) - x_{11}(t) - x_{12}(t) + h, \\
g_2(p(t)) - x_{21}(t) - x_{22}(t) &= p_2(t) - x_{21}(t) - x_{22}(t) + k, \\
-f_1(q(t)) + x_{11}(t) + x_{21}(t) &= -q_1(t) + x_{11}(t) + x_{21}(t), \\
-f_2(q(t)) + x_{12}(t) + x_{22}(t) &= -q_1(t) + q_2(t) + x_{12}(t) + x_{22}(t) - h,
\end{aligned}
$$

$$
\begin{aligned}
p_1(t) + c_{11}(x(t)) - q_1(t) &= p_1(t) + x_{11}(t) - q_1(t) + 1, \\
p_1(t) + c_{12}(x(t)) - q_2(t) &= p_1(t) + x_{12}(t) - q_2(t) + 1, \\
p_2(t) + c_{21}(x(t)) - q_1(t) &= p_2(t) + x_{21}(t) - q_1(t), \\
p_2(t) + c_{22}(x(t)) - q_2(t) &= p_2(t) + x_{22}(t) - q_2(t) + 1.
\end{aligned}
$$

Solving the system

$$\begin{cases} v(u(t)) = 0 \\ u(t) \in \mathbb{K}, \end{cases}$$

and taking into account that $f_2(q_1(t), q_2(t))$ is requested to be non-negative, which means $h + k - 1 \geq 0$, then, if h and k are non-negative parameters such that $h + 5k - 5 \geq 0$, we get the following solutions:

$$x_{11}(t) = \frac{2h + 4k - 4}{3}, \quad x_{12}(t) = \frac{2h + k - 1}{3},$$

$$x_{21}(t) = \frac{h + 5k - 2}{3}, \quad x_{22}(t) = \frac{h + 2k - 2}{3},$$

$$p_1(t) = \frac{h + 5k - 5}{3}, \quad p_2(t) = \frac{2h + 4k - 4}{3},$$

$$q_1(t) = h + 3k - 2, \quad q_2(t) = h + 2k - 1,$$

and

$$g_1(p(t)) = \frac{4h + 5k - 5}{3}, \quad g_2(p(t)) = \frac{2h + 7k - 4}{3},$$

$$f_1(q(t)) = h + 3k - 2, \quad f_2(q(t)) = h + k - 1,$$

$$c_{11}(x(t)) = \frac{2h + 4k - 1}{3}, \quad c_{12}(x(t)) = \frac{2h + k + 2}{3},$$

$$c_{21}(x(t)) = \frac{h + 5k - 2}{3}, \quad c_{22}(x(t)) = \frac{h + 2k + 1}{3},$$

with

$$s_1(t) = s_2(t) = d_1(t) = d_2(t) = 0.$$

If $h + 5k - 5 < 0$, then we must check in which face of the boundary the solution lies. After straightforward calculations, we are led to study the face obtained by the intersection of $\mathbb{K}$ with the conditions $p_1(t) = 0$ and $x_{11}(t) = 0$, where we must solve the new system, namely:

$$\begin{cases} p_2(t) - x_{21}(t) - x_{22}(t) + k = 0 \\ -q_1(t) + x_{21}(t) = 0 \\ -q_1(t) + q_2(t) + x_{12}(t) + x_{22}(t) - h = 0 \\ x_{12}(t) - q_2(t) + 1 = 0 \\ p_2(t) + x_{21}(t) - q_1(t) = 0 \\ p_2(t) + x_{22}(t) - q_2(t) + 1 = 0 \end{cases} \Longleftrightarrow \begin{cases} x_{12}(t) = \dfrac{h + k - 1}{4} \\ x_{21}(t) = \dfrac{-h + 3k + 1}{4} \\ x_{22}(t) = \dfrac{h + k - 1}{4} \\ p_2(t) = 0 \\ q_1(t) = \dfrac{-h + 3k + 1}{4} \\ q_2(t) = \dfrac{h + k + 3}{4}. \end{cases}$$

The solution we have found in the boundary is a solution to the problem in the whole convex set $\mathbb{K}$ if and only if the following conditions are satisfied:

$$\begin{cases} p_1(t) - x_{11}(t) - x_{12}(t) + h > 0 & \Longleftrightarrow \quad 3h - k + 1 > 0 \\ p_1(t) + x_{11}(t) - q_1(t) + 1 > 0 & \Longleftrightarrow \quad h - 3k + 3 > 0. \end{cases} \tag{3.46}$$

Since under condition $h + 5k - 5 < 0$ the conditions (3.46) are fulfilled, then the solution to the problem is:

$$\begin{cases} x_{11}(t) = 0, & p_1(t) = 0, \\ x_{12}(t) = \dfrac{h + k - 1}{4}, & p_2(t) = 0, \\ x_{21}(t) = \dfrac{-h + 3k + 1}{4}, & q_1(t) = \dfrac{-h + 3k + 1}{4}, \\ x_{22}(t) = \dfrac{h + k - 1}{4}, & q_2(t) = \dfrac{h + k + 3}{4}. \end{cases}$$

It is worth remarking that in this case there is a supply excess:

$$s_1(t) = g_1(p(t)) - x_{11}(t) - x_{12}(t) = \frac{3h - k + 1}{4},$$

and there is no equilibrium in the trade between P_1 and Q_1 because

$$p_1(t) + c_{11}(x(t)) - q_1(t) = \frac{h - 3k + 3}{4}.$$

Example 3.1.2 (The discretization method)

Let us consider the network in Figure 3.2 consisting of two supply markets and one demand market. The supply functions and the demand function depend on two non-negative functions $h(t)$ and $k(t)$, by means of which it is possible to control the production and the demand. The supply and demand functions and the transportation cost functions are given as follows:

$$\begin{aligned} g_1(p_1(t), p_2(t)) &= p_1(t) + h(t), & g_2(p_1(t), p_2(t)) &= p_2(t) + k(t); \\ f_1(q_1(t), q_2(t)) &= k(t) - q_1(t); & & \\ c_{11}(x(t)) &= x_{11}(t), & c_{21}(x(t)) &= x_{21}(t) + 1; \end{aligned}$$

where $t \in \left[0, \dfrac{1}{2}\right]$.

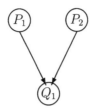

Figure 3.2: Network with two supply and one demand markets

The set $\mathbb{K}$ is defined as follows:

$$\mathbb{K} = \left\{ u(t) = (p(t), q(t), x(t)) \in \right.$$

$$L^2\left(\left[0, \frac{1}{2}\right], \mathbb{R}^2\right) \times L^2\left(\left[0, \frac{1}{2}\right], \mathbb{R}\right) \times L^2\left(\left[0, \frac{1}{2}\right], \mathbb{R}^2\right) :$$

$$0 \le p_1(t) \le h(t) + k(t) + 1, \ 0 \le p_2(t) \le h(t) + k(t) + 1,$$

$$0 \le q_1(t) \le h(t) + k(t) + 1, \ 0 \le x_{11}(t) \le h(t) + k(t) + 1,$$

$$\left. 0 \le x_{21}(t) \le h(t) + k(t) + 1 \right\}.$$

Before applying the discretization method, let us solve the problem by means of the direct method, in order to be able to make a comparison between the two methods. Hence, the operator $v(u(t))$ has the following components:

$$
\begin{aligned}
g_1(p(t)) - x_{11}(t) &= p_1(t) - x_{11}(t) + h(t), \\
g_2(p(t)) - x_{21}(t) &= p_2(t) - x_{21}(t) + k(t), \\
-f_1(q(t)) + x_{11}(t) + x_{21}(t) &= q_1(t) + x_{11}(t) + x_{21}(t) - k(t), \\
p_1(t) + c_{11}(x(t)) - q_1(t) &= p_1(t) + x_{11}(t) - q_1(t), \\
p_2(t) + c_{21}(x(t)) - q_1(t) &= p_2(t) + x_{21}(t) - q_1(t) + 1.
\end{aligned}
$$

Solving the system

$$\begin{cases} v(u(t)) = 0 \\ u(t) \in \mathbb{K}, \end{cases}$$

we find:

$$
\begin{cases}
p_1(t) - x_{11}(t) + h(t) = 0 \\
p_2(t) - x_{21}(t) + k(t) = 0 \\
q_1(t) + x_{11}(t) + x_{21}(t) - k(t) = 0 \\
p_1(t) + x_{11}(t) - q_1(t) = 0 \\
p_2(t) + x_{21}(t) - q_1(t) + 1 = 0
\end{cases}
\iff
\begin{cases}
p_1(t) = \dfrac{-5h(t) + k(t) + 1}{8} \\[2mm]
p_2(t) = \dfrac{-h(t) - 3k(t) - 3}{8} \\[2mm]
q_1(t) = \dfrac{-h(t) + k(t) + 1}{4} \\[2mm]
x_{11}(t) = \dfrac{3h(t) + k(t) + 1}{8} \\[2mm]
x_{21}(t) = \dfrac{-h(t) + 5k(t) - 3}{8}.
\end{cases}
$$

Since the conditions

$$
\begin{cases}
k(t) \geq 5h(t) - 1 \qquad k(t) \leq \dfrac{-h(t) - 3}{3} \\[3mm]
k(t) \geq h(t) - 1 \qquad k(t) \geq \dfrac{h(t) + 3}{5} \qquad k(t) \geq -3h(t) - 1
\end{cases}
$$

are never fulfilled simultaneously, then we have to search for the solution in the boundary of the set $\mathbb{K}$. After simple calculations, we are led to study the face obtained by the intersection of $\mathbb{K}$ with the constraint $p_2(t) = 0$. Solving the new system, namely:

$$
\begin{cases}
p_1(t) - x_{11}(t) + h(t) = 0 \\
q_1(t) + x_{11}(t) + x_{21}(t) - k(t) = 0 \\
p_1(t) + x_{11}(t) - q_1(t) = 0 \\
x_{21}(t) - q_1(t) + 1 = 0
\end{cases}
\iff
\begin{cases}
p_1(t) = \dfrac{-3h(t) + k(t) + 1}{5} \\[2mm]
q_1(t) = \dfrac{-h(t) + 2k(t) + 2}{5} \\[2mm]
x_{11}(t) = \dfrac{2h(t) + k(t) + 1}{5} \\[2mm]
x_{21}(t) = \dfrac{-h(t) + 2k(t) - 3}{5},
\end{cases}
$$

we obtain that the conditions

$$\begin{cases} k(t) \geq 3h(t) - 1 \\ k(t) \geq \dfrac{h(t) - 2}{2} \\ k(t) \geq -2h(t) - 1 \\ k(t) \geq \dfrac{h(t) + 3}{2} \end{cases}$$

together with the necessary and sufficient condition to have the solution in the whole set $\mathbb{K}$, namely

$$-x_{21}(t) + k(t) > 0 \Longleftrightarrow h(t) + 3k(t) + 3 > 0$$

are fulfilled simultaneously if and only if $h(t)$ and $k(t)$ are non-negative functions such that

$$\begin{cases} -3h(t) + k(t) + 1 \geq 0 \\ -h(t) + 2k(t) - 3 \geq 0. \end{cases}$$

Therefore, in this case the solution is

$$p_1(t) = \frac{-3h(t) + k(t) + 1}{5}, \qquad p_2(t) = 0,$$

$$q_1(t) = \frac{-h(t) + 2k(t) + 2}{5},$$

$$x_{11}(t) = \frac{2h(t) + k(t) + 1}{5}, \qquad x_{21}(t) = \frac{-h(t) + 2k(t) - 3}{5},$$

$$g_1(p(t)) = \frac{2h(t) + k(t) + 1}{5}, \qquad g_2(p(t)) = k(t),$$

$$f_1(q(t)) = \frac{h(t) + 3k(t) - 2}{5},$$

$$c_{11}(x(t)) = \frac{2h(t) + k(t) + 1}{5}, \qquad c_{21}(x(t)) = \frac{-h(t) + 2k(t) + 2}{5},$$

and there is a supply excess

$$s_2(t) = g_2(t) - x_{21}(t) = \frac{h(t) + 3k(t) + 3}{5}.$$

We pass now to the discretization procedure, assuming $h(t) = \dfrac{t}{2}$ and $k(t) = t + \dfrac{8}{7}$. To this end, we must rewrite the variational inequality

$$\ll v(u), u - u^* \gg \geq 0, \qquad \forall u \in \mathbb{K}$$

in the form

$$\int_0^{\frac{1}{2}} \langle Au^*(t) + b(t), u(t) - u^*(t) \rangle \, dt \geq 0, \qquad \forall u(t) \in \mathbb{K}$$

where A is a constant matrix and $b(t)$ is a time-dependent vector defined by

$$A = \begin{bmatrix} 1 & 0 & 0 & -1 & 0 \\ 0 & 1 & 0 & 0 & -1 \\ 0 & 0 & 1 & 1 & 1 \\ 1 & 0 & -1 & 1 & 0 \\ 0 & 1 & -1 & 0 & 1 \end{bmatrix} \quad \text{and } b(t) = \begin{bmatrix} h(t) \\ k(t) \\ -k(t) \\ 0 \\ 1 \end{bmatrix}.$$

It is possible to verify that the matrix $A(t)$ is positive definite, since the characteristic polynomial is

$$(1 - t) \cdot (t^4 - 4t^3 + 8t^2 - 10t + 8).$$

For each partition of the time interval $\left[0, \dfrac{1}{2}\right]$ by means of the points

$$0 < \frac{1}{2n} < \dots < \frac{j-1}{2n} < \frac{j}{2n} < \dots < \frac{1}{2},$$

we are led to consider the set

$$\mathbb{K}_j^n = \left\{ u_j^n = (p_{j1}^n, p_{j2}^n, q_{j1}^n, x_{j11}^n, x_{j21}^n) \in \mathbb{R}^5 : \right.$$

$$0 \leq p_{j1}^n \leq 2n \int_{(j-1)/2n}^{j/2n} (h(t) + k(t) + 1) \, dt,$$

$$0 \leq p_{j2}^n \leq 2n \int_{(j-1)/2n}^{j/2n} (h(t) + k(t) + 1) \, dt,$$

$$0 \leq q_{j1}^n \leq 2n \int_{(j-1)/2n}^{j/2n} (h(t) + k(t) + 1) \, dt,$$

$$0 \leq x_{j11}^n \leq 2n \int_{(j-1)/2n}^{j/2n} (h(t) + k(t) + 1) \, dt,$$

$$0 \le x_{j2}^n \le 2n \left. \int_{(j-1)/2n}^{j/2n} (h(t) + k(t) + 1) \, dt \right\},$$

that is

$$\mathbb{K}_j^n = \left\{ u_j^n = \left(p_{j1}^n, p_{j2}^n, q_{j1}^n, x_{j11}^n, x_{j21}^n \right) \in \mathbb{R}^5 : \right.$$

$$0 \le p_{j1}^n \le \frac{6j-3}{8n} + \frac{15}{7}, \quad 0 \le p_{j2}^n \le \frac{6j-3}{8n} + \frac{15}{7},$$

$$0 \le q_{j1}^n \le \frac{6j-3}{8n} + \frac{15}{7}, \quad 0 \le x_{j11}^n \le \frac{6j-3}{8n} + \frac{15}{7},$$

$$\left. 0 \le x_{j21}^n \le \frac{6j-3}{8n} + \frac{15}{7} \right\},$$

since

$$2n \int_{(j-1)/2n}^{j/2n} (h(t) + k(t) + 1) \, dt$$

$$= 2n \int_{(j-1)/2n}^{j/2n} \left(\frac{3}{2} t + \frac{15}{7} \right) dt = \frac{6j-1}{8n} + \frac{15}{7}.$$

Then the variational inequality we have to solve is

$$\langle A \left(u_j^n \right)^* + b_j^n, u_j^n - \left(u_j^n \right)^* \rangle \ge 0 \quad \forall u_j^n \in \mathbb{K}_j^n,$$

where

$$b_j^n = \begin{bmatrix} \dfrac{2j-1}{8n} \\[2ex] \dfrac{2j-1}{4n} + \dfrac{8}{7} \\[2ex] -\dfrac{2j-1}{4n} - \dfrac{8}{7} \\[1ex] 0 \\[1ex] 1 \end{bmatrix}$$

since

$$2n \int_{(j-1)/2n}^{j/2n} h(t) \, dt = \frac{2j-1}{8n} \quad \text{and} \quad 2n \int_{(j-1)/2n}^{j/2n} k(t) \, dt = \frac{2j-1}{4n} + \frac{8}{7}.$$

Taking into account the solution obtained by means of the direct method, we note that the system

$$\begin{cases} Au_j^n + b_j^n = 0 \\ u_j^n \in \mathbb{K}_j^n \end{cases}$$

does not admit solutions, whereas in the boundary $\mathbb{K}_j^n \cap \{p_{j2}^n = 0\}$ the system

$$\begin{cases} Au_j^n + b_j^n = 0 \\ p_{j2}^n = 0 \end{cases}$$

admits the solution

$$p_{j1}^n = \frac{-2j+1}{40\,n} + \frac{3}{7}, \qquad p_{j2}^n = 0,$$

$$q_{j1}^n = \frac{6j-3}{40\,n} + \frac{6}{7},$$

$$x_{j11}^n = \frac{2j-1}{10\,n} + \frac{3}{7}, \qquad x_{j21}^n = \frac{6j-3}{40\,n} - \frac{1}{7}.$$

The necessary and sufficient condition to have the solution in the whole convex set $\mathbb{K}$, namely

$$p_{j2}^n - x_{j21}^n + 2n \int_{(j-1)/2n}^{j/2n} k(t)\,dt > 0 \iff 26j - 13 > 0,$$

is obviously satisfied. Moreover, we have also:

$$g_{j1}^n(p) = \frac{2j-1}{10\,n} + \frac{3}{7}, \qquad g_{j2}^n(p) = \frac{2j-1}{4\,n} + \frac{8}{7},$$

$$f_{j1}^n(q) = \frac{14j-7}{40\,n} + \frac{2}{7},$$

$$c_{j11}^n(x) = \frac{2j-1}{10\,n} + \frac{3}{7}, \qquad c_{j21}^n(x) = \frac{6j-3}{40\,n} + \frac{6}{7},$$

and an excess

$$s_{j2}^n = \frac{14j-7}{40\,n} + \frac{6}{7}.$$

Finally, on the convex set $\mathbb{K}^n = \cap \mathbb{K}^n_j$ the solution is given by

$$u_n(t) = \sum_{j=1}^n \chi \left(\frac{j-1}{2n}, \frac{j}{2n} \right) u^n_j.$$

3.2 The Quantity Formulation

3.2.1 The Dynamic Model

In this section we are concerned with the spatial price equilibrium problem in the case of the quantity formulation, under the assumption that the data evolve in time (see [130] and [108] for the static case). We shall prove that the time-dependent equilibrium conditions can be incorporated directly into an evolutionary variational inequality for which an existence theorem is provided in a suitable Lebesgue class of functions. This fact means that, in order to obtain existence results, regularity assumptions with respect to time are not required. The same variational inequality formulation also is useful in order to perform a stability analysis of the equilibrium pattern.

Let us consider n supply markets P_i, $i = 1, 2, \ldots n$ and m demand markets Q_j, $j = 1, 2, \ldots m$ involved in the production and in the consumption respectively of a commodity during a period of time $[0, T]$, $T > 0$. Let $g_i(t)$, $t \in [0, T]$, $i = 1, 2, \ldots, n$ denote the supply of the commodity associated with supply market i at time $t \in [0, T]$ and let $p_i(t)$, $t \in [0, T]$, $i = 1, 2, \ldots, n$ denote the supply price of the commodity associated with supply market i at the same time $t \in [0, T]$. Let $f_j(t)$ $t \in [0, T]$, $j = 1, 2, \ldots, m$ denote the demand associated with the demand market j at time $t \in [0, T]$ and let $q_j(t)$ $t \in [0, T]$, $j = 1, 2, \ldots, m$ denote the demand price associated with the demand market j at time $t \in [0, T]$. Let $x_{ij}(t)$, $t \in [0, T]$, $i = 1, 2, \ldots, n$, $j = 1, 2, \ldots, m$ denote the non-negative commodity shipment between the supply and demand pair (P_i, Q_j) at time $t \in [0, T]$ and let $c_{ij}(t)$ $t \in [0, T]$, $i = 1, 2, \ldots, n$, $j = 1, 2, \ldots, m$ denote the non-negative unit transportation cost associated with trading the commodity between (P_i, Q_j) at the same time $t \in [0, T]$.

Assuming that we are in the presence of excesses on the supply and on the demand (see also [52]), denoted by $s_i(t)$ and $d_j(t)$ respectively, then the following feasibility conditions must hold for every $i = 1, \ldots, n$

and $j = 1, \ldots, m$ and a.e. in $[0, T]$:

$$g_i(t) = \sum_{j=1}^{m} x_{ij}(t) + s_i(t), \tag{3.47}$$

$$f_j(t) = \sum_{i=1}^{n} x_{ij}(t) + d_j(t). \tag{3.48}$$

Let us assume, for technical reasons, that the functional setting for the trajectories $w(t) = (g(t), f(t), x(t), s(t), d(t))$ is still the Hilbert space:

$$\tilde{L} = L^2\left([0, T], \mathbb{R}^n\right) \times L^2\left([0, T], \mathbb{R}^m\right) \times L^2\left([0, T], \mathbb{R}^{nm}\right)$$

$$\times L^2\left([0, T], \mathbb{R}^n\right) \times L^2\left([0, T], \mathbb{R}^m\right).$$

We recall (see also [37]) that, if z is an element of the Euclidean space $\mathbb{R}^k$, we denote by $\|z\|_k$ the usual Euclidean norm; then, if $z(t)$ is an element of $L^2([0, T], \mathbb{R}^k)$, we set

$$\|z\|_{L^2([0,T],\mathbb{R}^k)} = \left(\int_0^T \|z(t)\|_k^2 \, dt\right)^{\frac{1}{2}}.$$

We shall omit the index k and we shall denote $\|z\|_{L^2([0,T],\mathbb{R}^k)}$ briefly by $\|z\|_{L^2}$ if there is no possibility of confusion. If $(z_1, z_2, z_3) \in L^2([0, T], \mathbb{R}^{k_1}) \times L^2([0, T], \mathbb{R}^{k_2}) \times L^2([0, T], \mathbb{R}^{k_3})$, we set

$$\|(z_1, z_2, z_3)\|_{L^2} = \left(\|z_1\|_{L^2([0,T],\mathbb{R}^{k_1})}^2 + \|z_2\|_{L^2([0,T],\mathbb{R}^{k_2})}^2 + \|z_3\|_{L^2([0,T],\mathbb{R}^{k_3})}^2\right)^{\frac{1}{2}},$$

and in particular if $w(t) = (g(t), f(t), x(t), s(t), d(t)) \in \tilde{L}$, then

$$\begin{aligned}\|w(t)\|_{\tilde{L}} &= \left(\|g(t)\|_{L^2([0,T],\mathbb{R}^n)}^2 + \|f(t)\|_{L^2([0,T],\mathbb{R}^m)}^2 + \|x(t)\|_{L^2([0,T],\mathbb{R}^{nm})}^2\right.\\ &\quad + \left.\|s(t)\|_{L^2([0,T],\mathbb{R}^n)}^2 + \|d(t)\|_{L^2([0,T],\mathbb{R}^m)}^2\right)^{\frac{1}{2}}.\end{aligned}$$

Furthermore, we assume that the feasible vector $w(t)$ satisfies the condition:

$$w(t) \geq 0 \text{ a.e. in } [0, T]. \tag{3.49}$$

Hence, taking into account (3.47), (3.48), (3.49), the set of feasible vectors $w(t)$ is

$$\tilde{\mathbb{K}} = \left\{ w(t) = (g(t), f(t), x(t), s(t), d(t)) \in \tilde{L} : \right.$$

$$w(t) \geq 0 \text{ a.e. in } [0, T],$$

$$g_i(t) = \sum_{j=1}^{m} x_{ij} + s_i(t), \quad i = 1, \ldots, n,$$

$$\left. f_j(t) = \sum_{i=1}^{n} x_{ij} + d_j(t), \quad j = 1, \ldots, m, \text{ a.e. in } [0, T] \right\}. \quad (3.50)$$

It is easily seen that $\mathbb{K}$ is a convex, closed, not bounded subset of the Hilbert space $\tilde{L}$. Furthermore, we are given the mappings:

$$p : L^2([0, T], \mathbb{R}^n_+) \to L^2([0, T], \mathbb{R}^n_+)$$
$$q : L^2([0, T], \mathbb{R}^m_+) \to L^2([0, T], \mathbb{R}^m_+), \quad (3.51)$$

which assign to each supply $g(t)$ the supply price $p(g(t))$ and to each demand $f(t)$ the demand price $q(f(t))$.

Finally, we assume also that capacity constraints on p, q and c are added and are expressed by:

$$\underline{p}(t) \leq p(g(t)) \leq \overline{p}(t), \ \underline{q}(t) \leq q(f(t)) \leq \overline{q}(t), \ \underline{c}(t) \leq c(x(t)) \leq \overline{c}(t).$$

Then the dynamic market equilibrium conditions in the case of the quantity formulation take the following form.

Definition 3.2.1 $w^*(t) = (g^*(t), f^*(t), x^*(t), s^*(t), d^*(t)) \in \tilde{\mathbb{K}}$ *is a dynamic market equilibrium if and only if for each* $i = 1, \ldots, n$ *and* $j = 1, \ldots, m$ *and a.e. in* $[0, T]$ *there holds:*

$$\begin{cases} \text{if } s_i^*(t) > 0, & \text{then } p_i(g^*(t)) = \underline{p}_i(t); \\ \text{if } \underline{p}_i(t) < p_i(g^*(t)), & \text{then } s_i^*(t) = 0; \end{cases} \quad (3.52)$$

$$\begin{cases} \text{if } d_j^*(t) > 0, & \text{then } q_j(f^*(t)) = \overline{q}_j(t); \\ \text{if } q_j(f^*(t)) < \overline{q}_j(t), & \text{then } d_j^*(t) = 0; \end{cases} \quad (3.53)$$

$$\begin{cases} \text{if } x_{ij}^*(t) > 0, \quad \text{then } p_i(g^*(t)) + c_{ij}(x^*(t)) = q_j(f^*(t)); \\ \text{if } p_i(g^*(t)) + c_{ij}(x^*(t)) > q_j(f^*(t)), \quad \text{then } x_{ij}^*(t) = 0. \end{cases} \quad (3.54)$$

Condition (3.52) states that if in the supply market P_i there is a supply excess at time t, then the supply price in P_i must be equal to the minimal price in P_i at time t; if the supply price in P_i is greater than the minimal price at time t, then in P_i there is no supply excess at time t. Analogous is the meaning of condition (3.53) for the demand markets. Condition (3.54) states that if there is trade between a pair (P_i, Q_j) at time t, then the supply price of the supply market P_i plus the transportation cost between P_i and Q_j at the same time t must be equal to the demand price of the market Q_j at time t; whereas if the supply price plus the transportation cost at time t exceeds the demand price, then there is no shipment between P_i and Q_j at time t.

Let us consider now the following variational inequality:

Find $w^*(t) \in \tilde{\mathbb{K}}$ such that

$$\int_0^T \Big\{ p(g^*(t)) \cdot (g(t) - g^*(t)) - q(f^*(t)) \cdot (f(t) - f^*(t))$$
$$+ c(x^*(t)) \cdot (x(t) - x^*(t)) - \underline{p}(t)(s(t) - s^*(t))$$
$$+ \bar{q}(t)(d(t) - d^*(t)) \Big\} dt \geq 0, \quad \forall w(t) \in \tilde{\mathbb{K}}. \quad (3.55)$$

If we denote by L and $\mathbb{K}$ the following sets

$$L = L^2([0,T], \mathbb{R}^{nm}) \times L^2([0,T], \mathbb{R}^n) \times L^2([0,T], \mathbb{R}^m),$$

$$\mathbb{K} = \{u(t) = (x(t), s(t), d(t)) \in L : u(t) \geq 0\}$$

and by $p(x(t), s(t))$ and $q(x(t), d(t))$ the following functions

$$p(x(t), s(t)) = p\left(\sum_{j=1}^m x_{1j}(t) + s_1(t), \ldots, \sum_{j=1}^m x_{nj}(t) + s_n(t) \right),$$

$$q(x(t), d(t)) = q\left(\sum_{i=1}^n x_{i1}(t) + d_1(t), \ldots, \sum_{i=1}^n x_{im}(t) + d_m(t) \right),$$

then, taking into account the feasibility conditions (3.47) and (3.48), the variational inequality (3.55) can be rewritten in an equivalent way as follows (see [105]):

$$\text{Find } u^*(t) \in \mathbb{K} \text{ such that}$$
$$\ll v(u^*(t)), \ u(t) - u^*(t) \gg$$
$$= \int_0^T \Big\{ p(x^*(t), s^*(t)) - q(x^*(t), d^*(t)) + c(x^*(t)) \cdot (x(t) - x^*(t))$$
$$+ \left[p(x^*(t), s^*(t)) - \underline{p}(t) \right] (s(t) - s^*(t))$$
$$- \left[q(x^*(t), d^*(t)) - \overline{q}(t) \right] (d(t) - d^*(t)) \Big\} \, dt \geq 0,$$
$$\forall u(t) \in \mathbb{K}. \tag{3.56}$$

We are now able to characterize the time-dependent market equilibrium in terms of the variational inequality (3.56) (and hence (3.55)), by means of the following theorem (see also [105]).

Theorem 3.2.1 $u^* = (x^*, s^*, d^*) \in \mathbb{K}$ *is a dynamic market equilibrium if and only if u^* is a solution to the variational inequality (3.56).*

Proof: Let $u^*(t) = (x^*(t), s^*(t), d^*(t))$ be a market equilibrium. For every $x(t) \geq 0$ we have:

$$\int_0^T \left[p(x^*(t), s^*(t)) - q(x^*(t), d^*(t)) + c(x^*(t)) \right] \cdot \left[x(t) - x^*(t) \right] \, dt \geq 0.$$

In fact, if $x_{ij}^*(t) > 0$, then by (3.54) we have:

$$p_i(x^*(t), s^*(t)) - q_j(x^*(t), d^*(t)) + c_{ij}(x^*(t)) = 0$$

and the product vanishes. On the contrary, if $x_{ij}^*(t) = 0$, then, from (3.54), we have:

$$p_i(x^*(t), s^*(t)) - q_j(x^*(t), d^*(t)) + c_{ij}(x^*(t)) \geq 0$$

and the product is non-negative a.e. in $[0, T]$. Hence the integral is non-negative. By similar procedures, one obtains that each product in the second and third sum is non-negative. As a consequence the second and

the third integral are non-negative and it proves that $u^*(t)$ is a solution
to (3.56).

Conversely, let the variational inequality (3.56) hold and let us prove
that also the equilibrium conditions hold. Let us suppose first that (3.54)
is not satisfied, that is there exists a set $E \subset [0, T]$ with positive measure
and there exist i^* and j^* such that for each $t \in E$:

$$p_{i^*}(x^*(t), s^*(t)) - q_{j^*}(x^*(t), d^*(t)) + c_{i^* j^*}(x^*(t)) < 0.$$

If we choose $\bar{x} \in L^2([0, T], \mathbb{R}^{nm})$ such that

$$\bar{x}(t) = x^*(t) \quad \forall t \in [0, T] \setminus E,$$

and

$$\bar{x}_{ij}(t) \begin{cases} = x_{ij}^*(t) & \forall (i, j) \neq (i^*, j^*), \ t \in E \\ > x_{ij}^*(t) & t \in E, \end{cases}$$

then, assuming in (3.56) $x(t) = \bar{x}(t)$, $s(t) = s^*(t)$, $d(t) = d^*(t)$, we get:

$$\ll v(u^*), u - u^* \gg$$

$$= \int_0^T [p(x^*(t), s^*(t)) - q(x^*(t), d^*(t)) + c(x^*(t))] \cdot [\bar{x}(t) - x^*(t)] \, dt$$

$$= \int_{[0,T] \setminus E} [p(x^*(t), s^*(t)) - q(x^*(t), d^*(t)) + c(x^*(t))] \cdot [\bar{x}(t) - x^*(t)] \, dt$$

$$+ \int_E [p(x^*(t), s^*(t)) - q(x^*(t), d^*(t)) + c(x^*(t))] \cdot [\bar{x}(t) - x^*(t)] \, dt$$

$$= \int_E [p_{i^*}(x^*(t), s^*(t)) - q_{j^*}(x^*(t)d^*(t)) + c_{i^* j^*}(x^*(t))]$$

$$\cdot \left[\bar{x}_{i^* j^*}(t) - x_{i^* j^*}^*(t) \right] \, dt.$$

So we have proved that

$$p_i(x^*(t), s^*(t)) - q_j(x^*(t), d^*(t)) + c_{ij}(x^*(t)) \geq 0, \quad \text{a.e. in } [0, T].$$

Let us prove now that if $x_{ij}^*(t) > 0$, then

$$p_i(x^*(t), s^*(t)) + c_{ij}(x^*(t)) = q_j(x^*(t), d^*(t)), \quad \text{a.e. in } [0, T].$$

Let us suppose *ad absurdum* that there exists a set $E \subset [0, T]$ with
positive measure and there exist i^*, j^* such that

$$p_{i^*}(x^*(t), s^*(t)) - q_{j^*}(x^*(t), d^*(t)) + c_{i^* j^*}(x^*(t)) > 0.$$

If we choose

$$\bar{x}_{ij} \begin{cases} = x_{ij}^*(t) & \text{in } [0,T] \setminus E, \quad \forall(i,j) \neq (i^*,j^*) \\ = x_{ij}^*(t) & \forall(i,j) \neq (i^*,j^*), \quad t \in E \\ < x_{i^*j^*}^*(t) & t \in E, \end{cases}$$

assuming in (3.56) $x(t) = \bar{x}(t)$, $s(t) = s^*(t)$, $d(t) = d^*(t)$, then we have

$$\ll v(u^*), u - u^* \gg$$
$$= \int_E [p_{i^*}(x^*(t), s^*(t)) - q_{j^*}(x^*(t), d^*(t)) + c_{i^*j^*}(x^*(t))]$$
$$\cdot [\bar{x}_{i^*j^*}(t) - x_{i^*j^*}^*(t)] \, dt < 0.$$

It remains to prove that if a.e. in $[0,T]$

$$p_{i^*}(x^*(t), s^*(t)) + c_{i^*j^*}(x^*(t)) > q_{j^*}(x^*(t), d^*(t)),$$

then $x_{ij}^*(t) = 0$, $\forall i, j$. Let us suppose *ad absurdum* that there exists a set $E \subset [0,T]$ with positive measure and there exist i^*, j^* such that

$$p_{i^*}(x^*(t), s^*(t)) + c_{i^*j^*}(x^*(t)) > q_{j^*}(x^*(t), d^*(t)) \text{ in } E$$

and $x_{i^*j^*}^* > 0$. Using the previous arguments, it is easy to get a contradiction and hence $x_{ij}^*(t) = 0$ for all i and j.

Finally, let us prove that condition (3.52) is verified. Let us suppose *ad absurdum* that there exists a set $E \subset [0,T]$ with positive measure and there exist i^* such that $s_{i^*}^*(t) > 0$ and $p_{i^*}(x^*(t), s^*(t)) > \underline{p}_{i^*}(t)$ in E. If we choose

$$\bar{s}_i(t) \begin{cases} = s_i^*(t) & \forall t \in [0,T] \setminus E, \quad \forall i = 1,\dots,n \\ = s_i^*(t) & \forall i \neq i^*, \quad \forall t \in E \\ < s_{i^*}^*(t) & i = i^*, \quad \forall t \in E, \end{cases}$$

assuming $x(t) = x^*(t)$, $s(t) = \bar{s}(t)$, $d(t) = d^*(t)$, then from (3.56) we get

$$\ll v(u^*), u - u^* \gg = \int_E \left[p_{i^*}(x^*(t), s^*(t)) - \underline{p}_{i^*} \right] \cdot [\bar{s}_{i^*}(t) - s_{i^*}(t)] \, dt < 0.$$

Analogously, if we suppose *ad absurdum* that there exists a set $E \subset [0,T]$ with positive measure and there exists i^* such that:

if $s_{i^*}^*(t) > 0$, then $p_{i^*}(x^*(t), s^*(t)) > \underline{p}_{i^*}(t)$ in E,

we get a contradiction. So all the equilibrium conditions are satisfied. $\square$

Remark 3.2.1 As in Remark 3.1.2, the variational inequality (3.56) is equivalent to

$$\langle v(u^*(t), u(t) - u^*(t)) \rangle \geq 0, \quad \forall u(t) \in \mathbb{K}, \text{ a.e. in } [0, T].$$

3.2.2 Existence Results

Adapting a classical existence theorem (see Theorems D.5 and D.6) for the solution to a variational inequality to our problem, we will have the following theorem, which provides existence with or without pseudomonotonicity assumptions. Moreover, since the convex $\mathbb{K}$ is unbounded, we need coercivity assumptions, which we use in a generalized version (see [108] for the usual coercivity condition).

Theorem 3.2.2 *Each of the following conditions is sufficient to ensure the existence of the solution to (3.56):*

1. $v(u) = v(x(t), s(t), d(t))$ *is hemicontinuous with respect to the strong topology and there exist $A \subseteq \mathbb{K}$ compact and $B \subseteq \mathbb{K}$ compact, convex with respect to the strong topology such that*

$$\forall u_1 \in \mathbb{K} \setminus A \quad \exists u_2 \in B : \ \langle v(u_1), u_2 - u_1 \rangle < 0;$$

2. *v is pseudomonotone, v is hemicontinuous along line segments and there exist $A \subseteq \mathbb{K}$ compact and $B \subseteq \mathbb{K}$ compact, convex with respect to the weak topology such that*

$$\forall u_1 \in \mathbb{K} \setminus A \quad \exists u_2 \in B : \ \langle v(u_1), u_2 - u_1 \rangle < 0;$$

3. *v is hemicontinuous on $\mathbb{K}$ with respect to the weak topology, and there exist $A \subseteq \mathbb{K}$ compact and $B \subseteq \mathbb{K}$ compact, convex with respect to the weak topology such that*

$$\forall u_1 \in \mathbb{K} \setminus A \quad \exists u_2 \in B : \ \langle v(u_1), u_2 - u_1 \rangle < 0.$$

3.2.3 Stability analysis of the equilibrium patterns

We want to examine now the sensitivity analysis of the quantity model governed by the variational inequality (3.56). Let us assume that the supply price functions change from $p'(\cdot)$ to $p^*(\cdot)$, the demand price functions change from $q'(\cdot)$ to $q^*(\cdot)$ and the transportation cost functions change from $c'(\cdot)$ to $c^*(\cdot)$ and let us establish the relation between the corresponding equilibrium patterns (x', s', d') and (x^*, s^*, d^*).

Let us require that the following strict monotonicity conditions hold:

$$\forall u_1 = (x_1, s_1, d_1), \ u_2 = (x_2, s_2, d_2) \in L$$

- $\Big[p'(x_1(t), s_1(t)) - q'(x_1(t), d_1(t)) + c'(x_1(t))$

  $- (p'(x_2(t), s_2(t)) - q'(x_2(t), d_2(t)) + c'(x_2(t))) \Big]$

  $\cdot [x_1(t) - x_2(t)] \geq \beta \|x_1(t) - x_2(t)\|^2_{\mathbb{R}^{nm}},$

- $\Big[p'(x_1(t), s_1(t)) - p'(x_2(t), s_2(t)) \Big] \cdot [s_1(t) - s_2(t)]$

  $\geq \gamma \|s_1(t) - s_2(t)\|^2_{\mathbb{R}^{n}},$

- $\Big[q'(x_2(t), d_2(t)) - q'(x_1(t), d_1(t)) \Big] \cdot [d_1(t) - d_2(t)]$

  $\geq \delta \|d_1(t) - d_2(t)\|^2_{\mathbb{R}^{m}},$

  a.e. in $[0, T]$ and $\beta, \gamma, \delta \in \mathbb{R}^+ \setminus \{0\}$. $\hspace{2cm}$ (3.57)

Now, keeping in mind the previous notation, $\forall u = (x, s, d) \in L$ let us set:

$$v'(u) = \big(p'(x, s) - q'(x, d) + c'(x), p'(x, s) - \underline{p}', \overline{q}' - q'(x, d) \big),$$

$$v^*(u) = \big(p^*(x, s) - q^*(x, d) + c^*(x), p^*(x, s) - \underline{p}^*, \overline{q}^* - q^*(x, d) \big).$$

We can observe that from conditions (3.57) the strong monotonicity condition on v' holds, namely there exists $\alpha = \min\{\beta, \gamma, \delta\} > 0$ such that $\forall u_1, \ u_2 \in L$:

$$\langle v'(u_1) - v'(u_2), u_1 - u_2 \rangle \geq \alpha \|u_1 - u_2\|^2_{\mathbb{R}^{n+m+nm}}. \hspace{1cm} (3.58)$$

The following theorem establishes that small changes in the supply and demand price and transportation cost functions induce small changes in the supplies, demands, and commodity shipment patterns.

Theorem 3.2.3 *Let us consider the spatial price equilibrium problem with two supply price functions $p'(t)$ and $p^*(t)$, two demand price functions $q'(t)$ and $q^*(t)$ and two transportation cost functions $c'(t)$ and $c^*(t)$,* *and let $u'(t) \equiv (x'(t), s'(t), d'(t))$ and $u^*(t) \equiv (x^*(t), s^*(t), d^*(t))$ be the corresponding dynamic market equilibrium patterns. Then, under the assumptions (3.57), we have:*

$$\|u'(t) - u^*(t)\| \leq \frac{1}{\alpha} \|v'(u'(t)) - v^*(u^*(t))\|, \, a.e. \, \text{ in } [0, T].$$

Proof: First, we observe that, by virtue of Remark 3.2.1, the dynamic markets equilibria $u'(t)$ and $u^*(t)$ satisfy the variational inequality (3.56), namely the following conditions hold:

$$\langle v'(u'(t)), u(t) - u'(t) \rangle \geq 0 \quad \text{and} \quad \langle v^*(u^*(t)), u(t) - u^*(t) \rangle \geq 0 \quad \forall u(t) \in \mathbb{K}.$$

Choosing $u(t) = u^*(t)$ and $u(t) = u'(t)$, respectively, and adding the two inequalities we have:

$$\langle v^*(u^*(t)) - v'(u'(t)), u'(t) - u^*(t) \rangle \geq 0. \tag{3.59}$$

From (3.59) we derive:

$$\langle v^*(u^*(t)) - v'(u^*(t)), u'(t) - u^*(t) \rangle$$
$$\geq \langle v'(u'(t)) - v'(u^*(t)), u'(t) - u^*(t) \rangle. \tag{3.60}$$

Taking into account the monotonicity conditions (3.57) and using the Schwartz inequality we get:

$$\alpha \|u'(t) - u^*(t)\|^2_{\mathbb{R}^{n+m+nm}} \leq \langle v^*(u^*(t)) - v'(u^*(t)), u'(t) - u^*(t) \rangle$$

$$\leq \|v^*(u^*(t)) - v'(u^*(t))\| \, \|u'(t) - u^*(t)\|_{\mathbb{R}^{n+m+nm}}.$$

Hence:

$$\|u'(t) - u^*(t)\| \leq \frac{1}{\alpha} \|v^*(u^*(t)) - v'(u'(t))\|, \quad \text{a.e. in } [0, T]$$

and the assertion is proved. □

Theorem 3.2.4 *Under the same assumptions of Theorem 3.2.3, let us assume also that in the supply market i the supply price is increased* *[decreased] passing from* $p'_i(x^*(t), s^*(t))$ *to* $p^*_i(x^*(t), s^*(t))$, *whereas all the other supply price functions remain unchanged, namely:*

$$\begin{cases} p^*_i(x^*(t), s^*(t)) > p'_i(x^*(t), s^*(t)), \\ p^*_k(x^*(t), s^*(t)) = p'_k(x^*(t), s^*(t)), \; \forall k \neq i \end{cases} \quad a.e. \; in \; [0, T]. \quad (3.61)$$

Moreover, let us assume that the minimum supply price is fixed, namely:

$$\underline{p}^*(t) = \underline{p}'(t) \quad a.e. \; in \; [0, T]. \quad (3.62)$$

Let us suppose also that, for each $(x(t), s(t))$ *and a.e. in* $[0, T]$, *we have:*

$$\frac{\partial p'_k(x(t), s(t))}{\partial x_{hj}} = 0 \quad \forall k \neq i, \; h = 1, \dots, n, \; j = 1, \dots, m;$$

$$\frac{\partial p'_k(x(t), s(t))}{\partial s_h} = 0 \quad \forall k \neq i, \; h = 1, \dots, n. \quad (3.63)$$

Further, we suppose that the demand functions for all markets and the transportation cost functions in $(x^*(t), d^*(t))$ *remain unchanged, namely a.e. in* $[0, T]$:

$$\begin{aligned} q^*_j(x^*(t), d^*(t)) &= q'_j(x^*(t), d^*(t)), \quad j = 1, \dots, m, \\ c^*_{kj}(x^*(t)) &= c'_{kj}(x^*(t)), \quad k = 1, \dots, n, \; j = 1, \dots, m, \end{aligned} \quad (3.64)$$

then:

$$\begin{cases} \sum_{j=1}^{m} x^*_{ij}(t) + s^*_i(t) \leq \sum_{j=1}^{m} x'_{ij}(t) + s'_i(t), \;\; a.e. \; in \; [0, T] \\ s^*_i(t) \leq s'_i(t), \;\; a.e. \; in \; [0, T] \\ p^*_i(x^*(t), s^*(t)) \geq p'_i(x'(t), s'(t)) \;\; a.e. \; in \; [0, T]. \end{cases} \quad (3.65)$$

Proof: From (3.60) we derive:

$$\langle v^*(u^*) - v'(u^*), u' - u^* \rangle \geq \langle v'(u') - v'(u^*), u' - u^* \rangle \geq \alpha \left\| u' - u^* \right\|^2_{\mathbb{R}^{n+m+nm}}$$

and

$$\langle v^*(u^*) - v'(u^*), u^* - u' \rangle \leq 0.$$

This inequality can be rewritten in the following form:

$$\sum_{k=1}^{n}\sum_{j=1}^{m}\Big[\left(p_k^*(x^*(t),s^*(t))-q_j^*(x^*(t),d^*(t))+c_{kj}^*(x^*(t))\right)$$

$$-\left(p'_k(x^*(t),s^*(t))-q'_j(x^*(t),d^*(t))+c'_{kj}(x^*(t))\right)\Big]$$

$$\cdot\left[x_{kj}^*(t)-x'_{kj}(t)\right]+\sum_{k=1}^{n}\Big[\left(p_k^*(x^*(t),s^*(t))-\underline{p}_k^*(t)\right)$$

$$-\left(p'_k(x^*(t),s^*(t))-\underline{p}'_k(t)\right)\Big]\cdot[s_k^*(t)-s'_k(t)]$$

$$+\sum_{j=1}^{m}\big[\left(\overline{q}_j^*(t)-q_j^*(x^*(t),d^*(t))\right)$$

$$-\left(\overline{q}'_j(t)-q'_j(x^*(t),d^*(t))\right)\big]\cdot[d_j^*(t)-d'_j(t)]\leq 0,$$
$$\text{a.e. in }[0,T]. \tag{3.66}$$

From (3.66), by assumptions (3.61), (3.62) and (3.63), we derive a.e. in $[0,T]$:

$$\sum_{j=1}^{m}\Big[p_i^*(x^*(t),s^*(t))-p'_i(x^*(t),s^*(t))\Big]\cdot\left[x_{ij}^*(t)-x'_{ij}(t)\right]$$

$$+\left[p_i^*(x^*(t),s^*(t))-p'_i(x^*(t),s^*(t))\right]\cdot[s_i^*(t)-s'_i(t)]\leq 0,$$

that is

$$[p_i^*(x^*(t),s^*(t))-p'_i(x^*(t),s^*(t))]$$

$$\cdot\left[\left(\sum_{j=1}^{m}x_{ij}^*(t)+s_i^*(t)\right)-\left(\sum_{j=1}^{m}x'_{ij}(t)+s'_i(t)\right)\right]\leq 0.$$

Hence, because of:

$$p_i^*(x^*(t),s^*(t))-p'_i(x^*(t),s^*(t))>0\quad\text{a.e. in }[0,T],$$

it results that

$$\sum_{j=1}^{m}x_{ij}^*(t)-s_i^*(t)\leq\sum_{j=1}^{m}x'_{ij}(t)-s'_i(t)\quad\text{a.e. in }[0,T].$$

Let us prove now that:

$$s_i^*(t) \leq s_i'(t), \quad \text{a.e. in } [0,T]. \tag{3.67}$$

In fact, we have:

$$
\begin{aligned}
&[p^*(x^*(t), s^*(t)) - p'(x^*(t), s^*(t))] \cdot (s'(t) - s^*(t)) \\
&= [p^*(x^*(t), s^*(t)) - p'(x^*(t), s^*(t))]\, s'(t) \\
&\quad - [p^*(x^*(t), s^*(t)) - p'(x^*(t), s^*(t))]\, s^*(t) \\
&= [(p^*(x^*(t), s^*(t)) - p'(x^*(t), s^*(t))]\, s'(t) \\
&\quad - \left[p^*(x^*(t), s^*(t)) - \underline{p}^*(t) \right] s^*(t) + \left[p'(x^*(t), s^*(t)) - \underline{p}'(t) \right] s^*(t).
\end{aligned}
$$

From the equilibrium conditions (3.52) we get:

$$\left[p^*(x^*(t), s^*(t)) - \underline{p}^*(t) \right] s^* = \beta^* \cdot s^* = 0;$$

moreover, by assumption (3.61), it results that:

$$[p^*(x^*(t), s^*(t)) - p'(x^*(t), s^*(t))]\, s'(t)$$

$$= [p_i^*(x^*(t), s^*(t)) - p_i'(x^*(t), s^*(t))]\, s_i'(t) \geq 0;$$

and, because $p'(x^*(t), s^*(t)) \geq \underline{p}'(t)$ and $s^*(t) \geq 0$ a.e. in $[0,T]$, we obtain:

$$\left[p'(x^*(t), s^*(t)) - \underline{p}'(t) \right] s^*(t) \geq 0, \ \text{a.e. in } [0,T].$$

As a consequence, a.e. in $[0,T,]$ it results that:

$$[p_i^*(x^*(t), s^*(t)) - p_i'(x^*(t), s^*(t))] \cdot [s_i'(t) - s_i^*(t)] \geq 0, \tag{3.68}$$

because, from the equilibrium condition (3.52), we have:

$$s_i^*(t) \left[p_i^*(x^*(t), s^*(t)) - \underline{p}_i(t) \right] = 0; \tag{3.69}$$

moreover

$$s_i^*(t) \left[p_i'(x^*(t), s^*(t)) - \underline{p}_i'(t) \right] \geq 0. \tag{3.70}$$

Summing now (3.69) and the opposite of (3.70), we get:

$$s_i^*(t) \left[p_i^*(x^*(t), s^*(t)) - \underline{p}_i(t) - p_i'(x^*(t), s^*(t)) + \underline{p}_i'(t) \right] \leq 0,$$

that is

$$-s_i^*(t)\left[p_i^*(x^*(t),s^*(t)) - p_i'(x^*(t),s^*(t))\right] \geq 0, \text{ a.e. in } [0,T],$$

hence (3.68) holds. Since, by assumption,

$$p_i^*(x^*(t),s^*(t)) - p_i'(x^*(t),s^*(t)) > 0, \text{ a.e. in } [0,T],$$

then it must be that

$$s_i(t) \geq s_i^*(t) \text{ a.e. in } [0,T].$$

It remains to prove now the last line of (3.65). We have:

$$[p^*(x^*(t),s^*(t)) - p'(x'(t),s'(t))]\cdot[s'(t) - s^*(t)]$$
$$= [p^*(x^*(t),s^*(t)) - \underline{p}^*(t)]\cdot[s'(t) - s^*(t)]$$
$$- [p'(x'(t),s'(t)) - \underline{p}'(t)]\cdot[s'(t) - s^*(t)].$$

Then, taking into account the inequality (3.59), we obtain:

$$[p^*(x^*(t),s^*(t)) - p'(x'(t),s'(t))]\cdot[s'(t) - s^*(t)] \geq 0,$$

that is:

$$[p^*(x^*(t),s^*(t)) - p'(x'(t),s'(t))]\cdot[s'(t) - s^*(t)]$$
$$= [p_i^*(x^*(t),s^*(t)) - p_i'(x'(t),s'(t))]\cdot[s_i'(t) - s_i^*(t)]$$
$$+ \sum_{k\neq i}[p_k^*(x^*(t),s^*(t)) - p_k'(x'(t),s'(t))]\cdot[s_k'(t) - s_k^*(t)] \geq 0. \quad (3.71)$$

By means of assumption (3.61) and of the Lagrange theorem, applied in

$$\left[\sum_{j=1}^m x_{ij}^*(t) + s_i^*(t), \sum_{j=1}^m x_{ij}'(t) + s_i'(t)\right],$$

we have:

$$\forall k = 1,\ldots,n, \quad k \neq i :$$
$$p_k^*(x^*(t),s^*(t)) - p_k'(x'(t),s'(t))$$
$$= p_k'(x^*(t),s^*(t)) - p_k'(x'(t),s'(t))$$
$$= \sum_{h=1}^n \sum_{j=1}^m \frac{\partial p_k'(\overline{x}(t),\overline{s}(t))}{\partial x_{hj}} \cdot \left[x_{hj}^*(t) - x_{hj}'(t)\right]$$
$$+ \sum_{h=1}^n \frac{\partial p_k'(\overline{x}(t),\overline{s}(t))}{\partial s_h} \cdot \left[s_h^*(t) - s_h'(t)\right]. \quad (3.72)$$

From (3.72), by assumption (3.63), we deduce:

$$\sum_{h=1}^{n}\sum_{j=1}^{m}\frac{\partial p_{k}'(\overline{x}(t),\overline{s}(t))}{\partial x_{hj}}\cdot\left[x_{hj}^{*}(t)-x_{hj}'(t)\right]$$

$$+\sum_{h=1}^{n}\frac{\partial p_{k}'(\overline{x}(t),\overline{s}(t))}{\partial s_{h}}[s_{h}^{*}(t)-s_{h}'(t)]=0,$$

for all $k=1,\ldots,n$, $k\neq i$.

Then from (3.71) we get:

$$[p^{*}(x^{*}(t),s^{*}(t))-p'(x'(t),s'(t))]\cdot[s'(t)-s^{*}(t)]$$

$$=[p_{i}^{*}(x^{*}(t),s^{*}(t))-p_{i}'(x'(t),s'(t))]\cdot[s_{i}'(t)-s_{i}^{*}(t)]\geq 0.$$

Hence, by (3.67), also the last line of (3.65) holds. $\square$

3.3 Economic Model for Demand–Supply Markets

This model encompasses two phases. In the first phase, we consider an economy in which, during the time interval $[0,T]$, a commodity m_1 is produced by n supply markets $P_1,\ldots,P_n$ and is purchased by m demand markets $Q_1,\ldots,Q_m$. Then, in a second phase, starting after a period of time Δ, the previous demand markets $Q_1,\ldots,Q_m$ become supply markets of a new commodity m_2 using the commodity m_1. In the time interval $[\Delta,T+\Delta]$ the commodity m_2 is requested by the markets $P_1,\ldots,P_n$. We shall describe these models for more general data.

3.3.1 First Phase

The structure of the model remains the same as in Section 3.1.2. Only now we consider more general supply, demand and cost functions. In fact, we suppose that the following functions are given:

$$g=g(t,p(t)):[0,T]\times\mathbb{K}_{1}\rightarrow L^{2}([0,T],\mathbb{R}^{n}),$$
$$f=f(t,q(t)):[0,T]\times\mathbb{K}_{2}\rightarrow L^{2}([0,T],\mathbb{R}^{m}),$$
$$c=c(t,x(t)):[0,T]\times\mathbb{K}_{3}\rightarrow L^{2}([0,T],\mathbb{R}^{nm}),$$

which are of Carathéodory type, namely they are measurable with respect to t and continuous with respect to the other variables and such that

$$\|g(t, p(t))\|_{\mathbb{R}^n} \leq g(t) + \alpha(t) \|p(t)\|_{\mathbb{R}^n};$$
$$\|f(t, q(t))\|_{\mathbb{R}^m} \leq f(t) + \beta(t) \|q(t)\|_{\mathbb{R}^m};$$
$$\|c(t, x(t))\|_{\mathbb{R}^{nm}} \leq c(t) + \sigma(t) \|x(t)\|_{\mathbb{R}^{nm}}, \qquad (3.73)$$

with $g(t)$, $f(t)$, $c(t) \in L^2([0, T])$ and $\alpha(t)$, $\beta(t)$, $\sigma(t) \in L^\infty([0, T])$. Of course, by means of well-known results, we get that

$$g \in L^2([0, T], \mathbb{R}^n), \quad f \in L^2([0, T], \mathbb{R}^m), \quad c \in L^2([0, T], \mathbb{R}^{nm}).$$

Hence, we obtain, for the first phase, the following evolutionary variational inequality (see [35]):

$$\ll v(u), \tilde{u} - u \gg = \int_0^T \langle v(t, u(t)), \tilde{u}(t) - u(t) \rangle \, dt,$$
$$\forall \tilde{u} = (\tilde{p}, \tilde{q}, \tilde{x}) \in \mathbb{K}, \qquad (3.74)$$

where

$$v(t, u(t)) = \left(\left(g_i(t, p(t)) - \sum_{j=1}^m x_{ij}(t) \right)_{i=1,\dots,n}, \qquad (3.75) \right.$$

$$\left(f_j(t, q(t)) - \sum_{i=1}^n x_{ij}(t) \right)_{j=1,\dots,m}, \left. (p_i(t) + c_{ij}(t, x(t)) - q_j(t))_{\substack{i=1,\dots,n \\ j=1,\dots,m}} \right).$$

For such a variational inequality, we may provide some existence theorems under general assumptions, making use of (3.73).

Theorem 3.3.1 *Each of the following conditions is sufficient for the existence of a solution to the variational inequality:*

1. *There exist $A_1 \subseteq \mathbb{K}_1$, $A_2 \subseteq \mathbb{K}_2$, $A_3 \subseteq \mathbb{K}_3$ compact and $B_1 \subseteq \mathbb{K}_1$, $B_2 \subseteq \mathbb{K}_2$, $B_3 \subseteq \mathbb{K}_3$ convex and compact such that $\forall u_1 = (p_1, q_1, x_1) \in (\mathbb{K}_1 \setminus A_1) \times (\mathbb{K}_2 \setminus A_2) \times (\mathbb{K}_3 \setminus A_3) \, \exists u_2 = (p_2, q_2, x_2) \in B_1 \times B_2 \times B_3$ such that $\ll v(u_1), u_2 - u_1 \gg < 0$;*

2. *$v(u)$ is pseudomonotone;*

3. $v(u)$ *is an affine operator on* $\mathbb{K}$.

Proof:
1. If we endow $L^2([0,T],\mathbb{R}^n) \times L^2([0,T],\mathbb{R}^m) \times L^2([0,T],\mathbb{R}^{nm})$ with the strong topology, $\mathbb{K}$ is not a compact set and so we need to use condition (i) of Theorem 2.3.1. Then, taking into account that the assumption (3.73) ensures that the operator

$$\ll v(u), w - u \gg$$

is a Neminskii operator (see [62]), the strong continuity of the operator holds, namely: if u_n converges to u strongly in $\mathbb{K}$, then

$$\ll v(u_n), w - u_n \gg \text{ converges to } \ll v(u), w - u \gg,$$

by virtue of statements (i) and (ii) of Theorem 2.3.1, the first assertion of Theorem 3.3.1 follows.
2. Condition (3.73) allows us to show that $v(u)$ is hemicontinuous along line segments. We give a direct proof. In fact, let $\lambda_0 \in [0,1]$ and $\{\lambda_n\} \subseteq [0,1]$ such that $\lambda_n \to \lambda_0$ in $\mathbb{R}$ and let us prove that

$$\ll v(\lambda_n u_1 + (1 - \lambda_n)u_2), u_2 - u_1 \gg$$

converges to

$$\ll v(\lambda_0 u_1 + (1 - \lambda_0)u_2), u_2 - u_1 \gg,$$

that is to prove that

$$\int_0^T \langle v(t, \lambda_n u_1(t) + (1 - \lambda_n)u_2(t)), u_2(t) - u_1(t) \rangle \, dt$$

converges to

$$\int_0^T v(t, \lambda_0 u_1(t) + (1 - \lambda_0)u_2(t)) \cdot (u_2(t) - u_1(t)) \, dt.$$

Since $v(t, u(t))$, by virtue of assumption (3.73), is a Carathéodory function, then we obtain that

$$v(t, \lambda_n u_1(t) + (1 - \lambda_n)u_2(t)) \cdot (u_2(t) - u_1(t))$$

converges to

$$v(t, \lambda_0 u_1(t) + (1 - \lambda_0)u_2(t)) \cdot (u_2(t) - u_1(t)) \text{ a.e. in } [0, T].$$

Moreover, we have:

$$|\langle v(t, \lambda_n u_1(t) + (1 - \lambda_n)u_2(t)), u_2(t) - u_1(t)\rangle|_{\mathbb{R}^{n+m+nm}}$$

$$\leq \overline{\alpha}(t) + C\left(\lambda_n \|u_1(t)\|_{\mathbb{R}^{n+m+nm}} + (1 - \lambda_n)\|u_2(t)\|_{\mathbb{R}^{n+m+nm}}\right) \cdot$$

$$\|u_2(t) - u_1(t)\|_{\mathbb{R}^{n+m+nm}}$$

$$\leq \overline{\alpha}(t) + C\left(\|u_1(t)\|_{\mathbb{R}^{n+m+nm}} + \|u_2(t)\|_{\mathbb{R}^{n+m+nm}}\right)$$

$$\cdot \|u_2(t) - u_1(t)\|_{\mathbb{R}^{n+m+nm}} \text{ a.e. in } [0, T],$$

where $\overline{\alpha}(t)$ is a $L^2([0, T])$ function depending on g, f and c, and C is a constant, which depends on the supremum of $\alpha(t)$, $\beta(t)$, $\sigma(t)$, n and m. Applying the Theorem of Lebesgue, we obtain the hemicontinuity of the operator $v(t, u(t))$.

This result holds with any kind of topology we use. Then, since $\mathbb{K}$ is a convex, closed, and bounded set, $\mathbb{K}$ results to be weakly compact and, if we endow $L^2([0, T], \mathbb{R}^n) \times L^2([0, T], \mathbb{R}^m) \times L^2([0, T], \mathbb{R}^{nm})$ with the weak topology, then the first condition of Theorem 2.3.1 is automatically satisfied by choosing $A_1 = \mathbb{K}_1$, $A_2 = \mathbb{K}_2$, $A_3 = \mathbb{K}_3$ and $B_1 = B_2 = B_3 = \emptyset$. Hence, by virtue of the first and the third conditions of Theorem 2.3.1, the assertion 2. is proved.

3. If $v(t, u(t))$ is an affine operator, namely $v(t, u(t)) = A(t)u(t) + B(t)$, where

$$A(t) \in L^\infty\left([0, T], \mathbb{R}^{(n+m+nm)\times(n+m+nm)}\right)$$

and

$$B(t) \in L^2\left([0, T], \mathbb{R}^{n+m+nm}\right),$$

then $\ll v(u), u_2 - u_1 \gg$ is hemicontinuous with respect to the weak topology, because it results in a quadratic form. Moreover, $\mathbb{K}$ is compact with respect to the weak topology and we can choose $A_1 = \mathbb{K}_1$, $A_2 = \mathbb{K}_2$, $A_3 = \mathbb{K}_3$ and $B_1 = B_2 = B_3 = \emptyset$. We are led to assume the operator v is affine in condition 3., because of the results due to De Giorgi [47] and Landes [88] on the relationship between the weakly semicontinuous operators and the affine operators. $\quad\square$

3.3.2 Second Phase

Let us assume now that the markets $Q_1, \ldots, Q_m$, using the commodity m_1, produce another commodity m_2 which is required by the markets $P_1, \ldots, P_n$. Now the markets will be considered at all time $t \in [\Delta, T+\Delta]$. For each time $t \in [\Delta, T + \Delta]$, we have a total supply vector $\gamma(t + \Delta) \in \mathbb{R}^m$, a supply price vector $\pi(t + \Delta) \in \mathbb{R}^m$, the total demand vector $\varphi(t + \Delta) \in \mathbb{R}^n$, the demand price vector $\rho(t + \Delta) \in \mathbb{R}^n$, the flow vector $y(t + \Delta) \in \mathbb{R}^{nm}$ and the unit cost vector $c(t + \Delta) \in \mathbb{R}^{nm}$.

The feasible vectors $w(t + \Delta) = (\pi(t + \Delta), \rho(t + \Delta), y(t + \Delta))$ have to satisfy the time-dependent bounds on prices and transportation flows, namely that, almost everywhere on $[\Delta, T + \Delta]$,

$$w(t + \Delta) \in \prod_{j=1}^{m} [\underline{\pi}_j(t + \Delta), \overline{\pi}_j(t + \Delta)] \times \prod_{i=1}^{n} [\underline{\rho}_i(t + \Delta), \overline{\rho}_i(t + \Delta)]$$

$$\times \prod_{i=1}^{n} \prod_{j=1}^{m} [\underline{y}_{ij}(t + \Delta), \overline{y}_{ij}(t + \Delta)]$$

where $\underline{\pi}_j(t + \Delta)$, $\overline{\pi}_j(t + \Delta)$, $\underline{\rho}_i(t + \Delta)$, $\overline{\rho}_i(t + \Delta)$, $\underline{y}_{ij}(t + \Delta)$, $\overline{y}_{ij}(t + \Delta)$ are given.

The functional setting for the trajectories $w(t + \Delta)$ is the Hilbert space:

$$L^2([\Delta, T + \Delta], \mathbb{R}^m) \times L^2([\Delta, T + \Delta], \mathbb{R}^n) \times L^2([\Delta, T + \Delta], \mathbb{R}^{nm})$$

which we abbreviate by

$$\overline{L} = \overline{L}_1 \times \overline{L}_2 \times \overline{L}_3.$$

The set of feasible vectors $w(t + \Delta) = (\pi(t + \Delta), \rho(t + \Delta), y(t + \Delta))$ is given by

$$\Xi = \Xi_1 \times \Xi_2 \times \Xi_3$$
$$= \{\pi \in \overline{L}_1 : \underline{\pi}(t + \Delta) \leq \pi(t + \Delta) \leq \overline{\pi}(t + \Delta) \text{ a.e. on } [\Delta, T + \Delta]\}$$
$$\times \{\rho \in \overline{L}_2 : \underline{\rho}(t + \Delta) \leq \rho(t + \Delta) \leq \overline{\rho}(t + \Delta) \text{ a.e. on } [\Delta, T + \Delta]\}$$
$$\times \{y \in \overline{L}_3 : \underline{y}(t + \Delta) \leq y(t + \Delta) \leq \overline{y}(t + \Delta) \text{ a.e. on } [\Delta, T + \Delta]\}.$$

It is easily seen that Ξ is a convex, closed, and bounded set. Furthermore, we are given the mappings:

$$\gamma : [\Delta, T + \Delta] \times \Xi_1 \to \overline{L}_1, \quad \varphi : [\Delta, T + \Delta] \times \Xi_2 \to \overline{L}_2,$$

$$c : [\Delta, T + \Delta] \times \Xi_3 \to \overline{L}_3$$

which assign to each of the price trajectories $\pi \in \Xi_1$ and $\rho \in \Xi_2$ the supply $\gamma \in \overline{L}_1$ and the demand $\varphi \in \overline{L}_2$, respectively, and to the flow trajectory $y \in \Xi_3$ the cost $c \in \overline{L}_3$.

Introducing the supply excesses $\sigma_j(t + \Delta)$ and the demand excesses $\tau_i(t + \Delta)$ we must have:

$$\gamma_j(t + \Delta, \pi(t + \Delta)) = \sum_{i=1}^{n} y_{ij}(t + \Delta) + \sigma_j(t + \Delta) \quad j = 1, 2, \ldots, m \quad (3.76)$$

$$\varphi_i(t + \Delta, \rho(t + \Delta)) = \sum_{j=1}^{m} y_{ij}(t + \Delta) + \tau_i(t + \Delta) \quad i = 1, 2, \ldots, n. \quad (3.77)$$

Obviously $\sigma \in \overline{L}_1$ and $\tau \in \overline{L}_2$. Dynamic market equilibrium conditions take the following form (see [35]).

Definition 3.3.1 $\omega(t + \Delta) = (\pi(t + \Delta), \rho(t + \Delta), y(t + \Delta)) \in \overline{L}$ *is a dynamic market equilibrium if and only if for each* $j = 1, 2, \ldots, m$ *and* $i = 1, 2, \ldots, n$ *and a.e. on* $[\Delta, T + \Delta]$ *there hold:*

$$\sigma_j(t + \Delta) > 0 \Rightarrow \pi_j(t + \Delta) = \underline{\pi}_j(t + \Delta),$$
$$\underline{\pi}_j(t + \Delta) < \pi_j(t + \Delta) < \overline{\pi}_j(t + \Delta) \Rightarrow \sigma_j(t + \Delta) = 0;$$
$$j = 1, \ldots, m \quad (3.78)$$

$$\tau_i(t + \Delta) > 0 \Rightarrow \rho_i(t + \Delta) = \overline{\rho}_i(t + \Delta),$$
$$\underline{\rho}_i(t + \Delta) < \rho_i(t + \Delta) < \overline{\rho}_i(t + \Delta) \Rightarrow \tau_i(t + \Delta) = 0;$$
$$i = 1, \ldots, n \quad (3.79)$$

$$\pi_j(t + \Delta) + \\ + c_{ij}(t + \Delta, y(t + \Delta)) \begin{cases} \geq \rho_i(t + \Delta) & if \quad y_{ij}(t + \Delta) = \underline{y}_{ij}(t + \Delta) \\ = \rho_i(t + \Delta) & if \quad \underline{y}_{ij}(t + \Delta) \leq y_{ij}(t + \Delta) \\ & \qquad \leq \overline{y}_{ij}(t + \Delta) \\ \leq \rho_i(t + \Delta) & if \quad y_{ij}(t + \Delta) = \overline{y}_{ij}(t + \Delta) \end{cases}$$
$$j = 1, \ldots, m \quad i = 1, \ldots, n. \quad (3.80)$$

Let $\nu : \Xi \to \overline{L}$ be the operator defined by setting

$$\nu = \nu(t + \Delta, \pi(t + \Delta), \rho(t + \Delta), y(t + \Delta))$$

$$= \left((\gamma_j(t + \Delta, \pi(t + \Delta)) - \sum_{i=1}^{n} y_{ij}(t + \Delta))_{j=1,\dots,m}, \right.$$

$$(\varphi_i(t + \Delta, \rho(t + \Delta)) - \sum_{j=1}^{m} y_{ij}(t + \Delta))_{i=1,\dots,n},$$

$$\left. (\pi_j(t + \Delta) + c_{ij}(t + \Delta, y(t + \Delta)) - \rho_i(t + \Delta))_{\substack{j=1,\dots,m \\ i=1,\dots,n}} \right).$$

Let us assume that $\gamma(t + \Delta, \pi(t + \Delta)) \in \mathbb{R}^m$, $\varphi(t + \Delta, \rho(t + \Delta)) \in \mathbb{R}^n$, $c(t + \Delta, y(t + \Delta)) \in \mathbb{R}^{nm}$ are Carathéodory functions satisfying the following conditions:

$$\|\gamma(t + \Delta, \pi(t + \Delta))\|_{\mathbb{R}^m} \leq \gamma(t + \Delta) + \alpha_1(t + \Delta) \|\pi(t + \Delta)\|_{\mathbb{R}^m};$$
$$\|\varphi(t + \Delta, \rho(t + \Delta))\|_{\mathbb{R}^n} \leq \varphi(t + \Delta) + \beta_1(t + \Delta) \|\rho(t + \Delta)\|_{\mathbb{R}^n};$$
$$\|c(t + \Delta, y(t + \Delta))\|_{\mathbb{R}^{nm}} \leq c(t + \Delta) + \sigma_1(t + \Delta) \|y(t + \Delta)\|_{\mathbb{R}^{nm}}, \quad (3.81)$$

with $\gamma(t+\Delta)$, $\varphi(t+\Delta)$, $c(t+\Delta) \in L^2([\Delta, T + \Delta])$ and $\alpha_1(t+\Delta)$, $\beta_1(t+\Delta)$, $\sigma_1(t + \Delta) \in L^\infty([\Delta, T + \Delta])$.

The following characterization holds.

Theorem 3.3.2 *Suppose that for each $i = 1, 2, \dots, n$ and $j = 1, 2, \dots, m$ there hold*

1. $\rho_i(t + \Delta) = \underline{\rho}_i(t + \Delta)$ *on a set $E \subseteq [0, T]$ having positive measure*

$$\Rightarrow \varphi_i(t + \Delta, \rho(t + \Delta)) \geq 0 \ in \ E;$$

2. $y_{ij}(t + \Delta) > \underline{y}_{ij}(t + \Delta)$ *on a set $E \subseteq [0, T]$ having positive measure*
$\Rightarrow c_{ij}(t + \Delta, y(t + \Delta)) > 0 \ in \ E.$

Then $\omega(t + \Delta) = (\pi(t + \Delta), \rho(t + \Delta), y(t + \Delta)) \in \Xi$ is a dynamic *market equilibrium if and only if $\omega(t + \Delta)$ is a solution to*

$$\ll \nu(\omega), \tilde{\omega} - \omega \gg = \int_{\Delta}^{T+\Delta} \langle \nu(\omega(t+\Delta)), \tilde{\omega}(t+\Delta) - \omega(t+\Delta) \rangle \, dt$$

$$= \int_{\Delta}^{T+\Delta} \Bigg\{ \sum_{j=1}^{m} \Big(\gamma_j(t + \Delta, \pi(t+\Delta)) - \sum_{i=1}^{n} y_{ij}(t+\Delta) \Big)$$

$$\cdot (\tilde{\pi}_j(t+\Delta) - \pi_j(t+\Delta))$$

$$- \sum_{i=1}^{n} \Big(\varphi_i(t+\Delta, \rho(t+\Delta)) - \sum_{j=1}^{m} y_{ij}(t+\Delta) \Big)$$

$$\cdot (\tilde{\rho}_i(t+\Delta) - \rho_i(t+\Delta))$$

$$+ \sum_{j=1}^{m} \sum_{i=1}^{n} \Big(\pi_j(t+\Delta) + c_{ij}(t+\Delta, y(t+\Delta)) - \rho_i(t+\Delta) \Big)$$

$$\cdot (\tilde{y}_{ij}(t+\Delta) - y_{ij}(t+\Delta)) \Bigg\} \, dt \geq 0 \quad \forall \tilde{\omega} = (\tilde{\pi}, \tilde{\rho}, \tilde{y}) \in \Xi. \quad (3.82)$$

Proof: The proof is the same as for Theorem 3.1.4. $\square$

The existence theorems for the variational inequality (3.82) are analogous to the ones related to the first phase.

Theorem 3.3.3 *Each of the following conditions is sufficient for the existence of a solution to the variational inequality (3.82):*

1. *There exist $A_1 \subseteq \Xi_1$, $A_2 \subseteq \Xi_2$, $A_3 \subseteq \Xi_3$ compact and $B_1 \subseteq \Xi_1$, $B_2 \subseteq \Xi_2$, $B_3 \subseteq \Xi_3$ convex and compact such that $\forall \omega_1 = (\pi_1, \rho_1, y_1) \in (\Xi_1 \setminus A_1) \times (\Xi_2 \setminus A_2) \times (\Xi_3 \setminus A_3) \; \exists \omega_2 = (\pi_2, \rho_2, y_2) \in B_1 \times B_2 \times B_3$ such that $\ll \nu(\omega_1), \omega_2 - \omega_1 \gg < 0$;*

2. *$\nu(\omega)$ is pseudomonotone;*

3. *$\nu(\omega)$ is an affine operator on Ξ.*

3.3.3   The Dependence of the Second Phase on the First Phase

We now introduce additional constraints on $\omega(t+\Delta)$, because the production $\omega(t+\Delta)$ of m_2 depends upon the availability of the commodity m_1, namely upon $u(t)$. We assume that these constraints can be collectively described by the requirement $\omega \in D$, where $D \subseteq L$. We assume that D is convex and

$$\Xi \cap \operatorname{qi} D \neq \emptyset. \tag{3.83}$$

Two examples of set D could be

$$D = \{\omega(t + \Delta) \in \Xi : \omega(t + \Delta) \leq b(t, v(u(t))) \text{ a.e. on } [\Delta, T + \Delta]\},$$

and

$$D = \{\omega(t + \Delta) \in \Xi : b(\omega(t + \Delta), v(t, u(t))) \leq 0 \text{ a.e. on } [0, T]\},$$

where Ξ remains the same as in the previous section, $u(t)$ is the solution to (3.74) and b is a smooth function of its arguments. The presence of these additional constraints leads to an equilibrium condition expressed by the following variational inequality:

$$\omega \in \Xi \cap D \text{ and } \ll \nu(\omega), \tilde{\omega} - \omega \gg \geq 0 \quad \forall \tilde{\omega} \in \Xi \cap D, \tag{3.84}$$

for which the existence Theorem 3.3.3 holds.

We want to prove the following characterization which shows how the constraints depending on the first phase quantities of m_1 influence the quantities of m_2 produced.

Theorem 3.3.4 $\omega \in \Xi \cap D$ *is a solution to (3.84) if and only if there exists $\mu \in L^*$ such that*

$$\ll \mu, \tilde{\omega} - \omega \gg \geq 0 \qquad \forall \tilde{\omega} \in D, \tag{3.85}$$
$$\ll \nu(\omega) - \mu, \tilde{\omega} - \omega \gg \geq 0 \quad \forall \tilde{\omega} \in \Xi. \tag{3.86}$$

Proof: If (3.85) and (3.86) are satisfied, then it is clear that

$$\ll \nu(\omega), \tilde{\omega} - \omega, \gg \geq \ll \nu(\omega) - \mu, \tilde{\omega} - \omega \gg \geq 0 \quad \forall \tilde{\omega} \in \Xi \cap D,$$

and ω is an equilibrium in the sense of (3.84).

Conversely, let ω satisfy (3.84). We apply the separation theorem to the sets

$$A := \{(\tilde{\omega}, \gamma) \in D \times \mathbb{R} \mid \gamma < 0\},$$
$$B := \{(\tilde{\omega}, \gamma) \in \Xi \times \mathbb{R} \mid \ll \nu(\omega), \tilde{\omega} - \omega \gg \leq \gamma\}.$$

Then, A and B are nonempty, convex subsets of $L \times \mathbb{R}$; they are disjoint because of (3.84). Moreover, A has nonempty relative interior, since D has nonempty relative interior. So, from the separation theorem for convex sets, there exist $(\mu, k) \in L^* \times \mathbb{R}$, $(\mu, k) \neq (0,0)$, and $\alpha \in \mathbb{R}$ such that

$$\ll \mu, \tilde{\omega} \gg + k\gamma \leq \alpha \quad \forall (\tilde{\omega}, \gamma) \in A, \tag{3.87}$$

$$\ll \mu, \tilde{\omega} \gg + k\gamma \geq \alpha \quad \forall (\tilde{\omega}, \gamma) \in B. \tag{3.88}$$

It follows from (3.87) or (3.88) that $k \geq 0$. Assume, for contradiction, that $k = 0$. Choose $\omega_0 \in \Xi \cap \text{qi}\, D$, which is possible because of (3.83). Then from (3.87) and (3.88) follows $\ll \mu, \omega_0 \gg = \alpha$, and since now $\mu \neq 0$, there exists $\tilde{\omega} \in \text{ri}\, D$ with $\ll \mu, \tilde{\omega} \gg > \alpha$, which contradicts (3.87). Thus $k > 0$, and setting $\mu = -\overline{\mu} k$ and dividing by k, we obtain:

$$\ll -\overline{\mu}, \tilde{\omega} \gg + \gamma \leq \frac{\alpha}{k}.$$

Then we get, choosing γ arbitrarily close to zero in (3.87),

$$- \ll \overline{\mu}, \tilde{\omega} \gg \leq \frac{\alpha}{k} \quad \forall \tilde{\omega} \in D, \tag{3.89}$$

and, setting $\gamma := \ll \nu(\omega), \tilde{\omega} - \omega \gg$ in (3.88),

$$- \ll \overline{\mu} k, \tilde{\omega} \gg + k \ll \nu(\omega), \tilde{\omega} - \omega \gg \geq \alpha \quad \forall \tilde{\omega} \in \Xi,$$

from which:

$$- \ll \overline{\mu}, \tilde{\omega} \gg + \ll \nu(\omega), \tilde{\omega} - \omega \gg \geq \frac{\alpha}{k} \quad \forall \tilde{\omega} \in \Xi, \tag{3.90}$$

In particular, choosing $\tilde{\omega} = \omega$ in (3.89) and (3.90), we obtain

$$- \ll \overline{\mu}, \omega \gg = \alpha.$$

Substituting for α in (3.89) and (3.90) gives (3.85) and (3.86). $\quad\square$

Remark 3.3.1 From the variational inequality (3.86) it appears clear that the presence of additional constraints produces a worsening of the operator ν, according to the fact that the production of commodity m_2 depends on the availability (which has a cost) of commodity m_1.

3.3.4 General Model

Resuming, the model that describes the supply–demand market problem can be synthesized in the following way.

Theorem 3.3.5 *The first and second phase equilibrium problems are equivalent to the problem:*

$$\text{Find } U = (u, \omega) \in \mathbb{K}^* = \mathbb{K} \times (\Xi \cap D):$$
$$\ll V(U), \tilde{U} - U \gg =$$
$$\ll v(u), \tilde{u} - u \gg + \ll \nu(\omega), \tilde{\omega} - \omega \gg \geq 0 \quad \forall \tilde{U} \in \mathbb{K}^*, \qquad (3.91)$$

where $V(U) = (v(u), \nu(\omega))$.

Proof: Let us assume that u is a solution to (3.74) and ω is a solution to (3.82), then

$$\langle v(u), \tilde{u} - u \rangle \geq 0 \quad \forall \tilde{u} \in \mathbb{K}$$
$$\ll \nu(\omega), \tilde{\omega} - \omega \gg \geq 0 \quad \forall \tilde{\omega} \in \Xi \cap D,$$

from which we get

$$\ll V(U), \tilde{U} - U \gg = \ll v(u), \tilde{u} - u \gg + \ll \nu(\omega), \tilde{\omega} - \omega \gg \geq 0 \quad \forall \tilde{U} \in \mathbb{K}^*.$$

Vice versa, let us choose $\tilde{\omega} = \omega$ and $\tilde{u} = u$ in (3.91) respectively, then we obtain:

$$\langle v, \tilde{u} - u \rangle \geq 0 \quad \forall \tilde{u} \in \mathbb{K}$$

and

$$\ll \nu(\omega), \tilde{\omega} - \omega \gg \geq 0 \quad \forall \tilde{\omega} \in \Xi \cap D$$

and the assertion holds. $\square$

The existence theorem related to the previous variational inequality can be formulated in the following way.

Theorem 3.3.6 *Assuming that V verifies the Carathédory conditions (3.73) and (3.81), then each of the following conditions is sufficient for the existence of a solution to the variational inequality (3.91):*

1. *There exist $A \subseteq \mathbb{K}^*$ compact and $B \subseteq \mathbb{K}^*$ convex and compact such that $\forall U_1 \in (\mathbb{K}^* \setminus A) \; \exists U_2 \in B$ such that $\ll V(U_1), U_2 - U_1 \gg < 0$;*

2. $V(U)$ is pseudomonotone;

3. $V(U)$ is an affine operator on $\mathbb{K}^*$.

Example 3.3.1

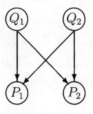

Figure 3.3: Supply and demand markets a.e. in $[\Delta, 1 + \Delta]$

Let us now examine a numerical example of an economy consisting of two supply markets P_1 and P_2 and two demand markets Q_1 and Q_2. In the first phase, which develops during the time interval $[0, 1]$, let us assume we have the same network as that presented in Example 3.1.1. So the supply, demand, and cost functions are:

$$g_1(p_1(t), p_2(t)) = p_1(t) + h(t), \qquad g_2(p_1(t), p_2(t)) = p_2(t) + k(t);$$
$$f_1(q_1(t), q_2(t)) = q_1(t), \qquad f_2(q_1(t), q_2(t)) = q_1(t) - q_2(t) + h(t);$$
$$c_{11}(x(t)) = x_{11}(t) + 1, \qquad c_{12}(x(t)) = x_{12}(t) + 1,$$
$$c_{21}(x(t)) = x_{21}(t), \qquad c_{22}(x(t)) = x_{22}(t) + 1.$$

By means of the direct method, we find that, if $h(t) + 5k(t) - 5 \geq 0$, then the solution is:

$$
\left\{
\begin{array}{ll}
x_{11}(t) = \dfrac{2h(t) + 4k(t) - 4}{3}, & x_{12}(t) = \dfrac{2h(t) + k(t) - 1}{3}, \\[2.5ex]
x_{21}(t) = \dfrac{h(t) + 5k(t) - 2}{3}, & x_{22}(t) = \dfrac{h(t) + 2k(t) - 2}{3}, \\[2.5ex]
p_1(t) = \dfrac{h(t) + 5k(t) - 5}{3}, & p_2(t) = \dfrac{2h(t) + 4k(t) - 4}{3}, \\[2.5ex]
q_1(t) = h(t) + 3k(t) - 2, & q_2(t) = h(t) + 2k(t) - 1,
\end{array}
\right.
$$

and, if $h(t) + 5k(t) - 5 < 0$, then the solution is:

$$
\begin{cases}
x_{11}(t) = 0 & x_{12}(t) = \dfrac{h(t) + k(t) - 1}{4} \\[2mm]
x_{21}(t) = \dfrac{-h(t) + 3k(t) + 1}{4} & x_{22}(t) = \dfrac{h(t) + k(t) - 1}{4} \\[2mm]
p_1(t) = 0 & p_2(t) = 0 \\[2mm]
q_1(t) = \dfrac{-h(t) + 3k(t) + 1}{4} & q_2(t) = \dfrac{h(t) + k(t) + 3}{4}.
\end{cases}
$$

In the second phase, which develops in the time interval $[\Delta, 1 + \Delta]$, the problem consists of two supply markets Q_1, Q_2 and two demand markets P_1, P_2, as shown in Figure 3.3. Q_1 and Q_2 now produce the commodity m_2 which is required by the markets P_1 and P_2 at time $t + \Delta$. The supply functions and the demand functions depend on two non-negative functions $\alpha(t + \Delta)$ and $\beta(t + \Delta)$, by means of which it is possible to control the production and the demand.

Let us assume that the supply, demand, and cost functions are:

$$
\begin{cases}
\gamma_1(\pi(t + \Delta)) = \pi_1(t + \Delta) + \alpha(t + \Delta), \\
\gamma_2(\pi(t + \Delta)) = \pi_2(t + \Delta) + \beta(t + \Delta);
\end{cases}
$$

$$
\begin{cases}
\varphi_1(\rho(t + \Delta)) = \rho_1(t + \Delta), \\
\varphi_2(\rho(t + \Delta)) = \rho_1(t + \Delta) - \rho_2(t + \Delta) + \alpha(t + \Delta);
\end{cases}
$$

$$
\begin{cases}
c_{11}(y(t + \Delta)) = y_{11}(t + \Delta) + 1, & c_{12}(y(t + \Delta)) = y_{12}(t + \Delta) + 1, \\
c_{21}(y(t + \Delta)) = y_{21}(t + \Delta), & c_{22}(y(t + \Delta)) = y_{22}(t + \Delta) + 1,
\end{cases}
$$

where

$$
\begin{aligned}
\pi(t + \Delta) &= (\pi_1(t + \Delta), \pi_2(t + \Delta)), \\
\rho(t + \Delta) &= (\rho_1(t + \Delta), \rho_2(t + \Delta)), \\
y(t + \Delta) &= (y_{11}(t + \Delta), y_{12}(t + \Delta), y_{21}(t + \Delta), y_{22}(t + \Delta)).
\end{aligned}
$$

The components of the operator $\nu = \nu(\omega(t + \Delta))$ are:

$$
\sum_{j=1}^{m}\left(\gamma_j - \sum_{i=1}^{n} y_{ij}\right), \quad \sum_{i=1}^{n}\left(\varphi_i - \sum_{j=1}^{m} y_{ij}\right), \quad \sum_{j=1}^{m}\sum_{i=1}^{n}(\pi_j + c_j - \rho_i),
$$

namely

$$
\begin{cases}
\pi_1(t+\Delta) - y_{11}(t+\Delta) - y_{21}(t+\Delta) + \alpha(t+\Delta), \\
\pi_2(t+\Delta) - y_{12}(t+\Delta) - y_{22}(t+\Delta) + \beta(t+\Delta), \\
\rho_1(t+\Delta) - y_{11}(t+\Delta) - y_{12}(t+\Delta), \\
\rho_1(t+\Delta) - \rho_2(t+\Delta) - y_{21}(t+\Delta) - y_{22}(t+\Delta) + \alpha(t+\Delta), \\
\pi_1(t+\Delta) + y_{11}(t+\Delta) - \rho_1(t+\Delta) + 1, \\
\pi_1(t+\Delta) + y_{21}(t+\Delta) - \rho_2(t+\Delta), \\
\pi_2(t+\Delta) + y_{12}(t+\Delta) - \rho_1(t+\Delta) + 1, \\
\pi_2(t+\Delta) + y_{22}(t+\Delta) - \rho_2(t+\Delta) + 1.
\end{cases}
$$

Solving the system: $\begin{cases} \nu(\omega) = 0 \\ \omega \in \Xi, \end{cases}$ where

$$
\Xi = \{\omega(t+\Delta) = (\pi(t+\Delta), \rho(t+\Delta), y(t+\Delta)) \in
$$
$$
L^2([\Delta, 1+\Delta], \mathbb{R}^2) \times L^2([\Delta, 1+\Delta], \mathbb{R}^2) \times L^2([\Delta, 1+\Delta], \mathbb{R}^4) :
$$
$$
\pi(t+\Delta) \geq 0, \ \rho(t+\Delta) \geq 0, \ y(t+\Delta) \geq 0\},
$$

then we find the following equilibrium supply prices, demand prices, and shipments:

$$
\begin{cases}
\pi_1(t+\Delta) = \dfrac{\alpha(t+\Delta) + 5\beta(t+\Delta) - 13}{3}, \\[4mm]
\pi_2(t+\Delta) = \dfrac{2\alpha(t+\Delta) + 4\beta(t+\Delta) - 14}{3} \\[4mm]
\rho_1(t+\Delta) = \alpha(t+\Delta) + 3\beta(t+\Delta) - 7, \\[4mm]
\rho_2(t+\Delta) = \alpha(t+\Delta) + 2\beta(t+\Delta) - 5, \\[4mm]
y_{11}(t+\Delta) = \dfrac{2\alpha(t+\Delta) + 4\beta(t+\Delta) - 11}{3}, \\[4mm]
y_{12}(t+\Delta) = \dfrac{\alpha(t+\Delta) + 5\beta(t+\Delta) - 10}{3}, \\[4mm]
y_{21}(t+\Delta) = \dfrac{2\alpha(t+\Delta) + \beta(t+\Delta) - 2}{3}, \\[4mm]
y_{22}(t+\Delta) = \dfrac{\alpha(t+\Delta) + 2\beta(t+\Delta) - 4}{3},
\end{cases}
$$

and

$$
\begin{cases}
\gamma_1(\pi(t+\Delta)) = \dfrac{4\alpha(t+\Delta) + 5\beta(t+\Delta) - 13}{3}, \\[2mm]
\gamma_2(\pi(t+\Delta)) = \dfrac{2\alpha(t+\Delta) + 7\beta(t+\Delta) - 14}{3}, \\[2mm]
\varphi_1(\rho(t+\Delta)) = \alpha(t+\Delta) + 3\beta(t+\Delta) - 7, \\[2mm]
\varphi_2(\rho(t+\Delta)) = \alpha(t+\Delta) + \beta(t+\Delta) - 2, \\[2mm]
c_{11}(t+\Delta) = \dfrac{2\alpha(t+\Delta) + 4\beta(t+\Delta) - 8}{3}, \\[2mm]
c_{12}(t+\Delta) = \dfrac{\alpha(t+\Delta) + 5\beta(t+\Delta) - 7}{3}, \\[2mm]
c_{21}(t+\Delta) = \dfrac{2\alpha(t+\Delta) + \beta(t+\Delta) - 2}{3}, \\[2mm]
c_{22}(t+\Delta) = \dfrac{\alpha(t+\Delta) + 2\beta(t+\Delta) - 1}{3},
\end{cases}
$$

if and only if

$$
\begin{cases}
\alpha(t+\Delta) + 5\beta(t+\Delta) - 13 \geq 0 \\
2\alpha(t+\Delta) + 4\beta(t+\Delta) - 14 \geq 0.
\end{cases}
\tag{3.92}
$$

Therefore, if conditions (3.92) are satisfied, then the solution lies in Ξ, otherwise we have to search the solution in the boundary of Ξ.

Let us introduce now as additional constraint the following:

$$
\sum_{j=1}^{2} \pi_j(t+\Delta) \leq \sum_{i=1}^{2} p_i(t),
$$

namely:

$$
\pi_1(t+\Delta) + \pi_2(t+\Delta) \leq p_1(t) + p_2(t),
$$

which means:

$$
\alpha(t+\Delta) \leq h(t) + 3k(t) - 3\beta(t+\Delta) + 6,
$$

under the assumptions

$$\begin{cases} h(t) + 5k(t) - 5 \geq 0 \\ \alpha(t + \Delta) + 5\beta(t + \Delta) - 13 \geq 0 \\ 2\alpha(t + \Delta) + 4\beta(t + \Delta) - 14 \geq 0. \end{cases}$$

Then we get:

$$\gamma_1(\pi(t + \Delta)) \leq \frac{4h(t) + 12k(t) - 7\beta(t + \Delta) + 11}{3},$$

$$\gamma_2(\pi(t + \Delta)) \leq \frac{2h(t) + 6k(t) + \beta(t + \Delta) - 2}{3},$$

$$\varphi_1(\rho(t + \Delta)) \leq h(t) + 3k(t) - 1,$$

$$\varphi_2(\rho(t + \Delta)) \leq h(t) + 3k(t) - 2\beta(t + \Delta) + 4. \tag{3.93}$$

Taking into account all the limitations, then we have the solution has represented by the system (3.93), if and only if the following conditions are satisfied:

$$\begin{cases} h(t) + 5k(t) - 5 \geq 0, \qquad \alpha(t + \Delta) + 5\beta(t + \Delta) - 13 \geq 0, \\ 2\alpha(t + \Delta) + 4\beta(t + \Delta) - 14 \geq 0, \qquad \beta \leq \dfrac{h(t) + 3k(t) + 6}{3}, \\ \alpha(t + \Delta) \leq h(t) + 3k(t) - 3\beta(t + \Delta) + 6. \end{cases}$$

3.4   Sources and Remarks

In [43] Daniele and Maugeri consider for the first time the time-dependent spatial price equilibrium in the case of price formulation and also provide existence results. In [35] and in [44] the authors study general models in two phases, which make clear that the evaluation of the economic phenomena is an essential feature of reality. Moreover the dependence of the second commodity m_2 on the availability of commodity m_1 is expressed by the introduction of additional constraints, whose effect is an increasing of the supply prices characterized by means of a Lagrangean variable.

The time-dependent model in the case of quantity formulation is studied in [37] and in the papers by Milasi and Vitanza [52] and [105] (see also [27] and [64]). Moreover in [37] and [52] the authors are also concerned with the study of sensitivity analysis.

Chapter 4

The Evolutionary Financial Model

In this chapter we propose an evolutionary model for the formulation and analysis of multi-sector, multi-instrument financial equilibrium problems. This new framework allows for the variance–covariance matrices associated with risk perception, the financial volumes held by the sectors, and the optimal portfolio compositions, as well as the instrument prices, all to be time-dependent.

We note that Nagurney, Dong, and Hughes (see [114]) were the first to develop a multi-sector, multi-instrument financial equilibrium model using variational inequality theory and recognized the network structure underlying the problem. That contribution was subsequently extended by Nagurney (see [109]) to include more general utility functions and by Nagurney and Siokos (see [119], [120]) to the international domain. Dong, Zhang, and Nagurney (see [54]) formulated a dynamic financial equilibrium model and analyzed it qualitatively using projected dynamical systems theory. Additional dynamic financial models, along with their variational inequality formulations at the equilibrium state (as well as their network structure), can be found in the book by Nagurney and Siokos (see [119]).

The model presented in this chapter builds upon the work of [114] but takes an alternative approach to that noted above, in that the dynamics are now modeled not using projected dynamical systems theory (see [127]) but, rather, *evolutionary variational inequalities*, and these are infinite - rather than finite-dimensional. In addition, the variance–covariance matrices (see also [93], [94]) which allow for risk minimization are now time-varying as are the financial volumes held by sectors.

Infinite-dimensional variational inequalities have been used previously in finance by Jaillet, Lamberton, and Lapeyre (see [86]) for the pricing of American options, and by Tourin and Zariphopoulou (see [156]) for single-agent investment modeling and computation. Stochastic variational inequalities, in turn, have been used by McLean (see [104]) for the non-linear portfolio choice problem and by Gurkan, Ozge, and Robinson (see [75]) for the pricing of American options. For additional background on finance and variational inequalities, see [110].

In this chapter we explicitly emphasize the importance of time in the study of financial decision-making and the interactions among financial sectors. The papers by Daniele and Maugeri (see [43]) and Daniele, Maugeri, and Oettli (see [45], [46]) discuss other time-dependent applications using the approach revealed here for the first time for financial equilibrium problems. Our research in other application settings has led us, in this chapter, to study financial equilibrium problems via an evolutionary model.

4.1   Quadratic Utility Function

This section is organized as follows. In subsection 4.1.1 we develop the model, provide the equilibrium conditions, and give the variational inequality formulation. We also identify the underlying network structure of the problem both out of and in the equilibrium state. In subsection 4.1.2 we provide some theoretical results, and in subsection 4.1.3 we give the proof of the variational inequality formulation and establish an existence result. In subsection 4.1.4, we propose a computational procedure, based on the subgradient method, which does not require discretization in time.

4.1.1   Statement of the Model

In this section we present the evolutionary financial model and give the variational inequality formulation of the equilibrium conditions. The functional setting in which we study this evolutionary model is the Lebesgue space $L^2([0,T],\mathbb{R}^p)$. The time dependence of the model in the $L^2([0,T])$ sense allows the model to follow the financial behavior, even in the presence of possibly very irregular evolution, whereas the equilibrium conditions are required to hold almost everywhere (see [43], [45], [46] for analogous problems). In this setting, the variance–covariance matrices associated with the sectors' risk perceptions will be required to have $L^\infty([0,T])$-entries.

Analytically, consider a financial economy consisting of m sectors, with a typical sector denoted by i, and with n instruments, with a typical financial instrument denoted by j, in the period $\mathcal{T} = [0,T]$. Examples of sectors include households, domestic businesses, banks, and other financial institutions, as well as state and local governments. Examples of financial instruments, in turn, are mortgages, mutual funds, savings deposits, money market funds, etc.

Let $s_i(t)$ denote the total financial volume held by sector i at time t, which is considered to depend on time $t \in [0,T]$. We emphasize the fact that in the presence of uncertainty and perceptions of risk, the volume s_i held by each sector cannot be considered stable and may decrease or increase depending on unfavorable or favorable economic conditions. As a consequence, the amounts of the assets and of the liabilities of the sectors will depend on time.

For this reason, at time t, denote the amount of instrument j held as an asset in sector i's portfolio by $x_{ij}(t)$ and the amount of instrument j held as a liability in sector i's portfolio by $y_{ij}(t)$. The assets in sector i's portfolio are grouped into the column vector $x_i(t) = [x_{i1}(t), x_{i2}(t), \ldots, x_{ij}(t), \ldots, x_{in}(t)]^T$ and the liabilities in sector i's portfolio are grouped into the column vector $y_i(t) = [y_{i1}(t), y_{i2}(t), \ldots, y_{ij}(t), \ldots, y_{in}(t)]^T$. Moreover, group the sector asset vectors into the matrix

$$x(t) \in L^2([0,T],\mathbb{R}^{nm})$$

and the sector liability vectors into the matrix

$$y(t) \in L^2([0,T],\mathbb{R}^{nm}).$$

In order to determine for each sector i the optimal composition of instruments held as assets and as liabilities, first we consider the influence due

to risk-aversion. Following the concept that assessment of risk is based
on a variance–covariance matrix denoting the sector's assessment of the
standard deviation of prices for each instrument, we use as a measure of
this aversion the $2n \times 2n$ variance–covariance matrix

$$Q^i(t) = \left[\begin{array}{cc} Q_{11}^i(t) & Q_{12}^i(t) \\ Q_{21}^i(t) & Q_{22}^i(t) \end{array} \right]$$

associated with sector i's assets and liabilities, which, in general, will
evolve in time as well and which we assume to be symmetric and positive
definite and with $L^\infty([0,T])$ entries. Further, denote by $[Q_{\alpha\beta}^i(t)]_j$ the
j-th column of $Q_{\alpha\beta}^i(t)$ with $\alpha = 1, 2$ and $\beta = 1, 2$. Then the aversion to
the risk at time $t \in [0,T]$ is given by:

$$\left[\begin{array}{c} x_i(t) \\ y_i(t) \end{array} \right]^T Q^i(t) \left[\begin{array}{c} x_i(t) \\ y_i(t) \end{array} \right].$$

The second component that we have to consider in the process of
optimization of each sector in the financial economy is their desire to
maximize the value of their asset holdings and to minimize the value of
their liabilities. These objectives depend on the prices of each instrument,
which, in turn, depend on time and appear as variables in our problem.
We denote the price of instrument j at time t by $r_j(t)$ and group the
instrument prices into the vector $r(t) = [r_1(t), r_2(t), \ldots, r_i(t), \ldots, r_n(t)]^T$.

Assuming as the functional setting the Lebesgue space $L^2([0,T], \mathbb{R}^p)$,
the set of feasible assets and liabilities becomes:

$$P_i = \Big\{ [x_i(t), y_i(t)]^T \in L^2([0,T], \mathbb{R}^{2n}) :$$

$$\sum_{j=1}^{n} x_{ij}(t) = s_i(t), \quad \sum_{j=1}^{n} y_{ij}(t) = s_i(t) \text{ a.e. in } [0,T],$$

$$x_{ij}(t) \geq 0, \quad y_{ij}(t) \geq 0, \text{ a.e. in } [0,T] \Big\}.$$

In Figure 4.1 we depict the network structure associated with the
above feasible set and the financial economy out of equilibrium. The set
of feasible assets and liabilities associated with each sector corresponds
to budget constraints.

We can now give the following definition of an equilibrium of the
financial model.

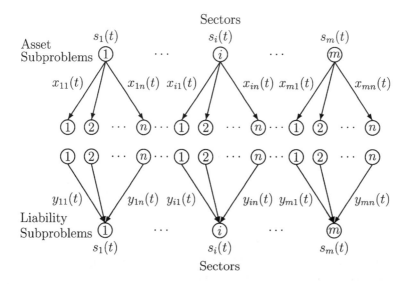

Figure 4.1: Multi-sector multi-instrument network a.e. in $[0, T]$

Definition 4.1.1 *A vector of sector assets, liabilities, and instrument prices* $(x^*(t),\ y^*(t),\ r^*(t)) \in \prod_{i=1}^{m} P_i \times L^2([0,T], \mathbb{R}^n_+)$ *is an equilibrium of the evolutionary financial model if and only if it satisfies simultaneously the system of inequalities*

$$2[Q^i_{11}(t)]^T_j\, x^*_i(t) + 2[Q^i_{21}(t)]^T_j\, y^*_i(t) - r^*_j(t) - \mu^{(1)}_i(t) \geq 0, \qquad (4.1)$$

and

$$2[Q^i_{12}(t)]^T_j\, x^*_i(t) + 2[Q^i_{22}(t)]^T_j\, y^*_i(t) + r^*_j(t) - \mu^{(2)}_i(t) \geq 0, \qquad (4.2)$$

and equalities

$$x^*_{ij}(t) \left[2[Q^i_{11}(t)]^T_j\, x^*_i(t) + 2[Q^i_{21}(t)]^T_j\, y^*_i(t) - r^*_j(t) - \mu^{(1)}_i(t)\right] = 0, \quad (4.3)$$

$$y^*_{ij}(t) \left[2[Q^i_{12}(t)]^T_j\, x^*_i(t) + 2[Q^i_{22}(t)]^T_j\, y^*_i(t) + r^*_j(t) - \mu^{(2)}_i(t)\right] = 0, \quad (4.4)$$

where $\mu_i^1(t)$, $\mu_i^2(t) \in L^2([0,T])$ are Lagrangean functionals, for all sectors i: $i = 1, 2, \ldots, m$, and for all instruments j: $j = 1, 2, \ldots, n$, and the condition

$$\begin{cases} \sum_{i=1}^{m} \left(x_{ij}^*(t) - y_{ij}^*(t)\right) \geq 0, & a.e. \ in \ [0,T] \\ \sum_{i=1}^{m} \left(x_{ij}^*(t) - y_{ij}^*(t)\right) r_j^*(t) = 0, & r^*(t) \in L^2([0,T], \mathbb{R}_+^n). \end{cases} \quad (4.5)$$

The meaning of this definition is the following: to each financial volume $s_i(t)$ invested by the sector i, we associate the functions $\mu_i^{(1)}(t)$ and $\mu_i^{(2)}(t)$ related, respectively, to the assets and to the liabilities and which represent the 'equilibrium disutilities' per unit of the sector i. The financial volume invested in the instrument j as assets $x_{ij}^*(t)$ is greater than or equal to zero if the j-th component

$$2[Q_{11}^i(t)]_j^T x_i^*(t) + 2[Q_{21}^i(t)]_j^T y_i^*(t) - r_j^*(t)$$

of the disutility is equal to $\mu_i^{(1)}(t)$, whereas if

$$2[Q_{11}^i(t)]_j^T x_i^*(t) + 2[Q_{21}^i(t)]_j^T y_i^*(t) - r_j^*(t) > \mu_i^{(1)}(t),$$

then $x_{ij}^*(t) = 0$. The same occurs for the liabilities. It is remarkable that the equilibrium definition is, in a sense, the same as that given by Wardrop's principle (see [157]), which states that in the case of user-optimization on congested transportation networks (see [28]) the user (which is a traveller in that case) rejects the less convenient (or more costly) choice (which, in the context of a transportation network, is a path or route).

The functions $\mu_i^{(1)}(t)$ and $\mu_i^{(2)}(t)$ are Lagrangean functionals associated with the constraints $\sum_{j=1}^{n} x_{ij}(t) - s_i(t) = 0$ and $\sum_{j=1}^{n} y_{ij}(t) - s_i(t) = 0$, respectively. The fact that they are unknown a priori has no influence because, as we shall see by means of Theorem 4.1.1, Definition 4.1.1 is equivalent to a variational inequality in which $\mu_i^{(1)}$ and $\mu_i^{(2)}$ do not appear. Nevertheless, by the use of Theorem 4.1.3, they can be obtained.

Conditions (4.5), which represent the equilibrium condition for the prices, express the equilibration of the total assets and the total liabilities of each instrument; namely, if the price of instrument j is positive, then the amount of the assets is equal to the amount of the liabilities; if there is a supply excess of an instrument in the economy, then its price must be zero.

Moreover, if we consider the group of conditions (4.1)–(4.4) for a fixed $r(t)$, then we realize that they are necessary and sufficient conditions to ensure that (x^*, y^*) is the minimum of the problem:

$$\min_{P_i} \int_0^T \left\{ \begin{bmatrix} x_i(t) \\ y_i(t) \end{bmatrix}^T Q^i(t) \begin{bmatrix} x_i(t) \\ y_i(t) \end{bmatrix} - r(t) \times [x_i(t) - y_i(t)] \right\} dt,$$

$$\forall \begin{bmatrix} x(t) \\ y(t) \end{bmatrix} \in \prod_{i=1}^m P_i. \tag{4.6}$$

Problem (4.6) means that each sector minimizes their risk while at the same time maximizing the value of their asset holdings and minimizing the value of their liabilities.

Since the feasible set P_i is a bounded, convex, and closed subset of the Hilbert space, then it is also weakly compact and, hence,

$$\min_{P_i} \int_0^T \left\{ \begin{bmatrix} x_i(t) \\ y_i(t) \end{bmatrix}^T Q^i(t) \begin{bmatrix} x_i(t) \\ y_i(t) \end{bmatrix} - r(t) \times [x_i(t) - y_i(t)] \right\} dt$$

exists, because the functional

$$U_i(x_i(t), y_i(t))$$

$$= \int_0^T \left\{ \begin{bmatrix} x_i(t) \\ y_i(t) \end{bmatrix}^T Q^i(t) \begin{bmatrix} x_i(t) \\ y_i(t) \end{bmatrix} - r(t) \times [x_i(t) - y_i(t)] \right\} dt$$

is weakly lower semicontinuous (see Lemma D.1 and Theorem D.9).

We now state the variational inequality formulation of the governing equilibrium conditions, the proof of which is given in Subsection 4.1.3.

Theorem 4.1.1 (Variational Inequality Formulation) *A vector of sector assets, liabilities and instrument prices*

$$(x^*(t),\ y^*(t),\ r^*(t)) \in \prod_{i=1}^m P_i \times L^2([0,T], \mathbb{R}_+^n)$$

is an evolutionary financial equilibrium if and only if it satisfies the following variational inequality:

$$Find \ (x^*(t), y^*(t), r^*(t)) \in \prod_{i=1}^{m} P_i \times L^2([0,T], \mathbb{R}_+^n)$$

$$\int_0^T \left\{ \sum_{i=1}^{m} \left[2[Q_{11}^i(t)]^T x_i^*(t) + 2[Q_{21}^i(t)]^T y_i^*(t) - r^*(t) \right] \times [x_i(t) - x_i^*(t)] \right.$$

$$+ \sum_{i=1}^{m} \left[2[Q_{12}^i(t)]^T x_i^*(t) + 2[Q_{22}^i(t)]^T y_i^*(t) + r^*(t) \right] \times [y_i(t) - y_i^*(t)]$$

$$\left. + \sum_{i=1}^{m} (x_i^*(t) - y_i^*(t)) \times [r(t) - r^*(t)] \right\} dt \geq 0,$$

$$\forall (x(t), y(t), r(t)) \in \prod_{i=1}^{m} P_i \times L^2([0,T], \mathbb{R}_+^n). \tag{4.7}$$

In the subsequent section we shall prove the equivalence between problem (4.6) and conditions (4.1)–(4.4). In addition, we shall establish the equivalence between condition (4.5) and an appropriate variational inequality.

In Figure 4.2 we depict the network structure of the financial economy in equilibrium. Observe, that due to conditions (4.5), in equilibrium, we have that for each financial instrument, its price times the total amount of the instrument as an asset minus the total amount as a liability is exactly equal to zero. Hence, the network structure of the financial economy, in equilibrium, is as given in Figure 4.2. The model thus depicts an evolution of the individual networks, as depicted in Figure 4.1, to the equilibrium network, as given in Figure 4.2. We note that Nagurney, Dong, and Hughes (see [114]) also identified the network structure of the financial equilibrium in their model which has the structure of the network in Figure 4.2, but that model was not time-dependent. Here we have also identified the evolution of the networks as depicted in Figure 4.1 through time to the equilibrium network of Figure 4.2.

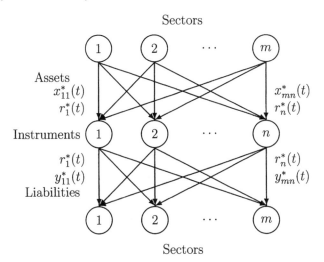

Figure 4.2: Multi-sector multi-instrument network at equilibrium

4.1.2 Some Theoretical Results

The proof of the equivalence between Definition 4.1.1 and the variational inequality formulation is obtained by showing that conditions (4.1)–(4.4) are equivalent to problem (4.6), which, in turn, is equivalent to a first variational inequality and that conditions (4.5) are equivalent to a second variational inequality. From these two variational inequalities, we then derive variational inequality (4.7).

We start by establishing the equivalence between problem (4.6) and a variational inequality. This proof is standard (see [151] for a similar argument), but we recall it for the reader's convenience.

Theorem 4.1.2 $[x_i^*(t), y_i^*(t)]$ *is a solution to (4.6) if and only if it is a solution to the variational inequality*

$$\int_0^T \sum_{i=1}^m \left[2[Q_{11}^i(t)]^T x_i^*(t) + [Q_{21}^i(t)]^T y_i^*(t) - r^*(t) \right] \times [x_i(t) - x_i^*(t)] \, dt$$

$$+ \int_0^T \sum_{i=1}^m \left[2[Q_{22}^i(t)]^T x_i^*(t) + [Q_{12}^i(t)]^T y_i^*(t) + r^*(t) \right]$$

$$\times [y_i(t) - y_i^*(t)]\, dt \geq 0, \quad \forall\, [x_i(t), y_i(t)] \in P_i \tag{4.8}$$

where $r_j^*(t)$ denotes the price for instrument j at time $t \in [0, T]$.

Proof: Let us assume that $[x_i^*(t), y_i^*(t)]$ is a solution to problem (4.6). Then for all $[x_i(t), y_i(t)] \in P_i$ the function

$$
\begin{aligned}
F(\lambda) = \int_0^T \sum_{i=1}^m \Big\{ & [\lambda x_i^*(t) + (1-\lambda)x_i(t)]^T\, Q_{11}^i(t)\, [\lambda x_i^*(t) + (1-\lambda)x_i(t)] \\
& + [\lambda y_i^*(t) + (1-\lambda)y_i(t)]^T\, Q_{21}^i(t)\, [\lambda x_i^*(t) + (1-\lambda)x_i(t)] \\
& + [\lambda x_i^*(t) + (1-\lambda)x_i(t)]^T\, Q_{12}^i(t)\, [\lambda y_i^*(t) + (1-\lambda)y_i(t)] \\
& + [\lambda y_i^*(t) + (1-\lambda)y_i(t)]^T\, Q_{22}^i(t)\, [\lambda y_i^*(t) + (1-\lambda)y_i(t)] \\
- r(t) \times & [\lambda x_i^*(t) + (1-\lambda)x_i(t) - \lambda y_i^*(t) - (1-\lambda)y_i(t)] \Big\}\, dt, \quad \lambda \in [0,1]
\end{aligned}
$$

admits the minimum solution when $\lambda = 1$ and $F'(1) \leq 0$. It follows then that:

$$F(\lambda) = \lambda^2 \int_0^T \sum_{i=1}^m [x_i^*(t)]^T Q_{11}^i(t) x_i^*(t)\, dt$$

$$+ \lambda(1-\lambda) \int_0^T \sum_{i=1}^m [x_i^*(t)]^T Q_{11}^i(t) x_i(t)\, dt$$

$$+ (1-\lambda)\lambda \int_0^T \sum_{i=1}^m [x_i(t)]^T Q_{11}^i(t) x_i^*(t)\, dt$$

$$+ (1-\lambda)^2 \int_0^T \sum_{i=1}^m [x_i(t)]^T Q_{11}^i(t) x_i(t)\, dt$$

$$+ \lambda^2 \int_0^T \sum_{i=1}^m [y_i^*(t)]^T Q_{21}^i(t) x_i^*(t)\, dt$$

$$+ \lambda(1-\lambda) \int_0^T \sum_{i=1}^m [y_i^*(t)]^T Q_{21}^i(t) x_i(t)\, dt$$

$$+ (1-\lambda)\lambda \int_0^T \sum_{i=1}^m [y_i(t)]^T Q_{21}^i(t) x_i^*(t)\, dt$$

$$+ (1 - \lambda)^2 \int_0^T \sum_{i=1}^m [y_i(t)]^T Q_{21}^i(t) x_i(t) \, dt$$

$$+ \lambda^2 \int_0^T \sum_{i=1}^m [x_i^*(t)]^T Q_{12}^i(t) y_i^*(t) \, dt$$

$$+ \lambda(1 - \lambda) \int_0^T \sum_{i=1}^m [x_i^*(t)]^T Q_{12}^i(t) y_i(t) \, dt$$

$$+ (1 - \lambda)\lambda \int_0^T \sum_{i=1}^m [x_i(t)]^T Q_{12}^i(t) y_i^*(t) \, dt$$

$$+ (1 - \lambda)^2 \int_0^T \sum_{i=1}^m [x_i(t)]^T Q_{12}^i(t) y_i(t) \, dt$$

$$+ \lambda^2 \int_0^T \sum_{i=1}^m [y_i^*(t)]^T Q_{22}^i(t) y_i^*(t) \, dt$$

$$+ \lambda(1 - \lambda) \int_0^T \sum_{i=1}^m [y_i^*(t)]^T Q_{22}^i(t) y_i(t) \, dt$$

$$+ (1 - \lambda)\lambda \int_0^T \sum_{i=1}^m [y_i(t)]^T Q_{22}^i(t) y_i^*(t) \, dt$$

$$+ (1 - \lambda)^2 \int_0^T \sum_{i=1}^m [y_i(t)]^T Q_{22}^i(t) y_i(t) \, dt$$

$$- \int_0^T \sum_{i=1}^m r(t) \times [\lambda x_i^*(t) + (1 - \lambda)x_i(t) - \lambda y_i^*(t) - (1 - \lambda)y_i(t)] \, dt.$$

Hence, we can consider the derivative of $F(\lambda)$ with respect to λ and we reach:

$$F'(\lambda) = \int_0^T \sum_{i=1}^m [x_i^*(t) - x_i(t)]^T Q_{11}^i(t) [\lambda x_i^*(t) + (1 - \lambda)x_i(t)] \, dt$$

$$+ \int_0^T \sum_{i=1}^m [\lambda x_i^*(t) + (1 - \lambda)x_i(t)]^T Q_{11}^i(t) [x_i^*(t) - x_i(t)] \, dt$$

$$+ \int_0^T \sum_{i=1}^m [y_i^*(t) - y_i(t)]^T Q_{21}^i(t) \left[\lambda x_i^*(t) + (1 - \lambda)x_i(t)\right] dt$$

$$+ \int_0^T \sum_{i=1}^m \left[\lambda y_i^*(t) + (1 - \lambda)y_i(t)\right]^T Q_{21}^i(t)[x_i^*(t) - x_i(t)] dt$$

$$+ \int_0^T \sum_{i=1}^m [x_i^*(t) - x_i(t)]^T Q_{12}^i(t) \left[\lambda y_i^*(t) + (1 - \lambda)y_i(t)\right] dt$$

$$+ \int_0^T \sum_{i=1}^m \left[\lambda x_i^*(t) + (1 - \lambda)x_i(t)\right]^T Q_{12}^i(t)[y_i^*(t) - y_i(t)] dt$$

$$+ \int_0^T \sum_{i=1}^m [y_i^*(t) - y_i(t)]^T Q_{22}^i(t) \left[\lambda y_i^*(t) + (1 - \lambda)y_i(t)\right] dt$$

$$+ \int_0^T \sum_{i=1}^m \left[\lambda y_i^*(t) + (1 - \lambda)y_i(t)\right]^T Q_{22}^i(t)[y_i^*(t) - y_i(t)] dt$$

$$- \int_0^T \sum_{i=1}^m r(t) \times [x_i^*(t) - x_i(t) - y_i^*(t) + y_i(t)] \ dt.$$

So we obtain:

$$F'(1) = \int_0^T \sum_{i=1}^m [x_i^*(t) - x_i(t)]^T Q_{11}^i(t)x_i^*(t) \, dt$$

$$+ \int_0^T \sum_{i=1}^m [x_i^*(t)]^T Q_{11}^i(t)[x_i^*(t) - x_i(t)] \, dt$$

$$+ \int_0^T \sum_{i=1}^m [y_i^*(t) - y_i(t)]^T Q_{21}^i(t)x_i^*(t) \, dt$$

$$+ \int_0^T \sum_{i=1}^m [y_i^*(t)]^T Q_{21}^i(t)[x_i^*(t) - x_i(t)] \, dt$$

$$+ \int_0^T \sum_{i=1}^m [x_i^*(t) - x_i(t)]^T Q_{12}^i(t)y_i^*(t) \, dt$$

$$+ \int_0^T \sum_{i=1}^m [x_i^*(t)]^T Q_{12}^i(t)[y_i^*(t) - y_i(t)] \, dt$$

$$+ \int_0^T \sum_{i=1}^m [y_i^*(t) - y_i(t)]^T Q_{22}^i(t) y_i^*(t) \, dt$$

$$+ \int_0^T \sum_{i=1}^m [y_i^*(t)]^T Q_{22}^i(t)[y_i^*(t) - y_i(t)] \, dt$$

$$- \int_0^T \sum_{i=1}^m r(t) \times [x_i^*(t) - x_i(t) - y_i^*(t) + y_i(t)] \, dt.$$

Then, taking into account the symmetry of the matrix $Q^i(t)$, we get:

$$F'(1)$$

$$= \int_0^T \sum_{i=1}^m \left[2[Q_{11}^i(t)]^T x_i^*(t) + 2[Q_{21}^i(t)]^T y_i^*(t) - r^*(t) \right] \times [x_i^*(t) - x_i(t)] \, dt$$

$$+ \int_0^T \sum_{i=1}^m \left[2[Q_{12}^i(t)]^T x_i^*(t) + 2[Q_{22}^i(t)]^T y_i^*(t) + r^*(t) \right] \times [y_i^*(t) - y_i(t)] \, dt \leq 0,$$

namely, the variational inequality (4.8).

Conversely, let us assume that $[x_i^*(t), y_i^*(t)]$ is a solution to problem (4.8). Since the function U_i is convex, then for all $[x_i(t), y_i(t)] \in P_i$ the following estimate holds:

$$U_i \begin{bmatrix} \lambda x_i(t) + (1 - \lambda) x_i^*(t) \\ \lambda y_i(t) + (1 - \lambda) y_i^*(t) \end{bmatrix} \leq \lambda U_i \begin{bmatrix} x_i(t) \\ y_i(t) \end{bmatrix} + (1 - \lambda) U_i \begin{bmatrix} x_i^*(t) \\ y_i^*(t) \end{bmatrix},$$

namely, $\forall \lambda \in (0, 1]$:

$$\frac{U_i \begin{bmatrix} x_i^*(t) + \lambda(x_i(t) - x_i^*(t)) \\ y_i^*(t) + \lambda(y_i(t) - y_i^*(t)) \end{bmatrix} - U_i \begin{bmatrix} x_i^*(t) \\ y_i^*(t) \end{bmatrix}}{\lambda}$$

$$\leq U_i \begin{bmatrix} x_i(t) \\ y_i(t) \end{bmatrix} - U_i \begin{bmatrix} x_i^*(t) \\ y_i^*(t) \end{bmatrix}. \tag{4.9}$$

When $\lambda \to 0$, the left-hand side of (4.9) converges to the left-hand side of the variational inequality (4.8), which is ≤ 0 and, hence, $[x_i^*(t), y_i^*(t)]$ is a solution to the problem (4.6). $\qquad\qquad\qquad\qquad\qquad\qquad\square$

Let $[x_i^*(t), y_i^*(t)]$ be the solution to problem (4.6) for a given $r^*(t)$ and, hence, to variational inequality (4.8). Now we can prove the following characterization of the solution.

Theorem 4.1.3 $[x_i^*(t), y_i^*(t)]$ *is a solution to (4.6) or to (4.8) if and only if a.e. in* $[0, T]$ *it satisfies the conditions:*

$$2[Q_{11}^i(t)]_j^T \, x_i^*(t) + 2[Q_{21}^i(t)]_j^T \, y_i^*(t) - r_j^*(t) - \mu_i^{(1)}(t) \geq 0, \qquad (4.1)$$

$$2[Q_{12}^i(t)]_j^T \, x_i^*(t) + 2[Q_{22}^i(t)]_j^T \, y_i^*(t) + r_j^*(t) - \mu_i^{(2)}(t) \geq 0, \qquad (4.2)$$

$$x_{ij}^*(t) \left[2[Q_{11}^i(t)]_j^T \, x_i^*(t) + 2[Q_{21}^i(t)]_j^T \, y_i^*(t) - r_j^*(t) - \mu_i^{(1)}(t) \right] = 0, \quad (4.3)$$

$$y_{ij}^*(t) \left[2[Q_{12}^i(t)]_j^T \, x_i^*(t) + 2[Q_{22}^i(t)]_j^T y_i^*(t) + r_j^*(t) - \mu_i^{(2)}(t) \right] = 0, \quad (4.4)$$

where $\mu_i^{(1)}(t)$, $\mu_i^{(2)}(t) \in L^2([0, T])$ *are Lagrangean functionals.*

Proof: The proof of this equivalence is based on the infinite-dimensional Lagrangean theory, which has proven to be a powerful tool in determining essential properties of optimization problems (see [32], [40], [85] and [103]). This theory proceeds in the following way.

Let us consider the function

$$\mathcal{L}\left(x_i(t), y_i(t), \lambda_i^{(1)}(t), \lambda_i^{(2)}(t), \mu_i^{(1)}(t), \mu_i^{(2)}(t)\right)$$

$$= \Psi(x_i(t), y_i(t)) - \int_0^T \sum_{j=1}^n \lambda_{ij}^{(1)}(t) x_{ij}(t) \, dt - \int_0^T \sum_{j=1}^n \lambda_{ij}^{(2)}(t) y_{ij}(t) \, dt$$

$$- \int_0^T \mu_i^{(1)}(t) \left(\sum_{j=1}^n x_{ij}(t) - s_i(t) \right) dt - \int_0^T \mu_i^{(2)}(t) \left(\sum_{j=1}^n y_{ij}(t) - s_i(t) \right) dt,$$

where

$$\Psi(x_i(t), y_i(t))$$

$$= \int_0^T \sum_{j=1}^n \left[2[Q_{11}^i(t)]_j^T x_i^*(t) + [Q_{21}^i(t)]_j^T y_i^*(t) - r_j^*(t)\right] \times [x_{ij}(t) - x_{ij}^*(t)]\, dt$$

$$+ \int_0^T \sum_{j=1}^n \left[2[Q_{22}^i(t)]_j^T x_i^*(t) + [Q_{12}^i(t)]_j^T y_i^*(t) + r_j^*(t)\right] \times [y_{ij}(t) - y_{ij}^*(t)]\, dt,$$

$$\begin{bmatrix} x_i(t) \\ y_i(t) \end{bmatrix} \in L^2([0,T], \mathbb{R}^{2n}) \quad \text{and} \quad (\lambda_i^1(t), \lambda_i^2(t), \mu_i^1(t), \mu_i^2(t)) \in \mathcal{C}$$

$$= \left\{ \lambda_i^{(1)}(t), \lambda_i^{(2)}(t) \in L^2([0,T], \mathbb{R}^n), \quad \lambda_i^{(1)}(t), \lambda_i^{(2)}(t) \geq 0, \right.$$

$$\left. \mu_i^{(1)}(t), \mu_i^{(2)}(t) \in L^2([0,T]); \quad i = 1, 2, \ldots, m \right\}.$$

By means of Lagrangean Theory (see [32], [40], [85] and [103]), it is possible to prove that there exist $\lambda_i^{(1)}(t)$, $\lambda_i^{(2)}(t)$, $\mu_i^{(1)}(t)$, $\mu_i^{(2)}(t)$, such that $\lambda_i^{(1)}(t) \geq 0$, $\lambda_i^{(2)}(t) \geq 0$ and

$$\int_0^T \sum_{j=1}^n \lambda_{ij}^{(1)}(t) x_{ij}^*(t)\, dt = 0 \;\Rightarrow\; \lambda_{ij}^{(1)}(t) x_{ij}^*(t) = 0 \text{ a.e. in } [0,T]$$

$$\int_0^T \sum_{j=1}^n \lambda_{ij}^{(2)}(t) y_{ij}^*(t)\, dt = 0 \;\Rightarrow\; \lambda_{ij}^{(2)}(t) y_{ij}^*(t) = 0 \text{ a.e. in } [0,T].$$

Moreover, using the characterization of the solution by means of a saddle point ([32], [40], [85] and [103]), we obtain:

$$\mathcal{L}\left(x_i(t), y_i(t), \lambda_i^{(1)}(t), \lambda_i^{(2)}(t), \mu_i^{(1)}(t), \mu_i^{(2)}(t)\right)$$

$$= \int_0^T \sum_{j=1}^n \left[2[Q_{11}^i(t)]_j^T x_i^*(t) + 2[Q_{21}^i(t)]_j^T y_i^*(t) - r_j^*(t) - \lambda_{ij}^{(1)}(t) - \mu_i^{(1)}(t)\right]$$

$$\times [x_{ij}(t) - x_{ij}^*(t)]\, dt$$

$$+ \int_0^T \sum_{j=1}^n \left[2[Q_{12}^i(t)]_j^T x_i^*(t) + 2[Q_{22}^i(t)]_j^T y_i^*(t) + r_j^*(t) - \lambda_{ij}^{(2)}(t) - \mu_i^{(2)}(t)\right]$$

$$\times [y_{ij}(t) - y_{ij}^*(t)]\, dt \geq 0, \quad \forall [x_i(t), y_i(t)] \in L^2([0,T], \mathbb{R}^{2n}). \quad (4.10)$$

If we set

$$\varepsilon_1(t) = 2[Q_{11}^i(t)]_j^T x_i^*(t) + 2[Q_{21}^i(t)]_j^T y_i^*(t) - r_j^*(t) - \lambda_{ij}^{(1)}(t) - \mu_i^{(1)}(t)$$

and

$$\varepsilon_2(t) = 2[Q_{12}^i(t)]_j^T x_i^*(t) + 2[Q_{22}^i(t)]_j^T y_i^*(t) - r_j^*(t) - \lambda_{ij}^{(1)}(t) - \mu_i^{(1)}(t),$$

by choosing

$$x_i(t) = x_i^*(t) + \varepsilon_1(t) \quad \text{and} \quad y_i(t) = y_i^*(t) + \varepsilon_2(t),$$

we get:

$$\int_0^T \sum_{j=1}^n \left[2[Q_{11}^i(t)]_j^T x_i^*(t) + 2[Q_{21}^i(t)]_j^T y_i^*(t) \right.$$
$$\left. - r_j^*(t) - \lambda_{ij}^{(1)}(t) - \mu_i^{(1)}(t) \right]^2 dt$$
$$+ \int_0^T \sum_{j=1}^n \left[2[Q_{12}^i(t)]_j^T x_i^*(t) + 2[Q_{22}^i(t)]_j^T y_i^*(t) \right.$$
$$\left. + r_j^*(t) - \lambda_{ij}^{(2)}(t) - \mu_i^{(2)}(t) \right]^2 dt \geq 0.$$

By choosing

$$x_i(t) = x_i^*(t) - \varepsilon_1(t) \quad \text{and} \quad y_i(t) = y_i^*(t) - \varepsilon_2(t),$$

we obtain:

$$- \int_0^T \sum_{j=1}^n \left[2[Q_{11}^i(t)]_j^T x_i^*(t) + 2[Q_{21}^i(t)]_j^T y_i^*(t) \right.$$
$$\left. - r_j^*(t) - \lambda_{ij}^{(1)}(t) - \mu_i^{(1)}(t) \right]^2 dt$$
$$- \int_0^T \sum_{j=1}^n \left[2[Q_{12}^i(t)]_j^T x_i^*(t) + 2[Q_{22}^i(t)]_j^T y_i^*(t) \right.$$
$$\left. + r_j^*(t) - \lambda_{ij}^{(2)}(t) - \mu_i^{(2)}(t) \right]^2 dt \geq 0.$$

Hence,

$$2[Q_{11}^i(t)]_j^T x_i^*(t) + 2[Q_{21}^i(t)]_j^T y_i^*(t) - r_j^*(t) - \mu_i^{(1)}(t) = \lambda_{ij}^{(1)}(t) \geq 0$$

and

$$2[Q_{12}^i(t)]_j^T x_i^*(t) + 2[Q_{22}^i(t)]_j^T y_i^*(t) + r_j^*(t) - \mu_i^{(2)}(t) = \lambda_{ij}^{(2)}(t) \geq 0.$$

Moreover, taking into account that $\lambda_i^{(1)}(t)x_i^*(t) = 0$, $\lambda_i^{(2)}(t)y_i^*(t) = 0$, we get:

$$x_{ij}^*(t)\left[2[Q_{11}^i(t)]_j^T x_i^*(t) + 2[Q_{21}^i(t)]_j^T y_i^*(t) - r_j^*(t) - \mu_i^{(1)}(t)\right] = 0$$

and

$$y_{ij}^*(t)\left[2[Q_{12}^i(t)]_j^T x_i^*(t) + 2[Q_{22}^i(t)]_j^T y_i^*(t) + r_j^*(t) - \mu_i^{(2)}(t)\right] = 0.$$

Conversely, if estimates (4.1)–(4.4) hold, then we show that the variational inequality (4.8) holds. From (4.1), we obtain:

$$\sum_{j=1}^n \left[2[Q_{11}^i(t)]_j^T x_i^*(t) + 2[Q_{21}^i(t)]_j^T y_i^*(t) - r_j^*(t) - \mu_i^{(1)}(t)\right]$$

$$\times [x_{ij}(t) - x_{ij}^*(t)] \geq 0,$$

and taking into account that $\sum_{j=1}^n x_{ij}(t) = s_i(t)$ and $\sum_{j=1}^n x_{ij}^*(t) = s_i(t)$ a.e. in $[0, T]$, we get:

$$\sum_{j=1}^n \left[2[Q_{11}^i(t)]_j^T x_i^*(t) + 2[Q_{21}^i(t)]_j^T y_i^*(t) - r_j^*(t)\right] \times [x_{ij}(t) - x_{ij}^*(t)] \geq 0,$$

and then

$$\int_0^T \sum_{j=1}^n \left[2[Q_{11}^i(t)]_j^T x_i^*(t) + 2[Q_{21}^i(t)]_j^T y_i^*(t) - r_j^*(t)\right]$$

$$\times [x_{ij}(t) - x_{ij}^*(t)]\, dt \geq 0. \tag{4.11}$$

Similarly, one obtains:

$$\sum_{j=1}^n \left[2[Q_{22}^i(t)]_j^T y_i^*(t) + 2[Q_{12}^i(t)]_j^T x_i^*(t) + r_j^*(t)\right] \times [y_{ij}(t) - y_{ij}^*(t)] \geq 0$$

and, subsequently,

$$\int_0^T \sum_{j=1}^n \left[2[Q_{22}^i(t)]_j^T y_i^*(t) + 2[Q_{12}^i(t)]_j^T x_i^*(t) + r_j^*(t)\right]$$

$$\times [y_{ij}(t) - y_{ij}^*(t)]\, dt \geq 0. \tag{4.12}$$

Summing now inequalities (4.11) and (4.12) for all i, we conclude that for $(x^*(t), y^*(t)) \in \prod_{i=1}^{m} P_i$:

$$\sum_{i=1}^{m} \int_0^T \sum_{j=1}^{n} \left[2[Q_{11}^i(t)]_j^T x_i^*(t) + 2[Q_{21}^i(t)]_j^T y_i^*(t) - r_j^*(t) \right] \times [x_{ij}(t) - x_{ij}^*(t)] \, dt$$

$$+ \int_0^T \sum_{j=1}^{n} \left[2[Q_{22}^i(t)]_j^T x_i^*(t) + 2[Q_{12}^i(t)]_j^T y_i^*(t) + r_j^*(t) \right] \times [y_{ij}(t) - y_{ij}^*(t)] \, dt \geq 0,$$

$$\forall [x_i(t), y_i(t)] \in P_i,$$

and the proof is complete. $\square$

We now describe the variational inequality associated with the instrument prices $r_j(t)$.

The equilibrium condition related to the prices of the instruments is

$$\begin{cases} \sum_{i=1}^{m} \left(x_{ij}^*(t) - y_{ij}^*(t) \right) \geq 0 & \text{a.e. in } [0,T] \\ \sum_{i=1}^{m} \left(x_{ij}^*(t) - y_{ij}^*(t) \right) r_j^*(t) = 0, & r^*(t) \in L^2([0,T], \mathbb{R}_+^n). \end{cases} \tag{4.5}$$

Let us prove the following theorem.

Theorem 4.1.4 *Condition (4.5) is equivalent to*

$$\begin{cases} \text{Find } r^*(t) \in L^2([0,T], \mathbb{R}_+^n) \text{ such that} \\ \int_0^T \sum_{i=1}^{m} \left[x_{ij}^*(t) - y_{ij}^*(t) \right] \times \left[r_j(t) - r_j^*(t) \right] \, dt \geq 0, \\ \forall r(t) \in L^2([0,T], \mathbb{R}_+^n). \end{cases} \tag{4.13}$$

Proof: Let us prove that condition (4.5) implies (4.13). Let us set

$$E_+ = \{ t \in [0,T] : r_j^*(t) > 0 \},$$

and let us show that in E_+ we have: $\sum_{i=1}^{m} [x_{ij}^*(t) - y_{ij}^*(t)] = 0.$ $\forall r(t) \in$ $L^2([0,T], \mathbb{R}_+^n)$, we get:

$$\int_{E_+} \sum_{i=1}^{m} [x_{ij}^*(t) - y_{ij}^*(t)] \times [r_j(t) - r_j^*(t)] \ dt \geq 0.$$

On the other hand, if we consider $E_0 = \{t \in [0,T] : r_j^*(t) = 0\}$, then in E_0 it follows that $\sum_{i=1}^{m} [x_{ij}^*(t) - y_{ij}^*(t)] \geq 0.$ Hence,

$$\int_0^T \sum_{i=1}^{m} [x_{ij}^*(t) - y_{ij}^*(t)] \times [r_j(t) - r_j^*(t)] \ dt$$

$$= \int_{E_0} \sum_{i=1}^{m} [x_{ij}^*(t) - y_{ij}^*(t)] \times r_j(t) \ dt$$

$$+ \int_{E_+} \sum_{i=1}^{m} [x_{ij}^*(t) - y_{ij}^*(t)] \times [r_j(t) - r_j^*(t)] \ dt \geq 0,$$

and (4.13) holds.

Let us prove now that (4.13) implies condition (4.5). From (4.13) it follows that:

$$\int_{E_0} \sum_{i=1}^{m} [x_{ij}^*(t) - y_{ij}^*(t)] \times r_j(t) \ dt$$

$$+ \int_{E_+} \sum_{i=1}^{m} [x_{ij}^*(t) - y_{ij}^*(t)] \times [r_j(t) - r_j^*(t)] \ dt \geq 0.$$

If $\sum_{i=1}^{m} [x_{ij}^*(t) - y_{ij}^*(t)] > 0$ in E_+ (or in a subset of E_+ with positive measure), then we choose

$$r_j(t) = \begin{cases} 0 & \text{in } E_0 \\ r_j^*(t) - \varepsilon(t) & \text{in } E_+, \end{cases}$$

where $0 < \varepsilon(t) < r_j^*(t)$ and we get:

$$\int_0^T \sum_{i=1}^m \left[x_{ij}^*(t) - y_{ij}^*(t)\right] \times \left[r_j(t) - r_j^*(t)\right] \, dt$$

$$= \int_{E_+} \sum_{i=1}^m \left[x_{ij}^*(t) - y_{ij}^*(t)\right] \times \left[-\varepsilon(t)\right] \, dt < 0,$$

which is an absurdity.

On the contrary, if $\displaystyle\sum_{i=1}^m \left[x_{ij}^*(t) - y_{ij}^*(t)\right] < 0$ in E_+ (or in a subset of E_+ with positive measure), then we choose

$$r_j(t) = \begin{cases} 0 & \text{in } E_0 \\ r_j^*(t) + \varepsilon(t) & \text{in } E_+, \end{cases}$$

where $\varepsilon(t) > 0$ and we get:

$$\int_0^T \sum_{i=1}^m \left[x_{ij}^*(t) - y_{ij}^*(t)\right] \times \left[r_j(t) - r_j^*(t)\right] \, dt$$

$$= \int_{E_+} \sum_{i=1}^m \left[x_{ij}^*(t) - y_{ij}^*(t)\right] \times \varepsilon(t) \, dt < 0,$$

which is also an absurdity.

Further, if we select

$$r_j(t) = \begin{cases} 0 & \text{in } E_+ \\ \varepsilon(t) & \text{in } E_0, \end{cases}$$

where $\varepsilon(t) > 0$, then, if $\displaystyle\sum_{i=1}^m \left[x_{ij}^*(t) - y_{ij}^*(t)\right] < 0$ in E_0 (or in a subset

of E_0 with positive measure), we get: $\displaystyle\int_{E_0} \sum_{i=1}^m \left[x_{ij}^*(t) - y_{ij}^*(t)\right] \varepsilon(t) \, dt < 0,$

which is an absurdity. $\square$

4.1.3 Variational Formulation and an Existence Theorem: Quadratic Utility Function

Following the proof of Theorem 4.1.3, we can now prove Theorem 4.1.1.

Proof: From the results of the preceding section, it immediately follows that if $(x^*(t), y^*(t), r^*(t)) \in \prod_{i=1}^{m} P_i \times L^2([0,T], \mathbb{R}^n_+)$ is a dynamic financial equilibrium, then it satisfies the variational inequalities (4.8) and (4.13), and hence the variational inequality (4.7), and vice versa. $\square$

We now establish the following existence theorem.

Theorem 4.1.5 (Existence) *If* $(x^*(t), y^*(t), r^*(t)) \in \prod_{i=1}^{m} P_i \times L^2([0,T], \mathbb{R}^n_+)$ *is an equilibrium, then the equilibrium asset and liability vector* $(x^*(t), y^*(t))$ *is a solution to the variational inequality:*

$$\sum_{i=1}^{m} \int_0^T \Big\{ \sum_{j=1}^{n} \big[2[Q^i_{11}(t)]_j^T x_i^*(t) + 2[Q^i_{21}(t)]_j^T y_i^*(t)\big] \times \big[x_{ij}(t) - x_{ij}^*(t)\big]$$

$$\sum_{j=1}^{n} \big[2[Q^i_{12}(t)]_j^T x_i^*(t) + 2[Q^i_{22}(t)]_j^T y_i^*(t)\big] \times \big[y_{ij}(t) - y_{ij}^*(t)\big] \Big\} \, dt \geq 0,$$

$$\forall (x(t), y(t)) \in S, \tag{4.14}$$

where

$$S \equiv \left\{ (x(t), y(t)) \in \prod_{i=1}^{m} P_i; \quad \sum_{i=1}^{m} (x_{ij}(t) - y_{ij}(t)) \geq 0, j = 1, 2, \ldots, n \right\}.$$

Conversely, if $(x^*(t), y^*(t))$ *is a solution to (4.14), then there exists* $r^*(t) \in L^2([0,T], \mathbb{R}^n_+)$ *such that* $(x^*(t), y^*(t), r^*(t))$ *is an equilibrium.*

Proof: Assume that $(x^*(t), y^*(t), r^*(t)) \in \prod_{i=1}^{m} P_i \times L^2([0,T], \mathbb{R}^n_+)$ is an equilibrium. Then $(x^*(t), y^*(t), r^*(t))$ satisfies (4.7). In (4.7) let us set:

$$x_i(t) = x_i^*(t), \ y_i(t) = y_i^*(t), \ r(t) = 0, \text{ a.e. in } [0,T] \text{ and } \forall i = 1, \ldots, m,$$

then we get:

$$-\sum_{i=1}^{m} \int_{0}^{T} \sum_{j=1}^{n} \left[x_{ij}^*(t) - y_{ij}^*(t) \right] \times r_j^*(t)\, dt \geq 0. \qquad (4.15)$$

Let us now set in (4.7) $r(t) = r^*(t)$ and we obtain:

$$\sum_{i=1}^{m} \int_{0}^{T} \left\{ \sum_{j=1}^{n} \left[2[Q_{11}^i(t)]_j^T\, x_i^*(t) + 2[Q_{21}^i(t)]_j^T\, y_i^*(t) \right] \times \left[x_{ij}(t) - x_{ij}^*(t) \right] \right.$$

$$\left. + \sum_{j=1}^{n} \left[2[Q_{12}^i(t)]_j^T\, x_i^*(t) + 2[Q_{22}^i(t)]_j^T\, y_i^*(t) \right] \times \left[y_{ij}(t) - y_{ij}^*(t) \right] \right\} dt$$

$$\geq \int_{0}^{T} \sum_{j=1}^{n} r_j^*(t) \left[\sum_{i=1}^{m} (x_{ij}(t) - y_{ij}(t)) - \sum_{i=1}^{m} (x_{ij}^*(t) - y_{ij}^*(t)) \right] dt. \quad (4.16)$$

But the right-hand side of inequality (4.16) is greater than or equal to 0, because of (4.15) and the constraint set S. Thus, we have established that $(x^*(t), y^*(t))$ satisfies (4.14).

Observe that there always exists an asset and liability pattern $(x^*(t), y^*(t))$ satisfying (4.14), because S is weakly compact and for each $(u(t), v(t)) \in S$ the operator

$$(x(t), y(t))$$

$$\rightarrow \sum_{i=1}^{m} \int_{0}^{T} \left\{ \sum_{j=1}^{n} \left[2[Q_{11}^i(t)]_j^T\, x_i^*(t) + 2[Q_{21}^i(t)]_j^T\, y_i^*(t) \right] \times \left[u_{ij}(t) - x_{ij}(t) \right] \right.$$

$$\left. + \sum_{j=1}^{n} \left[2[Q_{12}^i(t)]_j^T\, x_i^*(t) + 2[Q_{22}^i(t)]_j^T\, y_i^*(t) \right] \times \left[v_{ij}(t) - y_{ij}(t) \right] \right\} dt$$

is weakly upper semicontinuous (see Appendix B for more details). Now, in order to prove the existence of $r^*(t) \in L^2([0,T], \mathbb{R}_+^n)$ such that $(x^*(t), y^*(t), r^*(t))$ is an equilibrium, let us apply the Lagrange Multiplier Theorem (see [32], [40], [85] and [103]) to the function:

$$\mathcal{L}\left(x(t), y(t), \lambda^{(1)}(t), \lambda^{(2)}(t), \mu^{(1)}(t), \mu^{(2)}(t), r(t) \right)$$

$$= \Psi(x(t), y(t)) - \sum_{i=1}^{m} \int_{0}^{T} \sum_{j=1}^{n} \lambda_{ij}^{(1)}(t) x_{ij}(t)\, dt - \sum_{i=1}^{m} \int_{0}^{T} \lambda_{ij}^{(2)}(t) y_{ij}(t)\, dt$$

$$-\sum_{i=1}^{m} \int_{0}^{T} \mu_i^{(1)}(t) \left[\sum_{j=1}^{n} x_{ij}(t) - s_i(t) \right] dt$$

$$-\sum_{i=1}^{m} \int_{0}^{T} \mu_i^{(2)}(t) \left[\sum_{j=1}^{n} y_{ij}(t) - s_i(t) \right] dt$$

$$-\int_{0}^{T} \sum_{j=1}^{n} r_j(t) \left[\sum_{i=1}^{m} (x_{ij}(t) - y_{ij}(t)) \right] dt$$

where

$$\Psi(x(t), y(t))$$

$$= \sum_{i=1}^{m} \left\{ \int_{0}^{T} \sum_{j=1}^{n} \left[2[Q_{11}^i(t)]_j^T x_i^*(t) + [Q_{21}^i(t)]_j^T y_i^*(t) \right] \times [x_{ij}(t) - x_{ij}^*(t)] \, dt \right.$$

$$\left. + \int_{0}^{T} \sum_{j=1}^{n} \left[2[Q_{22}^i(t)]_j^T x_i^*(t) + [Q_{12}^i(t)]_j^T y_i^*(t) \right] \times [y_{ij}(t) - y_{ij}^*(t)] \right\} dt$$

and $\left(\lambda^{(1)}(t), \lambda^{(2)}(t), \mu^{(1)}(t), \mu^{(2)}(t), r(t) \right) \in \overline{C}$

$$= \left\{ \lambda^{(1)}(t), \ \lambda^{(2)}(t) \in L^2([0,T], \mathbb{R}^{nm}), \quad \lambda_{ij}^{(1)}(t), \ \lambda_{ij}^{(2)}(t) \geq 0, \right.$$

$$\mu^{(1)}(t), \ \mu^{(2)}(t) \in L^2([0,T], \mathbb{R}^m); \ r(t) \in L^2([0,T], \mathbb{R}^n),$$

$$\left. r(t) \geq 0 \text{ a.e. in } [0,T] \right\}.$$

We get that, besides $\lambda_i^{(1)}(t)$, $\lambda_i^{(2)}(t)$, $\mu_i^{(1)}(t)$ and $\mu_i^{(2)}(t)$, there exists an $r^*(t) \in L^2([0,T], \mathbb{R}_+^n)$ corresponding to the constraints defining S. For such a pattern $(x^*(t), y^*(t), r^*(t))$ we have:

$$2[Q_{11}^i(t)]_j^T x_i^*(t) + 2[Q_{21}^i(t)]_j^T y_i^*(t) - r_j^*(t) - \mu_i^{(1)}(t) = \lambda_{ij}^{(1)} \geq 0, \quad (4.1)$$

$$2[Q_{12}^i(t)]_j^T x_i^*(t) + 2[Q_{22}^i(t)]_j^T y_i^*(t) + r_j^*(t) - \mu_i^{(2)}(t) = \lambda_{ij}^{(2)} \geq 0, \quad (4.2)$$

$$x_{ij}^*(t) \left[2[Q_{11}^i(t)]_j^T x_i^*(t) + 2[Q_{21}^i(t)]_j^T y_i^*(t) - r_j^*(t) - \mu_i^{(1)}(t) \right] = 0, \quad (4.3)$$

$$y^*_{ij}(t) \left[2[Q^i_{12}(t)]^T_j \, x^*_i(t) + 2[Q^i_{22}(t)]^T_j y^*_i(t) + r^*_j(t) - \mu^{(2)}_i(t) \right] = 0, \quad (4.4)$$

and

$$
\begin{cases}
\displaystyle\sum_{i=1}^{m} \left(x^*_{ij}(t) - y^*_{ij}(t) \right) \geq 0 & \text{a.e. in } [0,T] \\[2mm]
\displaystyle\sum_{i=1}^{m} \left(x^*_{ij}(t) - y^*_{ij}(t) \right) r^*_j(t) = 0, & r^*(t) \in L^2([0,T], \mathbb{R}^n_+).
\end{cases}
\quad (4.5)
$$

From conditions (4.1)–(4.5), a.e. in $[0,T]$, we obtain:

$$
\sum_{i=1}^{m} \sum_{j=1}^{n} \left[2[Q^i_{11}(t)]^T_j \, x^*_i(t) + 2[Q^i_{21}(t)]^T_j \, y^*_i(t) - r^*_j(t) \right]
$$

$$
\times \left[x_{ij}(t) - x^*_{ij}(t) \right]
$$

$$
+ \sum_{i=1}^{m} \sum_{j=1}^{n} \left[2[Q^i_{12}(t)]^T_j \, x^*_i(t) 2[Q^i_{22}(t)]j^T \, y^*_i(t) + r^*_j(t) \right]
$$

$$
\times \left[y_{ij}(t) - y^*_{ij}(t) \right] \geq 0
\qquad (4.17)
$$

and

$$
\sum_{i=1}^{m} \sum_{j=1}^{n} \left[x^*_{ij}(t) - y^*_{ij}(t) \right] \times \left[r_j(t) - r^*_j(t) \right] \geq 0.
\qquad (4.18)
$$

Summing now (4.17) and (4.18) and integrating the result, we obtain:

$$
\sum_{i=1}^{m} \int_0^T \left\{ \sum_{j=1}^{n} \left[2[Q^i_{11}(t)]^T_j \, x^*_i(t) + 2[Q^i_{21}(t)]^T_j \, y^*_i(t) - r^*_j(t) \right] \times \left[x_{ij}(t) - x^*_{ij}(t) \right] \right.
$$

$$
+ \sum_{j=1}^{n} \left[2[Q^i_{12}(t)]^T_j \, x^*_i(t) + 2[Q^i_{22}(t)]^T_j \, y^*_i(t) + r^*_j(t) \right] \times \left[y_{ij}(t) - y^*_{ij}(t) \right]
$$

$$
\left. + \sum_{j=1}^{n} \left(x^*_{ij}(t) - y^*_{ij}(t) \right) \times \left[r_j(t) - r^*_j(t) \right] \right\} dt \geq 0,
$$

and the proof is complete.   □

4.1.4 Computational Procedure

We now present a computational procedure based on the subgradient method (see [136]) which does not require a discretization on time.

Let us set, for the sake of brevity, $u(t) = (x(t), y(t), r(t))$ and

$$U(u) = \begin{bmatrix} 2[Q_{11}^i(t)]_j^T x_i(t) + 2[Q_{21}^i(t)]_j^T y_i(t) - r_j(t) \\ 2[Q_{12}^i(t)]_j^T x_i(t) + 2[Q_{22}^i(t)]_j^T y_i(t) + r_j(t) \\ x_{ij}(t) - y_{ij}(t) \end{bmatrix}_{\substack{i=1,\ldots,m \\ j=1,\ldots,n}}.$$

Then, we have:

$$\ll U(u), \tilde{u} - u \gg$$

$$= \sum_{i=1}^{m} \int_0^T \left\{ \sum_{j=1}^{n} \left[2[Q_{11}^i(t)]_j^T x_i(t) + 2[Q_{21}^i(t)]_j^T y_i(t) - r_j(t) \right] \right.$$

$$\times (\tilde{x}_{ij}(t) - x_{ij}(t))$$

$$+ \sum_{j=1}^{n} \left[2[Q_{12}^i(t)]_j^T x_i(t) + 2[Q_{22}^i(t)]_j^T y_i(t) + r_j(t) \right] \times (\tilde{y}_{ij}(t) - y_{ij}(t))$$

$$\left. + \sum_{j=1}^{n} (x_{ij}(t) - y_{ij}(t)) \times (\tilde{r}_j(t) - r_j(t)) \right\} dt.$$

Let

$$\mathbb{K} = \left\{ \prod_{i=1}^{m} P_i \times L^2([0,T], \mathbb{R}_+^n) \right\}$$

and

$$B = \left\{ u(t) \in \prod_{i=1}^{m} L^2([0,T], \mathbb{R}_+^{2n}) \times L^2([0,T], \mathbb{R}_+^n) \right\}.$$

B is easy to handle and projections onto B are readily available. For each $u \in B$ let us set

$$\psi_1(u) = \max_{\tilde{u} \in \mathbb{K}} \ll U(\tilde{u}), u - \tilde{u} \gg,$$

$$\psi_2(u) = \sum_{i=1}^{m} \int_0^T \left\{ \left(\sum_{j=1}^{n} x_{ij}(t) - s_i(t) \right)^2 + \left(\sum_{j=1}^{n} y_{ij}(t) - s_i(t) \right)^2 \right\} dt.$$

It is easy to see that $\psi_1(u)$ is well-defined. Then the real-valued function

$$\psi(u) = \max\{\psi_1(u), \psi_2(u)\}$$

is a gap function for the variational inequality

$$\ll U(\tilde{u}), \tilde{u} - u \gg \geq 0, \quad \forall \tilde{u} \in \mathbb{K} \tag{4.19}$$

and, with $U(u)$ monotone, it is also a gap function for the variational inequality

$$\ll U(u), \tilde{u} - u \gg \geq 0, \quad \forall u \in \mathbb{K}. \tag{4.20}$$

In fact, we recall that if U is monotone, then variational inequalities (4.19) and (4.20) are equivalent.

Note that $\psi(u)$ is a gap function because $\psi(u) \geq 0 \quad \forall u \in \mathbb{K}$ and if $\psi(u) = 0$, then u solves (4.19) and, hence, (4.20).

The function $\psi_1(u)$, being the maximum of a family of continuous and affine functions, is convex and weakly lower semicontinuous. Then $\psi(u)$ is convex and weakly lower semicontinuous, too. The needed convexity of ψ is the main reason for considering (4.19) instead of (4.20).

We shall see below that the subdifferential

$$\partial\psi(u) = \left\{ \tau \in \prod_{i=1}^{m} L^2([0,T], \mathbb{R}^{2n}) \times L^2([0,T], \mathbb{R}^n) : \right.$$

$$\left. \psi(\tilde{u}) - \psi(u) \geq \ll \tau, \tilde{u} - u \gg, \quad \forall \tilde{u} \in B \right\}$$

is nonempty for all $u \in B$. Let us define $\Gamma = \{u \in B : \psi(u) = 0\}$. Because of the equivalence between (4.19) and (4.20), $u \in \prod_{i=1}^{m} L^2([0,T], \mathbb{R}^{2n}) \times L^2([0,T], \mathbb{R}^n)$ is a solution to (4.20) if and only if $u \in \Gamma$.

The subgradient method for finding an element of Γ can now be described as follows. Choose an arbitrary $u^0 \in B$ and given $u^n \in B$, $u^n \notin \Gamma$, let us set

$$u^{n+1} = \text{Proj}_B(u^n - \rho_n \tau_n),$$

where $\tau_n \in \partial\psi(H^n)$, $\rho_n = \dfrac{\psi(H^n)}{\|\tau_n\|^2}$, and Proj_B denotes the projection (see [108]) onto the set B.

Using the linearity of U, we shall see below that τ_n can be chosen in such a way that $\|\tau_n\|$ remains bounded. If $\|\tau_n\|$ remains bounded and $u^n \notin \Gamma$ for all n, then we have the following result.

Theorem 4.1.6 (Convergence) *It results that $\psi(u^n) \to 0$. The sequence $\{u^n\}$ has weak cluster points and every weak cluster point is in Γ. If the sequence $\{u^n\}$ has a strong cluster point $\bar{u}$, then $\bar{u}$ is unique and $\{u^n\}$ converges strongly to $\bar{u}$.*

Proof: See [46]. $\qquad\square$

We now have to prove the existence of the subdifferential τ. For a given $u \in B$, let us define $\tau^{(1)}(t) = U(\bar{u}(t))$ where $\bar{u}$ is a solution to $\max_{\tilde{u} \in \mathbb{K}} \ll U(\tilde{u}), u - \tilde{u} \gg$. As already observed, there exists $\tilde{u}$. Then $\tau^{(1)}(t) \in \partial \psi_1(t)$.

Let us define $\tau^{(2)}(t) = 2\left(\sum_{j=1}^{n} x_{ij}(t) - s_i(t)\right) + 2\left(\sum_{j=1}^{n} y_{ij}(t) - s_i(t)\right).$

It is easy to prove that $\tau^{(2)}(t) \in \partial \psi_2(t)$, because the estimate

$$\psi_2(\tilde{u}) - \psi_2(u) \geq \ll \tau^{(2)}(t), \tilde{u} - u \gg$$

leads to

$$\left(\sum_{j=1}^{n} \tilde{x}_{ij}(t) - s_i(t)\right)^2 + \left(\sum_{j=1}^{n} \tilde{y}_{ij}(t) - s_i(t)\right)^2$$

$$-\left(\sum_{j=1}^{n} x_{ij}(t) - s_i(t)\right)^2 - \left(\sum_{j=1}^{n} y_{ij}(t) - s_i(t)\right)^2$$

$$\geq 2\left(\sum_{j=1}^{n} x_{ij}(t) - s_i(t)\right)\left(\sum_{j=1}^{n} \tilde{x}_{ij}(t) - s_i(t)\right) - 2\left(\sum_{j=1}^{n} x_{ij}(t) - s_i(t)\right)^2$$

$$+2\left(\sum_{j=1}^{n} y_{ij}(t) - s_i(t)\right)\left(\sum_{j=1}^{n} \tilde{y}_{ij}(t) - s_i(t)\right) - 2\left(\sum_{j=1}^{n} y_{ij}(t) - s_i(t)\right)^2,$$

that is,

$$\left(\sum_{j=1}^{n}\tilde{x}_{ij}(t)-s_i(t)\right)^2 - 2\left(\sum_{j=1}^{n}x_{ij}(t)-s_i(t)\right)\left(\sum_{j=1}^{n}\tilde{x}_{ij}(t)-s_i(t)\right)$$

$$+\left(\sum_{j=1}^{n}x_{ij}(t)-s_i(t)\right)^2 + \left(\sum_{j=1}^{n}\tilde{y}_{ij}(t)-s_i(t)\right)^2$$

$$-2\left(\sum_{j=1}^{n}y_{ij}(t)-s_i(t)\right)\left(\sum_{j=1}^{n}\tilde{y}_{ij}(t)-s_i(t)\right)+\left(\sum_{j=1}^{n}y_{ij}(t)-s_i(t)\right)^2 \geq 0,$$

which always holds.

Now let us define

$$\tau = \begin{cases} \tau^{(1)} & \text{if} \quad \psi(u)=\psi_1(u) \\ \tau^{(2)} & \text{if} \quad \psi(u)=\psi_2(u). \end{cases}$$

Then $\tau \in \partial\psi(u)$ and it is easy to show that τ remains bounded if u varies in B.

4.2   General Utility Function

In Section 4.1 we studied an evolutionary financial equilibrium problem in the case of quadratic utility function

$$U_i(x_i(t), y_i(t))$$

$$= \int_0^T \left\{ \begin{bmatrix} x_i(t) \\ y_i(t) \end{bmatrix}^T Q^i(t) \begin{bmatrix} x_i(t) \\ y_i(t) \end{bmatrix} - r(t) \times [x_i(t)-y_i(t)] \right\} dt,$$

where $Q^i(t) = \begin{bmatrix} Q^i_{11}(t) & Q^i_{12}(t) \\ Q^i_{21}(t) & Q^i_{22}(t) \end{bmatrix}$ is a $2n \times 2n$ variance–covariance matrix. Now we intend to extend this particular model to a general case in which the utility function is given by

$$U_i(t, x_i(t), y_i(t), r(t)) = u_i(t, x_i(t), y_i(t)) + r(t)(x_i(t)-y_i(t)),$$

where $u_i(t, x_i(t), y_i(t))$ is a concave and differentiable function. The assumption of concavity on $u_i(t, x_i(t), y_i(t))$ is essential in order to obtain a characterization of the evolutionary financial equilibrium and also the existence of the financial equilibrium. This fact perfectly agrees with many other situations in which the concavity (or convexity) plays an essential role. This section is organized as follows. In subsection 4.2.1, we develop the model, provide the equilibrium conditions, and give the variational inequality formulation. We also identify the underlying network structure of the problem both out of and in the equilibrium state. In subsection 4.2.2, we provide some theoretical results, whereas in subsection 4.2.3 we give the proof of the variational inequality formulation and establish an existence result.

4.2.1 Statement of the Model

The structure of the problem remains unchanged from section 4.1 with a financial economy consisting of m sectors, with a typical sector denoted by i, and with n instruments, with a typical financial instrument denoted by j, in the period $\mathcal{T} = [0, T]$.

We generalize the quadratic financial model and we assume that each sector seeks to maximize its utility, where the utility function $U_i(t, x_i(t), y_i(t), r(t))$ is given by:

$$U_i(t, x_i(t), y_i(t), r(t)) = u_i(t, x_i(t), y_i(t)) + r(t)(x_i(t) - y_i(t)).$$

The quadratic financial model is a particular case of this general model which can be obtained by setting

$$-u_i(t, x_i(t), y_i(t)) = \begin{bmatrix} x_i(t) \\ y_i(t) \end{bmatrix}^T Q^i(t) \begin{bmatrix} x_i(t) \\ y_i(t) \end{bmatrix}.$$

Hence $-u_i(t, x_i(t), y_i(t))$ represents a general form of the aversion to risk.

We suppose that the sector's utility function $u_i(t, x_i(t), y_i(t))$ is defined on $[0, T] \times \mathbb{R}^n \times \mathbb{R}^n$, measurable in t and continuous with respect to x_i and y_i. Moreover, we assume that $\dfrac{\partial u_i}{\partial x_{ij}}$ and $\dfrac{\partial u_i}{\partial y_{ij}}$ exist and that they are measurable in t and continuous with respect to x_i and y_i. Further, we require that the following growth conditions hold:

$$|u_i(t, x, y)| \leq \alpha_i(t) \, \|x\| \, \|y\|,$$
$$\forall x, y \in \mathbb{R}^n, \text{ a.e. in } [0, T], \ \forall i = 1, \dots, n, \tag{4.21}$$

and

$$\left|\frac{\partial u_i(t,x,y)}{\partial x_{ij}}\right| \le \beta_{ij}(t)\,\|y\|, \quad \left|\frac{\partial u_i(t,x,y)}{\partial y_{ij}}\right| \le \gamma_{ij}(t)\,\|x\|, \qquad (4.22)$$

where α_i, β_{ij}, γ_{ij} are non-negative functions of $L^\infty([0,T])$. Finally, we suppose that the function $u_i(t, x_i(t), y_i(t))$ is concave.

Assuming as the functional setting the Lebesgue space $L^2([0,T], \mathbb{R}^p)$, the set of feasible assets and liabilities becomes:

$$P_i = \left\{ (x_i(t), y_i(t)) \in L^2([0,T], \mathbb{R}^{2n}) : \right.$$

$$\sum_{j=1}^{n} x_{ij}(t) = s_i(t), \quad \sum_{j=1}^{n} y_{ij}(t) = s_i(t) \text{ a.e. in } [0,T],$$

$$\left. x_{ij}(t) \ge 0, \quad y_{ij}(t) \ge 0, \text{ a.e. in } [0,T] \right\}.$$

We can now give the following definition of an equilibrium of the financial model.

Definition 4.2.1 *A vector of sector assets, liabilities, and instrument prices* $(x^*(t),\ y^*(t),\ r^*(t)) \in \prod_{i=1}^{m} P_i \times L^2([0,T], \mathbb{R}_+^n)$ *is an equilibrium of the evolutionary financial model if and only if it satisfies simultaneously the system of inequalities*

$$-\frac{\partial u_i(t, x_i^*(t), y_i^*(t))}{\partial x_{ij}} - r_j^*(t) - \mu_i^{(1)}(t) \ge 0, \qquad (4.23)$$

and

$$-\frac{\partial u_i(t, x_i^*(t), y_i^*(t))}{\partial y_{ij}} + r_j^*(t) - \mu_i^{(2)}(t) \ge 0, \qquad (4.24)$$

and equalities

$$x_{ij}^*(t)\left[-\frac{\partial u_i(t, x_i^*(t), y_i^*(t))}{\partial x_{ij}} - r_j^*(t) - \mu_i^{(1)}(t)\right] = 0, \qquad (4.25)$$

$$y_{ij}^*(t)\left[-\frac{\partial u_i(t, x_i^*(t), y_i^*(t))}{\partial y_{ij}} + r_j^*(t) - \mu_i^{(2)}(t)\right] = 0, \qquad (4.26)$$

where $\mu_i^1(t)$, $\mu_i^2(t) \in L^2([0,T])$ are Lagrangean functionals, for all sectors i: $i = 1, 2, \ldots, m$, and for all instruments j: $j = 1, 2, \ldots, n$, and the condition

$$\begin{cases} \displaystyle\sum_{i=1}^m \left(x_{ij}^*(t) - y_{ij}^*(t)\right) \geq 0, & a.e. \ in \ [0, T] \\ \displaystyle\sum_{i=1}^m \left(x_{ij}^*(t) - y_{ij}^*(t)\right) r_j^*(t) = 0, & r^*(t) \in L^2([0, T], \mathbb{R}_+^n). \end{cases} \qquad (4.27)$$

The meaning of Definition 4.2.1 is the following: to each financial volume $s_i(t)$ invested by the sector i, we associate the functions $\mu_i^{(1)}(t)$ and $\mu_i^{(2)}(t)$ related, respectively, to the assets and to the liabilities and which represent the 'equilibrium disutilities' per unit of the sector i. The financial volume invested in the instrument j as assets $x_{ij}^*(t)$ is greater than or equal to zero if the j-th component

$$-\frac{\partial u_i(t, x_i^*(t), y_i^*(t))}{\partial x_{ij}} - r_j^*(t)$$

of the utility is equal to $\mu_i^{(1)}(t)$, whereas if

$$-\frac{\partial u_i(t, x_i^*(t), y_i^*(t))}{\partial x_{ij}} - r_j^*(t) > \mu_i^{(1)}(t),$$

then $x_{ij}^*(t) = 0$. The same occurs for the liabilities. The functions $\mu_i^{(1)}(t)$ and $\mu_i^{(2)}(t)$ are the Lagrangean functionals associated with the constraints $\sum_{j=1}^n x_{ij}(t) - s_i(t) = 0$ and $\sum_{j=1}^n y_{ij}(t) - s_i(t) = 0$, respectively. But, as we have already observed, the fact that they are unknown a priori has no influence because, as we shall see by means of Theorem 4.2.1, Definition 4.2.1 is equivalent to a variational inequality in which $\mu_i^{(1)}$ and $\mu_i^{(2)}$ do not appear. Nevertheless, by the use of Theorem 4.2.3, they can be obtained.

Conditions (4.27) have the meaning already described and represent the equilibrium condition for the prices. They express the equilibration of the total assets and the total liabilities of each instrument; namely, if the price of instrument j is positive, then the amount of the assets is equal to the amount of the liabilities; if there is a supply excess of an instrument in the economy, then its price must be zero.

Moreover, if we consider the group of conditions (4.23)–(4.26) for a fixed $r(t)$, then we realize that they are necessary and sufficient conditions to ensure that (x_i^*, y_i^*) is the maximum of the problem:

$$\max_{P_i} \int_0^T \{u_i(t, x_i(t), y_i(t)) + r(t) \times [x_i(t) - y_i(t)]\} \, dt,$$

$$\forall (x_i(t), y_i(t)) \in P_i. \tag{4.28}$$

Problem (4.28) means that each sector maximizes their utility. The functional $u_i(t, x(t), y(t))$ is concave and, using assumption (4.21), it also belongs to $L^1([0, T])$, as does $r(t) \times [x_i(t) - y_i(t)]$. Moreover, since it is continuous by virtue of (4.21) (see [62]), it is also upper semicontinuous in the set P_i which is weakly compact, then such a maximum exists (see [85], Lemma 2.11, p. 15).

We now state the variational inequality formulation of the governing equilibrium conditions, the proof of which is given in Section 4.2.3.

Theorem 4.2.1 *A vector* $(x^*(t), y^*(t), r^*(t)) \in \displaystyle\prod_{i=1}^{m} P_i \times L^2([0, T], \mathbb{R}_+^n)$ *is an evolutionary financial equilibrium if and only if it satisfies the following variational inequality:*

$$Find \ (x^*(t), y^*(t), r^*(t)) \in \prod_{i=1}^{m} P_i \times L^2([0, T], \mathbb{R}_+^n) :$$

$$\sum_{i=1}^{m} \int_0^T \left\{ \sum_{j=1}^{n} \left[-\frac{\partial u_i(t, x_i^*(t), y_i^*(t))}{\partial x_{ij}} - r^*(t) \right] \times \left[x_{ij}(t) - x_{ij}^*(t) \right] \right.$$

$$+ \sum_{j=1}^{n} \left[-\frac{\partial u_i(t, x_i^*(t), y_i^*(t))}{\partial y_{ij}} + r^*(t) \right] \times \left[y_{ij}(t) - y_{ij}^*(t) \right]$$

$$\left. + \sum_{j=1}^{n} (x_i^*(t) - y_i^*(t)) \times [r(t) - r^*(t)] \right\} dt \geq 0,$$

$$\forall (x(t), y(t), r(t)) \in \prod_{i=1}^{m} P_i \times L^2([0, T], \mathbb{R}_+^n). \tag{4.29}$$

Such an integral exists as a consequence of condition (4.22).

In the subsequent section we shall prove the equivalence between problem (4.28) and conditions (4.23)–(4.26). In addition, we shall establish the equivalence between condition (4.27) and a suitable variational inequality. Observe that due to conditions (4.27), in equilibrium we have that for each financial instrument, its price times the total amount of the instrument as an asset minus the total amount as a liability is exactly equal to zero.

4.2.2   Some Theoretical Results

As in Section 4.1, the proof of the equivalence between Definition 4.2.1 and the variational inequality formulation is obtained by showing that conditions (4.23)–(4.26) are equivalent to problem (4.28), which, in turn, is equivalent to a first variational inequality and that conditions (4.27) are equivalent to a second variational inequality. From these two variational inequalities, we then derive variational inequality (4.29).

We start by establishing the equivalence between problem (4.28) and a variational inequality.

Theorem 4.2.2 $\left(x_i^*(t), y_i^*(t)\right)$ *is a solution to (4.28) if and only if* $\left(x_i^*(t), y_i^*(t)\right)$ *is a solution to the variational inequality*

$$\int_0^T -\sum_{j=1}^n \left[-\frac{\partial u_i(t, x_i^*(t), y_i^*(t))}{\partial x_{ij}} + r^*(t) \right] \times [x_{ij}(t) - x_{ij}^*(t)] \, dt$$

$$+ \int_0^T -\sum_{j=1}^n \left[-\frac{\partial u_i(t, x_i^*(t), y_i^*(t))}{\partial y_{ij}} - r^*(t) \right] \times [y_{ij}(t) - y_{ij}^*(t)] \, dt \geq 0,$$

$$\forall \left(x_i(t), y_i(t)\right) \in P_i \tag{4.30}$$

where $r_j^*(t)$ *denotes the price for instrument* j *at time* $t \in [0, T]$.

Proof: See subsection 4.1.2. □

Let $(x_i^*(t), y_i^*(t))$ be the solution to problem (4.28) for a given $r^*(t)$ and, hence, to variational inequality (4.30). Now we can prove the following characterization of the solution.

Theorem 4.2.3 $(x_i^*(t), y_i^*(t))$ *is a solution to (4.28) or to (4.30) if and only if a.e. in* $[0, T]$ *it satisfies the conditions:*

$$-\frac{\partial u_i(t, x_i^*(t), y_i^*(t))}{\partial x_{ij}} - r_j^*(t) - \mu_i^{(1)}(t) \geq 0, \qquad (4.23)$$

$$-\frac{\partial u_i(t, x_i^*(t), y_i^*(t))}{\partial y_{ij}} + r_j^*(t) - \mu_i^{(2)}(t) \geq 0, \qquad (4.24)$$

$$x_{ij}^*(t)\left[-\frac{\partial u_i(t, x_i^*(t), y_i^*(t))}{\partial x_{ij}} - r_j^*(t) - \mu_i^{(1)}(t)\right] = 0, \qquad (4.25)$$

$$y_{ij}^*(t)\left[-\frac{\partial u_i(t, x_i^*(t), y_i^*(t))}{\partial y_{ij}} + r_j^*(t) - \mu_i^{(2)}(t)\right] = 0, \qquad (4.26)$$

where $\mu_i^{(1)}(t)$, $\mu_i^{(2)}(t) \in L^2([0,T])$ *are Lagrangean functionals.*

Proof: The proof of this equivalence is based on the infinite-dimensional Lagrangean theory, which has proven to be a powerful tool in determining essential properties of optimization problems (see [32], [40], [85] and [103]). This theory proceeds in the following way.

Let us consider the function

$$\mathcal{L}\left(x_i(t), y_i(t), \lambda_i^{(1)}(t), \lambda_i^{(2)}(t), \mu_i^{(1)}(t), \mu_i^{(2)}(t)\right)$$

$$= \Psi(x_i(t), y_i(t)) - \int_0^T \sum_{j=1}^n \lambda_{ij}^{(1)}(t)x_{ij}(t)\, dt - \int_0^T \sum_{j=1}^n \lambda_{ij}^{(2)}(t)y_{ij}(t)\, dt$$

$$- \int_0^T \mu_i^{(1)}(t)\left(\sum_{j=1}^n x_{ij}(t) - s_i(t)\right) dt$$

$$- \int_0^T \mu_i^{(2)}(t)\left(\sum_{j=1}^n y_{ij}(t) - s_i(t)\right) dt,$$

where

$$\Psi(x_i(t), y_i(t))$$

$$= \int_0^T \sum_{j=1}^n \left[-\frac{\partial u_i(t, x_i(t), y_i(t))}{\partial x_{ij}} - r_j^*(t)\right] \times [x_{ij}(t) - x_{ij}^*(t)]\, dt$$

$$+ \int_0^T \sum_{j=1}^n \left[-\frac{\partial u_i(t, x_i(t), y_i(t))}{\partial y_{ij}} + r_j^*(t)\right] \times [y_{ij}(t) - y_{ij}^*(t)]\, dt,$$

$(x_i(t), y_i(t)) \in L^2([0,T], \mathbb{R}^{2n})$ and $\left(\lambda_i^{(1)}(t), \lambda_i^{(2)}(t), \mu_i^{(1)}(t), \mu_i^{(2)}(t) \right) \in \mathcal{C}$

$$= \Big\{ \lambda_i^{(1)}(t), \ \lambda_i^{(2)}(t) \in L^2([0,T], \mathbb{R}^n), \quad \lambda_i^{(1)}(t), \ \lambda_i^{(2)}(t) \geq 0,$$

$$\mu_i^{(1)}(t), \ \mu_i^{(2)}(t) \in L^2([0,T]); \ i = 1, 2, \ldots, m \Big\}.$$

By means of the Lagrangean Theory (see [32], [40], [85] and [103]), it is possible to prove that there exist $\lambda_i^{(1)}(t), \lambda_i^{(2)}(t), \mu_i^{(1)}(t), \mu_i^{(2)}(t)$, such that $\lambda_i^{(1)}(t) \geq 0, \lambda_i^{(2)}(t) \geq 0$ and

$$\int_0^T \sum_{j=1}^n \lambda_{ij}^{(1)}(t) x_{ij}^*(t) \, dt = 0 \Rightarrow \lambda_{ij}^{(1)}(t) x_{ij}^*(t) = 0 \text{ a.e. in } [0,T]$$

$$\int_0^T \sum_{j=1}^n \lambda_{ij}^{(2)}(t) y_{ij}^*(t) \, dt = 0 \Rightarrow \lambda_{ij}^{(2)}(t) y_{ij}^*(t) = 0 \text{ a.e. in } [0,T].$$

Moreover, using the characterization of the solution by means of a saddle point (see [32]), we obtain:

$$\mathcal{L}\left(x_i(t), y_i(t), \lambda_i^{(1)}(t), \lambda_i^{(2)}(t), \mu_i^{(1)}(t), \mu_i^{(2)}(t) \right)$$

$$= \int_0^T \sum_{j=1}^n \left[-\frac{\partial u_i(t, x_i^*(t), y_i^*(t))}{\partial x_{ij}} - r_j^*(t) - \lambda_{ij}^{(1)}(t) - \mu_i^{(1)}(t) \right]$$

$$\times [x_{ij}(t) - x_{ij}^*(t)] \, dt$$

$$+ \int_0^T \sum_{j=1}^n \left[-\frac{\partial u_i(t, x_i^*(t), y_i^*(t))}{\partial y_{ij}} + r_j^*(t) - \lambda_{ij}^{(2)}(t) - \mu_i^{(2)}(t) \right]$$

$$\times [y_{ij}(t) - y_{ij}^*(t)] \, dt \geq 0, \quad \forall \, (x_i(t), y_i(t)) \in L^2([0,T], \mathbb{R}^{2n}). \quad (4.31)$$

If we set

$$\varepsilon_1(t) = -\frac{\partial u_i(t, x_i^*(t), y_i^*(t))}{\partial x_{ij}} - r_j^*(t) - \lambda_{ij}^{(1)}(t) - \mu_i^{(1)}(t)$$

and

$$\varepsilon_2(t) = -\frac{\partial u_i(t, x_i^*(t), y_i^*(t))}{\partial y_{ij}} - r_j^*(t) - \lambda_{ij}^{(1)}(t) - \mu_i^{(1)}(t),$$

by choosing

$$x_i(t) = x_i^*(t) + \varepsilon_1(t) \quad \text{and} \quad y_i(t) = y_i^*(t) + \varepsilon_2(t),$$

we get:

$$\int_0^T \sum_{j=1}^n \left[-\frac{\partial u_i(t, x_i^*(t), y_i^*(t))}{\partial x_{ij}} - r_j^*(t) - \lambda_{ij}^{(1)}(t) - \mu_i^{(1)}(t) \right]^2 dt$$

$$+ \int_0^T \sum_{j=1}^n \left[-\frac{\partial u_i(t, x_i^*(t), y_i^*(t))}{\partial y_{ij}} + r_j^*(t) - \lambda_{ij}^{(2)}(t) - \mu_i^{(2)}(t) \right]^2 dt \geq 0.$$

By choosing

$$x_i(t) = x_i^*(t) - \varepsilon_1(t) \quad \text{and} \quad y_i(t) = y_i^*(t) - \varepsilon_2(t),$$

we obtain:

$$-\int_0^T \sum_{j=1}^n \left[-\frac{\partial u_i(t, x_i^*(t), y_i^*(t))}{\partial x_{ij}} - r_j^*(t) - \lambda_{ij}^{(1)}(t) - \mu_i^{(1)}(t) \right]^2 dt$$

$$-\int_0^T \sum_{j=1}^n \left[-\frac{\partial u_i(t, x_i^*(t), y_i^*(t))}{\partial y_{ij}} + r_j^*(t) - \lambda_{ij}^{(2)}(t) - \mu_i^{(2)}(t) \right]^2 dt \geq 0.$$

Hence,

$$-\frac{\partial u_i(t, x_i^*(t), y_i^*(t))}{\partial x_{ij}} - r_j^*(t) - \mu_i^{(1)}(t) = \lambda_{ij}^{(1)}(t) \geq 0$$

and

$$-\frac{\partial u_i(t, x_i^*(t), y_i^*(t))}{\partial y_{ij}} r_j^*(t) - \mu_i^{(2)}(t) = \lambda_{ij}^{(2)}(t) \geq 0.$$

Moreover, taking into account that $\lambda_i^{(1)}(t)x_i^*(t) = 0$, $\lambda_i^{(2)}(t)y_i^*(t) = 0$, we get:

$$x_{ij}^*(t) \left[-\frac{\partial u_i(t, x_i^*(t), y_i^*(t))}{\partial x_{ij}} - r_j^*(t) - \mu_i^{(1)}(t) \right] = 0$$

and

$$y_{ij}^*(t) \left[-\frac{\partial u_i(t, x_i^*(t), y_i^*(t))}{\partial y_{ij}} + r_j^*(t) - \mu_i^{(2)}(t) \right] = 0.$$

Conversely, if estimates (4.23)–(4.26) hold, then we show that the variational inequality (4.30) holds. From (4.23), we obtain:

$$\sum_{j=1}^{n} \left[-\frac{\partial u_i(t, x_i^*(t), y_i^*(t))}{\partial x_{ij}} - r_j^*(t) - \mu_i^{(1)}(t) \right] \times [x_{ij}(t) - x_{ij}^*(t)] \geq 0,$$

and taking into account that $\sum_{j=1}^{n} x_{ij}(t) = s_i(t)$ and $\sum_{j=1}^{n} x_{ij}^*(t) = s_i(t)$ a.e. in $[0, T]$, we get:

$$\sum_{j=1}^{n} \left[-\frac{\partial u_i(t, x_i^*(t), y_i^*(t))}{\partial x_{ij}} - r_j^*(t) \right] \times [x_{ij}(t) - x_{ij}^*(t)] \geq 0,$$

and then

$$\int_0^T \sum_{j=1}^{n} \left[-\frac{\partial u_i(t, x_i^*(t), y_i^*(t))}{\partial x_{ij}} - r_j^*(t) \right] \times [x_{ij}(t) - x_{ij}^*(t)] \, dt \geq 0. \quad (4.32)$$

Similarly, one obtains:

$$\sum_{j=1}^{n} \left[-\frac{\partial u_i(t, x_i^*(t), y_i^*(t))}{\partial y_{ij}} + r_j^*(t) \right] \times [y_{ij}(t) - y_{ij}^*(t)] \geq 0$$

and, subsequently,

$$\int_0^T \sum_{j=1}^{n} \left[-\frac{\partial u_i(t, x_i^*(t), y_i^*(t))}{\partial y_{ij}} + r_j^*(t) \right] \times [y_{ij}(t) - y_{ij}^*(t)] \, dt \geq 0. \quad (4.33)$$

Summing now inequalities (4.32) and (4.33) for all i, we conclude that for $(x^*(t), y^*(t)) \in \prod_{i=1}^{m} P_i$:

$$\sum_{i=1}^{m} \int_0^T \sum_{j=1}^{n} \left[-\frac{\partial u_i(t, x_i^*(t), y_i^*(t))}{\partial x_{ij}} - r_j^*(t) \right] \times [x_{ij}(t) - x_{ij}^*(t)] \, dt$$

$$+ \int_0^T \sum_{j=1}^{n} \left[-\frac{\partial u_i(t, x_i^*(t), y_i^*(t))}{\partial y_{ij}} + r_j^*(t) \right] \times [y_{ij}(t) - y_{ij}^*(t)] \, dt \geq 0,$$

$$\forall \, (x_i(t), y_i(t)) \in P_i,$$

and the proof is complete.   □

We now describe the variational inequality associated with the instrument prices $r_j(t)$.

The equilibrium condition related to the prices of the instruments is

$$\begin{cases} \sum_{i=1}^{m} \left(x_{ij}^*(t) - y_{ij}^*(t) \right) \geq 0 & \text{a.e. in } [0,T] \\ \sum_{i=1}^{m} \left(x_{ij}^*(t) - y_{ij}^*(t) \right) r_j^*(t) = 0, & r^*(t) \in L^2([0,T], \mathbb{R}_+^n). \end{cases} \qquad (4.27)$$

Following the same proof of [36], we get the following theorem.

Theorem 4.2.4 *Condition (4.27) is equivalent to*

$$\begin{cases} \text{Find } r^*(t) \in L^2([0,T], R_+^n) \text{ such that} \\ \int_0^T \sum_{i=1}^{m} \left[x_{ij}^*(t) - y_{ij}^*(t) \right] \times \left[r_j(t) - r_j^*(t) \right] \, dt \geq 0, \\ \forall r(t) \in L^2([0,T], \mathbb{R}_+^n). \end{cases} \qquad (4.34)$$

4.2.3   Variational Formulation and an Existence Theorem: General Utility Function

Following the proof of Theorem 4.2.3, we can now prove Theorem 4.2.1.
Proof: From the results of the preceding section, it immediately follows that if $(x^*(t), y^*(t), r^*(t)) \in \prod_{i=1}^{m} P_i \times L^2([0,T], \mathbb{R}_+^n)$ is a dynamical financial equilibrium, then it satisfies the variational inequalities (4.30) and (4.34), and hence the variational inequality (4.29), and vice versa.   □

We now establish the following existence theorem.

Theorem 4.2.5 (Existence) *If $(x^*(t), y^*(t), r^*(t)) \in \prod_{i=1}^{m} P_i \times L^2([0,T],$ $\mathbb{R}_+^n)$ is an equilibrium, then the equilibrium assets and liabilities vector*

$(x^*(t), y^*(t))$ *is a solution to the variational inequality:*

$$\sum_{i=1}^{m} \int_0^T \left\{ \sum_{j=1}^{n} \left[-\frac{\partial u_i(t, x_i^*(t), y_i^*(t))}{\partial x_{ij}} \right] \times \left[x_{ij}(t) - x_{ij}^*(t) \right] \right.$$

$$+ \sum_{j=1}^{n} \left[-\frac{\partial u_i(t, x_i^*(t), y_i^*(t))}{\partial y_{ij}} \right] \times \left[y_{ij}(t) - y_{ij}^*(t) \right] \right\} dt \geq 0,$$

$$\forall (x(t), y(t)) \in S, \tag{4.35}$$

where

$$S \equiv \left\{ (x(t), y(t)) \in \prod_{i=1}^{m} P_i; \ \sum_{i=1}^{m} (x_{ij}(t) - y_{ij}(t)) \geq 0, j = 1, 2, \ldots, n \right\}.$$

Conversely, if $(x^*(t), y^*(t))$ is a solution to (4.35), then there exists $r^*(t) \in L^2([0,T], \mathbb{R}_+^n)$ such that $(x^*(t), y^*(t), r^*(t))$ is an equilibrium.

Proof: Assume that $(x^*(t), y^*(t), r^*(t)) \in \prod_{i=1}^{m} P_i \times L^2([0,T], \mathbb{R}_+^n)$ is an equilibrium. Then $(x^*(t), y^*(t), r^*(t))$ satisfies (4.29). In (4.29) let us set:

$$x_i(t) = x_i^*(t), \ y_i(t) = y_i^*(t), \ r(t) = 0, \ \text{a.e. in } [0,T] \text{ and } \forall i = 1, \ldots, m,$$

then we get:

$$-\sum_{i=1}^{m} \int_0^T \sum_{j=1}^{n} \left[x_{ij}^*(t) - y_{ij}^*(t) \right] \times r_j^*(t) \, dt \geq 0. \tag{4.36}$$

Let us now set $r(t) = r^*(t)$ in (4.29) and we obtain:

$$\sum_{i=1}^{m} \int_0^T \left\{ -\frac{\partial u_i(t, x_i^*(t), y_i^*(t))}{\partial x_{ij}} \right] \times \left[x_{ij}(t) - x_{ij}^*(t) \right] \right.$$

$$+ \sum_{j=1}^{n} \left[-\frac{\partial u_i(t, x_i^*(t), y_i^*(t))}{\partial y_{ij}} \right] \times \left[y_{ij}(t) - y_{ij}^*(t) \right] \right\} dt$$

$$\geq \int_0^T \sum_{j=1}^{n} r_j^*(t) \left[\sum_{i=1}^{m} (x_{ij}(t) - y_{ij}(t)) - \sum_{i=1}^{m} (x_{ij}^*(t) - y_{ij}^*(t)) \right] dt. \tag{4.37}$$

But the right-hand side of inequality (4.37) is greater than or equal to 0, because of (4.36) and the constraint set S. Thus, we have established that $(x^*(t), y^*(t))$ satisfies (4.35).

Observe that $u_i(t, x_i(t), y_i(t))$ is concave, then $-u_i(t, x_i(t), y_i(t))$ is convex and its gradient is monotone. From assumption (4.22), it is also hemicontinuous along line segments and, hence, it is lower semicontinuous with respect to the strong and weak topology. By virtue of Corollary 5.1 in [46], the variational inequality (4.36) admits a solution.

Now, in order to prove the existence of $r^*(t) \in L^2([0, T], \mathbb{R}^n_+)$ such that $(x^*(t), y^*(t), r^*(t))$ is an equilibrium, let us apply the Lagrange Multiplier Theorem (see [32]) to the function:

$$\mathcal{L}\left(x(t), y(t), \lambda^{(1)}(t), \lambda^{(2)}(t), \mu^{(1)}(t), \mu^{(2)}(t), r(t)\right)$$

$$= \Phi(x(t), y(t)) - \sum_{i=1}^{m} \int_0^T \sum_{j=1}^{n} \lambda_{ij}^{(1)}(t) x_{ij}(t)\, dt - \sum_{i=1}^{m} \int_0^T \sum_{j=1}^{n} \lambda_{ij}^{(2)}(t) y_{ij}(t)\, dt$$

$$- \sum_{i=1}^{m} \int_0^T \mu_i^{(1)}(t) \left[\sum_{j=1}^{n} x_{ij}(t) - s_i(t) \right] dt$$

$$- \sum_{i=1}^{m} \int_0^T \mu_i^{(2)}(t) \left[\sum_{j=1}^{n} y_{ij}(t) - s_i(t) \right] dt$$

$$- \int_0^T \sum_{j=1}^{n} r_j(t) \left[\sum_{i=1}^{m} (x_{ij}(t) - y_{ij}(t)) \right] dt$$

where

$$\Phi(x(t), y(t)) = \sum_{i=1}^{m} \int_0^T \sum_{j=1}^{n} \left[-\frac{\partial u_i(t, x_i^*(t), y_i^*(t))}{\partial x_{ij}} \right] \times [x_{ij}(t) - x_{ij}^*(t)]\, dt$$

$$+ \int_0^T \sum_{j=1}^{n} \left[-\frac{\partial u_i(t, x_i^*(t), y_i^*(t))}{\partial y_{ij}} \right] \times [y_{ij}(t) - y_{ij}^*(t)]\, dt,$$

and

$$\left(\lambda_i^{(1)}(t), \lambda_i^{(2)}(t), \mu_i^{(1)}(t), \mu_i^{(2)}(t), r(t)\right) \in \overline{C}$$

$$= \left\{ \begin{array}{l} \lambda^{(1)}(t), \ \lambda^{(2)}(t) \in L^2([0,T], \mathbb{R}^{nm}), \quad \lambda_i^{(1)}(t), \ \lambda_i^{(2)}(t) \geq 0, \\[2mm] \mu_i^{(1)}(t), \ \mu_i^{(2)}(t) \in L^2([0,T]); \ i = 1, 2, \ldots, m; \\[2mm] r(t) \in L^2([0,T], \mathbb{R}^n), \quad r(t) \geq 0 \text{ a.e. in } [0,T] \end{array} \right\}.$$

We get that, besides $\lambda_i^{(1)}(t)$, $\lambda_i^{(2)}(t)$, $\mu_i^{(1)}(t)$ and $\mu_i^{(2)}(t)$, there exists an $r^*(t) \in L^2([0,T], \mathbb{R}_+^n)$ corresponding to the constraints defining S. For such a pattern $(x^*(t), y^*(t), r^*(t))$ we have:

$$-\frac{\partial u_i(t, x_i^*(t), y_i^*(t))}{\partial x_{ij}} - r_j^*(t) - \mu_i^{(1)}(t) = \lambda_{ij}^{(1)} \geq 0, \qquad (4.23)$$

$$-\frac{\partial u_i(t, x_i^*(t), y_i^*(t))}{\partial y_{ij}} + r_j^*(t) - \mu_i^{(2)}(t) = \lambda_{ij}^{(2)} \geq 0, \qquad (4.24)$$

$$x_{ij}^*(t) \left[-\frac{\partial u_i(t, x_i^*(t), y_i^*(t))}{\partial x_{ij}} - r_j^*(t) - \mu_i^{(1)}(t) \right] = 0, \qquad (4.25)$$

$$y_{ij}^*(t) \left[-\frac{\partial u_i(t, x_i^*(t), y_i^*(t))}{\partial y_{ij}} + r_j^*(t) - \mu_i^{(2)}(t) \right] = 0, \qquad (4.26)$$

and

$$\left\{ \begin{array}{ll} \displaystyle\sum_{i=1}^{m} \left(x_{ij}^*(t) - y_{ij}^*(t) \right) \geq 0 & \text{a.e. in } [0,T] \\[4mm] \displaystyle\sum_{i=1}^{m} \left(x_{ij}^*(t) - y_{ij}^*(t) \right) r_j^*(t) = 0, & r^*(t) \in L^2([0,T], \mathbb{R}_+^n). \end{array} \right. \qquad (4.27)$$

From conditions (4.23)–(4.27), a.e. in $[0,T]$, we obtain:

$$\sum_{i=1}^{m} \sum_{j=1}^{n} \left[-\frac{\partial u_i(t, x_i^*(t), y_i^*(t))}{\partial x_{ij}} - r_j^*(t) \right] \times \left[x_{ij}(t) - x_{ij}^*(t) \right]$$

$$+ \sum_{i=1}^{m} \sum_{j=1}^{n} \left[-\frac{\partial u_i(t, x_i^*(t), y_i^*(t))}{\partial y_{ij}} + r_j^*(t) \right] \times \left[y_{ij}(t) - y_{ij}^*(t) \right] \geq 0 \ (4.38)$$

and

$$\sum_{i=1}^{m} \sum_{j=1}^{n} \left[x_{ij}^*(t) - y_{ij}^*(t) \right] \times \left[r_j(t) - r_j^*(t) \right] \geq 0. \qquad (4.39)$$

Summing now (4.38) and (4.39) and integrating the result, we obtain:

$$\sum_{i=1}^{m} \int_0^T \left\{ \sum_{j=1}^{n} \left[-\frac{\partial u_i(t, x_i^*(t), y_i^*(t))}{\partial x_{ij}} - r_j^*(t) \right] \times \left[x_{ij}(t) - x_{ij}^*(t) \right] \right.$$

$$+ \sum_{j=1}^{n} \left[-\frac{\partial u_i(t, x_i^*(t), y_i^*(t))}{\partial y_{ij}} + r_j^*(t) \right] \times \left[y_{ij}(t) - y_{ij}^*(t) \right]$$

$$\left. + \sum_{j=1}^{n} \left(x_{ij}^*(t) - y_{ij}^*(t) \right) \times \left[r_j(t) - r_j^*(t) \right] \right\} dt \geq 0,$$

and the proof is complete.   □

4.3   Policy Intervention

In this section the general model of competitive financial equilibrium described in section 4.2 (see [38]) is generalized to allow for the incorporation of policy interventions in the form of taxes and price controls. From the aspect of policy interventions, denote the price ceiling associated with instrument j by $\bar{r}_j(t)$ and the price floor associated with instrument j by $\underline{r}_j(t)$. The meaning of this constraint is that to each investor a minimal price $\underline{r}_j$ for the assets held in the instrument j is guaranteed, whereas each investor is requested to pay for the liabilities in any case a minimal price $\underline{r}_j$. Analogously each investor cannot obtain for an asset a price greater than $\bar{r}_j$ and as a liability the price cannot exceed the maximum price $\bar{r}_j$. The social, economic and financial reasons which induce such an intervention are discussed in [53] and [108].

There is also another value we can assign to the prices $\underline{r}_j$ and $\bar{r}_j$: they can represent a tax which in any case must be paid for the assets or a discount applied to the liabilities. In this section we shall introduce a model with the first interpretation, whereas in the papers [41] and [74] the authors adopt the second interpretation.

Denote the given tax rate levied on sector i's net yield on financial instrument j, as $\tau_{ij}(t)$. Assume that the tax rates lie in the interval $[0, 1)$ and belong to $L^\infty(0, T)$. Therefore, the government in this model has the flexibility of levying a distinct tax rate across both sectors and instruments and the possibility of adjusting the tax rate following the evolution of the system.

Then if, at time t, $x_{ij}(t)$ still denotes the amount of instrument j held as an asset in sector i's portfolio, $y_{ij}(t)$ still denotes the amount of instrument j held as a liability in sector i's portfolio, the equilibrium condition for price $r_j(t)$ of instrument j is the following:

$$\sum_{i=1}^{m}(1 - \tau_{ij}(t))(x_{ij}(t) - y_{ij}(t)) \begin{cases} \leq 0 & \text{if} \quad r_j(t) = \overline{r}_j(t) \\ = 0 & \text{if} \quad \underline{r}_j(t) < r_j(t) < \overline{r}_j(t) \quad (4.40) \\ \geq 0 & \text{if} \quad r_j(t) = \underline{r}_j(t) \end{cases}$$

In other words, if there is an actual supply excess of an instrument in the economy, then its price must be the price floor. If the price of an instrument is positive, but not at the ceiling, then the market of that instrument must clear. Finally, if there is an actual demand excess for an instrument in the economy, then the price must be at the ceiling.

In this section we intend to study this new financial evolutionary problem, proving also that in this case the equilibrium conditions are equivalent to a variational inequality, from which an existence result follows.

4.3.1 Statement of the Problem and Main Results

In addition to the assumptions of sectors, instruments, financial volumes, assets and liabilities of Section 4.1.1, let us consider the instrument ceiling prices $\overline{r}_j(t)$ grouped into the column vector

$$\overline{r}_j(t) = [\overline{r}_1(t), \dots, \overline{r}_i(t), \dots, \overline{r}_m(t)]^T,$$

the instrument floor prices $\underline{r}_j(t)$ grouped into the column vector

$$\underline{r}_j(t) = [\underline{r}_1(t), \dots, \underline{r}_i(t), \dots, \underline{r}_m(t)]^T,$$

and the tax rates $\tau_{ij}(t)$ grouped into the matrix

$$
\tau(t) = \begin{bmatrix} \tau_{11}(t) & \cdots & \tau_{1j}(t) & \cdots & \tau_{1n}(t) \\ \cdots & & & & \\ \tau_{i1}(t) & \cdots & \tau_{ij}(t) & \cdots & \tau_{in}(t) \\ \cdots & & & & \\ \tau_{m1}(t) & \cdots & \tau_{mj}(t) & \cdots & \tau_{mn}(t) \end{bmatrix}.
$$

The set of feasible assets and liabilities remains unchanged:

$$
P_i = \left\{ [x_i(t), y_i(t)]^T \in L^2([0,T], \mathbb{R}^{2n}) : \sum_{j=1}^{n} x_{ij}(t) = s_i(t), \right.
$$

$$
\left. \sum_{j=1}^{n} y_{ij}(t) = s_i(t) \text{ a.e. in } [0,T], \ x_{ij}(t) \geq 0, y_{ij}(t) \geq 0 \text{ a.e. in } [0,T] \right\}
$$

and the set of feasible instrument prices becomes:

$$
\mathcal{R} = \left\{ r(t) \in L^2([0,T], \mathbb{R}^n) : \underline{r}_j(t) \leq r_j(t) \leq \overline{r}_j(t), \right.
$$
$$
\left. j = 1, \ldots, n, \text{ a.e. in } [0,T] \right\},
$$

where $\underline{r}(t), \overline{r}(t)$ are assumed to belong to $L^2([0,T]; \mathbb{R}^n)$.

We generalize the quadratic financial model and assume that each sector seeks to maximize its utility, where the utility function is given by:

$$
U_i(t, x_i(t), y_i(t), r(t))
$$
$$
= u_i(t, x_i(t), y_i(t)) + \sum_{j=1}^{n} r_j(t)(1 - \tau_{ij}) \left(x_{ij}(t) - y_{ij}(t) \right). \quad (4.41)
$$

Observe that the objective function (4.41) differs from the objective function in [38], in that the second addend now incorporates the tax rate through the presence of the $(1 - \tau_{ij})$ factor multiplying the $(r_j(t) - \underline{r}_j(t))$ $(x_{ij}(t) - y_{ij}(t))$ quantity, with the former term acting, actually, as a discount rate.

We can provide the following definition of an evolutionary financial equilibrium.

Definition 4.3.1 *A vector of sector assets, liabilities, and instrument prices* $(x^*(t), y^*(t), r^*(t)) \in \prod_{i=1}^{m} P_i \times \mathcal{R}$ *is an equilibrium of the evolutionary* *financial model if and only if it satisfies the system of inequalities*

$$-\frac{\partial u_i(t, x_i^*(t), y_i^*(t))}{\partial x_{ij}} - (1 - \tau_{ij}(t)) \, r_j^*(t) - \mu_i^{(1)}(t) \geq 0, \qquad (4.42)$$

and

$$-\frac{\partial u_i(t, x_i^*(t), y_i^*(t))}{\partial y_{ij}} + (1 - \tau_{ij}(t)) \, r_j^*(t) - \mu_i^{(2)}(t) \geq 0, \qquad (4.43)$$

and equalities

$$x_{ij}^*(t) \left[-\frac{\partial u_i(t, x_i^*(t), y_i^*(t))}{\partial x_{ij}} - (1 - \tau_{ij}(t)) \, r_j^*(t) - \mu_i^{(1)}(t) \right] = 0, \quad (4.44)$$

$$y_{ij}^*(t) \left[-\frac{\partial u_i(t, x_i^*(t), y_i^*(t))}{\partial y_{ij}} + (1 - \tau_{ij}(t)) \, r_j^*(t) - \mu_i^{(2)}(t) \right] = 0, \quad (4.45)$$

where $\mu_i^{(1)}(t)$, $\mu_i^{(2)}(t) \in L^2([0, T])$ are Lagrangean functionals, for all sectors i: $i = 1, 2, \ldots, m$, and for all instruments j: $j = 1, 2, \ldots, n$, and verifies condition (4.40) a.e. in $[0, T]$, namely

$$\sum_{i=1}^{m} (1 - \tau_{ij}(t))(x_{ij}^*(t) - y_{ij}^*(t)) \begin{cases} \leq 0 & if \quad r_j^*(t) = \bar{r}_j(t) \\ = 0 & if \quad \underline{r}_j(t) < r_j^*(t) < \bar{r}_j(t) \quad (4.46) \\ \geq 0 & if \quad r_j^*(t) = \underline{r}_j(t). \end{cases}$$

As explained in [38], the meaning of Definition 4.3.1 is the following: to each financial volume $s_i(t)$ held by the sector i, we associate the functions $\mu_i^{(1)}(t)$, $\mu_i^{(2)}(t)$, related, respectively, to the assets and to the liabilities and which represent the 'equilibrium disutilities' for one unit of the sector i. The financial volume invested in the instrument j as assets $x_{ij}^*(t)$ is greater than or equal to zero if the j-th component

$$-\frac{\partial u_i(t, x_i^*(t), y_i^*(t))}{\partial x_{ij}} - (1 - \tau_{ij}(t)) \, r_j^*(t)$$

of the disutility is equal to $\mu_i^{(1)}(t)$, whereas if

$$-\frac{\partial u_i(t, x_i^*(t), y_i^*(t))}{\partial x_{ij}} - (1 - \tau_{ij}(t)) \, r_j^*(t) > \mu_i^{(1)}(t),$$

then $x_{ij}^*(t) = 0$. The same occurs for the liabilities.

The functions $\mu_i^{(1)}(t)$, $\mu_i^{(2)}(t)$ are the Lagrangean functionals associated, respectively, with the constraints $\sum_{j=1}^{n} x_{ij}(t) - s_i(t) = 0$ and $\sum_{j=1}^{n} y_{ij}(t) - s_i(t) = 0$. They are unknown a priori, but this has no influence, since we shall prove later that Definition 4.3.1 is equivalent to a variational inequality in which $\mu_i^{(1)}(t)$, $\mu_i^{(2)}(t)$ do not appear.

Conditions (4.46), which represent the equilibrium condition for the prices, express the equilibrating of the total assets and the total liabilities of each instrument.

The proof of the variational inequality formulation of the governing equilibrium conditions is obtained in a few steps. First of all, we shall prove that the equilibrium conditions (4.42)–(4.45) are equivalent to a suitable maximum problem, which, in turn, is equivalent to a first variational inequality.

Theorem 4.3.1 $(x_i^*(t), y_i^*(t))$ *is a solution to*

$$\max_{P_i} \int_0^T \{u_i(t, x_i(t), y_i(t)) + (1 - \tau_{ij}(t))\, r_j(t) \times [x_i(t) - y_i(t)]\}\, dt,$$

$$\forall\, (x_i(t), y_i(t)) \in P_i. \tag{4.47}$$

if and only if it is a solution to the variational inequality

$$\int_0^T -\sum_{j=1}^{n} \left[-\frac{\partial u_i(t, x_i^*(t), y_i^*(t))}{\partial x_{ij}} + (1 - \tau_{ij}(t))\, r_j^*(t) \right]$$

$$\times [x_{ij}(t) - x_{ij}^*(t)]\, dt$$

$$+ \int_0^T -\sum_{j=1}^{n} \left[-\frac{\partial u_i(t, x_i^*(t), y_i^*(t))}{\partial y_{ij}} - (1 - \tau_{ij}(t))\, r_j^*(t) \right]$$

$$\times [y_{ij}(t) - y_{ij}^*(t)]\, dt \geq 0, \quad \forall\, (x_i(t), y_i(t)) \in P_i, \tag{4.48}$$

for a given $r^*(t) \in \mathcal{R}$.

Proof: Let us prove the necessary condition. Assume that $(x_i^*(t), y_i^*(t))$ is a solution to problem (4.47) and consider, $\forall\, (x_i(t), y_i(t)) \in P_i$, the function

$$F(\lambda) = \int_0^T \Big\{ u_i(t, \lambda x_i^*(t) + (1-\lambda)x_i(t), \lambda y_i^*(t) + (1-\lambda)y_i(t))$$
$$+ (1 - \tau_{ij}(t))\, r_j(t)$$
$$\times \left[\lambda x_i^*(t) + (1-\lambda)x_i(t) - \lambda y_i^*(t) - (1-\lambda)y_i(t) \right] \Big\}\, dt,$$
$$\lambda \in [0,1].$$

We have that $\lambda = 1$ is a maximum point for $F(\lambda)$ and then $F'(1) \geq 0$.

Hence, we can consider the derivative of $F(\lambda)$ with respect to λ and we obtain:

$$\frac{\partial}{\partial \lambda} \int_0^T \Big\{ u_i(t, \lambda x_i^*(t) + (1-\lambda)x_i(t), \lambda y_i^*(t) + (1-\lambda)y_i(t))$$

$$+ (1 - \tau_{ij}(t))\, r_j(t)$$

$$\times \left[\lambda x_i^*(t) + (1-\lambda)x_i(t) - \lambda y_i^*(t) - (1-\lambda)y_i(t) \right] \Big\}\, dt$$

$$= \int_0^T \Big\{ \sum_{j=1}^n \frac{\partial u_i(t, \lambda x_i^*(t) + (1-\lambda)x_i(t), \lambda y_i^*(t) + (1-\lambda)y_i(t))}{\partial x_{ij}}$$

$$\times [x_{ij}^*(t) - x_{ij}(t)]$$

$$+ \sum_{j=1}^n \frac{\partial u_i(t, \lambda x_i^*(t) + (1-\lambda)x_i(t), \lambda y_i^*(t) + (1-\lambda)y_i(t))}{\partial y_{ij}}$$

$$\times [y_{ij}^*(t) - y_{ij}(t)] \Big\}\, dt + \int_0^T \sum_{i=1}^m (1 - \tau_{ij}(t))\, r_j(t)$$

$$\times \left[x_{ij}^*(t) - x_{ij}(t) - y_{ij}^*(t) + y_{ij}(t) \right]\, dt.$$

Then

$$F'(1) = \int_0^T \Big\{ \sum_{j=1}^n \frac{\partial u_i(t, x_i^*(t), y_i^*(t))}{\partial x_{ij}} \cdot (x_{ij}^*(t) - x_{ij}(t))$$

$$+ \sum_{j=1}^n \frac{\partial u_i(t, x_i^*(t), y_i^*(t))}{\partial y_{ij}} \cdot (y_{ij}^*(t) - y_{ij}(t)) \Big\}\, dt$$

$$+ \int_0^T \sum_{i=1}^m (1 - \tau_{ij}(t))\, r_j(t) \times \left[x_{ij}^*(t) - x_{ij}(t) - y_{ij}^*(t) + y_{ij}(t) \right]\, dt \geq 0,$$

$$\forall\, (x_i(t), y_i(t)) \in P_i,$$

that is, the variational inequality (4.48).

Conversely, let us assume that $(x_i^*(t), y_i^*(t))$ is solution to problem (4.48). Since the function $\mathcal{U}_i(x_i(t), y_i(t)) = \int_0^T U_i(t, x_i(t), y_i(t), r(t)) \, dt$ is concave, then for all $(x_i^*(t), y_i^*(t)) \in P_i$ the following estimate holds:

$$-\mathcal{U}_i \left(\lambda x_i(t) + (1 - \lambda) x_i^*(t), \; \lambda y_i(t) + (1 - \lambda) y_i^*(t) \right)$$
$$\leq -\lambda \mathcal{U}_i \left(x_i(t), y_i(t) \right) - (1 - \lambda) \mathcal{U}_i \left(x_i^*(t), y_i^*(t) \right),$$

namely, $\forall \lambda \in (0, 1]$:

$$\frac{1}{\lambda} \left[-\mathcal{U}_i \left(x_i^*(t) + \lambda(x_i(t) - x_i^*(t)), \; y_i^*(t) + \lambda(y_i(t) - y_i^*(t)) \right) \right.$$
$$\left. + \mathcal{U}_i \left(x_i^*(t), \; y_i^*(t) \right) \right] \leq -\mathcal{U}_i \left(x_i(t), y_i(t) \right) + \mathcal{U}_i \left(x_i^*(t), y_i^*(t) \right). \quad (4.49)$$

When $\lambda \to 0$, the left-hand side of (4.49) converges to:

$$-\left[\frac{d}{d\lambda} \mathcal{U}_i \left(x_i^*(t) + \lambda(x_i(t) - x_i^*(t)), \; y_i^*(t) + \lambda(y_i(t) - y_i^*(t)) \right) \right]_{\lambda=0}$$
$$= -\int_0^T \sum_{j=1}^n \left\{ \frac{\partial u_i(t, x_i^*(t), y_i^*(t))}{\partial x_{ij}} \cdot (x_{ij}(t) - x_{ij}^*(t)) \right.$$
$$+ \frac{\partial u_i(t, x_i^*(t), y_i^*(t))}{\partial y_{ij}} \cdot (y_{ij}(t) - y_{ij}^*(t))$$
$$\left. + (1 - \tau_{ij}(t)) \, r_j^*(t)(x_{ij}(t) - x_{ij}^*(t) - y_{ij}(t) + y_{ij}^*(t)) \right\} dt,$$

that is the left-hand side of the variational inequality (4.48), which is greater than or equal to $0 \; \forall \, (x_i(t), y_i(t)) \in P_i$ and, hence,

$$0 \leq -\mathcal{U}_i \left(x_i(t), y_i(t) \right) + \mathcal{U}_i \left(x_i^*(t), y_i^*(t) \right), \quad \forall \, (x_i(t), y_i(t)) \in P_i.$$

It means that $(x_i^*(t), y_i^*(t))$ is solution to the problem (4.47). $\qquad \square$

Now we may prove the equivalence between problem (4.47) or problem (4.48) and the equilibrium conditions (4.42)–(4.45).

Theorem 4.3.2 $(x_i^*(t), y_i^*(t))$ *is a solution to (4.47) or to (4.48) if and only if it satisfies, a.e. in $[0, T]$, conditions (4.42)–(4.45), where $\mu_i^{(1)}(t)$, $\mu_i^{(2)}(t) \in L^2([0, T])$ are Lagrangean functionals.*

Proof: Let $(x_i^*(t), y_i^*(t))$ be a solution to (4.47). In order to obtain conditions (4.42)–(4.45) we use the infinite-dimensional Lagrangean theory (see [32], [40], [85] and [103]).

Let us consider the function

$$\mathcal{L}(x_i(t), y_i(t), \lambda_i^{(1)}(t), \lambda_i^{(2)}(t), \mu_i^{(1)}(t), \mu_i^{(2)}(t))$$

$$= \Psi(x_i(t), y_i(t)) - \int_0^T \sum_{j=1}^n \lambda_{ij}^{(1)}(t)x_{ij}(t)dt - \int_0^T \sum_{j=1}^n \lambda_{ij}^{(2)}(t)y_{ij}(t)dt$$

$$- \int_0^T \mu_i^{(1)}(t)\Big(\sum_{j=1}^n x_{ij}(t) - s_i(t)\Big)dt - \int_0^T \mu_i^{(2)}(t)\Big(\sum_{j=1}^n y_{ij}(t) - s_i(t)\Big)dt,$$

where

$$\Psi(x_i(t), y_i(t))$$

$$= \int_0^T \sum_{j=1}^n \left[-\frac{\partial u_i(t, x_i^*(t), y_i^*(t))}{\partial x_{ij}} - (1 - \tau_{ij}(t))\, r_j^*(t) \right] \times [x_{ij}(t) - x_{ij}^*(t)]\, dt$$

$$+ \int_0^T \sum_{j=1}^n \left[-\frac{\partial u_i(t, x_i^*(t), y_i^*(t))}{\partial y_{ij}} + (1 - \tau_{ij}(t))\, r_j^*(t) \right] \times [y_{ij}(t) - y_{ij}^*(t)]\, dt,$$

$(x_i(t), y_i(t)) \in L^2([0,T], \mathbb{R}^{2n})$ and $\left(\lambda_i^{(1)}(t), \lambda_i^{(2)}(t), \mu_i^{(1)}(t), \mu_i^{(2)}(t)\right) \in \mathcal{C}$

$$= \Big\{\lambda_i^{(1)}(t),\ \lambda_i^{(2)}(t) \in L^2([0,T], \mathbb{R}^n),\quad \lambda_i^{(1)}(t),\ \lambda_i^{(2)}(t) \geq 0,$$

$$\mu_i^{(1)}(t),\ \mu_i^{(2)}(t) \in L^2([0,T]);\ i = 1, 2, \ldots, m\Big\}.$$

Applying the Lagrange Multiplier Theorem [32], it is possible to prove that there exist $\lambda_i^{(1)}(t), \lambda_i^{(2)}(t), \mu_i^{(1)}(t), \mu_i^{(2)}(t) \in \mathcal{C}$ such that

$$\int_0^T \sum_{j=1}^n \lambda_{ij}^{(1)}(t)x_{ij}^*(t)\, dt = 0; \quad \int_0^T \sum_{j=1}^n \lambda_{ij}^{(2)}(t)y_{ij}^*(t)\, dt = 0,$$

from which it follows

$$\lambda_{ij}^{(1)}(t)x_{ij}^*(t) = 0, \quad \lambda_{ij}^{(2)}(t)y_{ij}^*(t) = 0 \quad \text{a.e. in } [0,T]. \tag{4.50}$$

Moreover, using the characterization of the solution by means of a saddle point (see [32]), we obtain

$$\mathcal{L}\left(x_i(t), y_i(t), \lambda_i^{(1)}(t), \lambda_i^{(2)}(t), \mu_i^{(1)}(t), \mu_i^{(2)}(t)\right)$$

$$= \int_0^T \sum_{j=1}^n \left[-\frac{\partial u_i(t, x_i^*(t), y_i^*(t))}{\partial x_{ij}} - (1 - \tau_{ij}(t))\, r_j^*(t) \right.$$

$$\left. -\lambda_{ij}^{(1)}(t) - \mu_i^{(1)}(t) \right] \times [x_{ij}(t) - x_{ij}^*(t)]\, dt$$

$$+ \int_0^T \sum_{j=1}^n \left[-\frac{\partial u_i(t, x_i^*(t), y_i^*(t))}{\partial y_{ij}} + (1 - \tau_{ij}(t))\, r_j^*(t) \right.$$

$$\left. -\lambda_{ij}^{(2)}(t) - \mu_i^{(2)}(t) \right] \times [y_{ij}(t) - y_{ij}^*(t)]\, dt \geq 0,$$

$$\forall\, (x_i(t), y_i(t)) \in L^2([0,T], \mathbb{R}^{2n}). \tag{4.51}$$

Choosing

$$x_i(t) = x_i^*(t) + \varepsilon_1(t), \quad y_i(t) = y_i^*(t) + \varepsilon_2(t),$$

with

$$\varepsilon_1(t) = -\frac{\partial u_i(t, x_i^*(t), y_i^*(t))}{\partial x_{ij}} - (1 - \tau_{ij}(t))\, r_j^*(t) - \lambda_{ij}^{(1)}(t) - \mu_i^{(1)}(t),$$

$$\varepsilon_2(t) = -\frac{\partial u_i(t, x_i^*(t), y_i^*(t))}{\partial y_{ij}} - (1 - \tau_{ij}(t))\, r_j^*(t) - \lambda_{ij}^{(1)}(t) - \mu_i^{(1)}(t),$$

(4.51) becomes:

$$\int_0^T \sum_{j=1}^n \left[-\frac{\partial u_i(t, x_i^*(t), y_i^*(t))}{\partial x_{ij}} - (1 - \tau_{ij}(t))\, r_j^*(t) - \lambda_{ij}^{(1)}(t) - \mu_i^{(1)}(t) \right]^2 dt$$

$$+ \int_0^T \sum_{j=1}^n \left[-\frac{\partial u_i(t, x_i^*(t), y_i^*(t))}{\partial y_{ij}} + (1 - \tau_{ij}(t))\, r_j^*(t) \right.$$

$$\left. -\lambda_{ij}^{(2)}(t) - \mu_i^{(2)}(t) \right]^2 dt \geq 0.$$

Similarly, choosing

$$x_i(t) = x_i^*(t) - \varepsilon_1(t), \quad y_i(t) = y_i^*(t) - \varepsilon_2(t),$$

we obtain

$$-\int_0^T \sum_{j=1}^n \left[-\frac{\partial u_i(t, x_i^*(t), y_i^*(t))}{\partial x_{ij}} - (1 - \tau_{ij}(t)) \, r_j^*(t) \right.$$

$$\left. - \lambda_{ij}^{(1)}(t) - \mu_i^{(1)}(t) \right]^2 dt$$

$$-\int_0^T \sum_{j=1}^n \left[-\frac{\partial u_i(t, x_i^*(t), y_i^*(t))}{\partial y_{ij}} + (1 - \tau_{ij}(t)) \, r_j^*(t) \right.$$

$$\left. - \lambda_{ij}^{(2)}(t) - \mu_i^{(2)}(t) \right]^2 dt \geq 0.$$

Hence we may conclude

$$\begin{cases} -\dfrac{\partial u_i(t, x_i^*(t), y_i^*(t))}{\partial x_{ij}} - (1 - \tau_{ij}(t)) \, r_j^*(t) - \mu_i^{(1)}(t) \\ \qquad\qquad = \lambda_{ij}^{(1)}(t) \geq 0 \\ -\dfrac{\partial u_i(t, x_i^*(t), y_i^*(t))}{\partial y_{ij}} + (1 - \tau_{ij}(t)) \, r_j^*(t) - \mu_i^{(2)}(t) \\ \qquad\qquad = \lambda_{ij}^{(2)}(t) \geq 0. \end{cases} \tag{4.52}$$

which are (4.42), (4.43).

Moreover, from (4.50) and (4.52), we get (4.44), (4.45).

Conversely, assuming that (4.42)–(4.45) are fulfilled, let us show that (4.48) holds. From (4.42) and (4.44) we have

$$\sum_{j=1}^n \left[-\frac{\partial u_i(t, x_i^*(t), y_i^*(t))}{\partial x_{ij}} - (1 - \tau_{ij}(t)) \, r_j^*(t) - \mu_i^{(1)}(t) \right]$$

$$\times [x_{ij}(t) - x_{ij}^*(t)] \geq 0.$$

Since $\sum\limits_{j=1}^{n} x_{ij}(t) = s_i(t)$, $\sum\limits_{j=1}^{n} x_{ij}^*(t) = s_i(t)$ a.e. in $[0, T]$, after integrating, we derive

$$\int_0^T \sum_{j=1}^{n} \left[-\frac{\partial u_i(t, x_i^*(t), y_i^*(t))}{\partial x_{ij}} - (1 - \tau_{ij}(t)) \, r_j^*(t) \right]$$
$$\times \left[x_{ij}(t) - x_{ij}^*(t) \right] dt \geq 0. \tag{4.53}$$

In a similar way we get

$$\int_0^T \sum_{j=1}^{n} \left[-\frac{\partial u_i(t, x_i^*(t), y_i^*(t))}{\partial y_{ij}} + (1 - \tau_{ij}(t)) \, (r_j^*(t) - \underline{r}_j(t)) \right]$$
$$\times \left[y_{ij}(t) - y_{ij}^*(t) \right] dt \geq 0. \tag{4.54}$$

Summing (4.53), (4.54) for all $i = 1, \ldots, m$, we obtain (4.48). □

Now we can show the following characterization of the equilibrium condition related to the instrument prices.

Theorem 4.3.3 *Condition (4.46) is equivalent to*

$$\left\{ \begin{array}{l} \text{Find } r^*(t) \in \mathcal{R} \text{ such that} \\ \int_0^T \sum_{i=1}^{m} (1 - \tau_{ij}(t)) \, \left[x_{ij}^*(t) - y_{ij}^*(t) \right] \times \left[r_j(t) - r_j^*(t) \right] \, dt \geq 0, \\ \forall r(t) \in \mathcal{R}. \end{array} \right. \tag{4.55}$$

Proof: Suppose $r^*(t)$ satisfies (4.46) and define

$$E_+ = \{ t \in [0, T] : \underline{r}_j(t) < r_j^*(t) < \overline{r}_j(t) \},$$
$$E_0 = \{ t \in [0, T] : r_j^*(t) = \underline{r}_j(t) \},$$
$$E^* = \{ t \in [0, T] : r_j^*(t) = \overline{r}_j(t) \}.$$

From condition (4.46) it follows that:

$$\sum_{i=1}^{m} (1 - \tau_{ij}(t)) \, \left[x_{ij}^*(t) - y_{ij}^*(t) \right] = 0, \text{ in } E_+,$$

$$\sum_{i=1}^{m}(1 - \tau_{ij}(t))\,[x_{ij}^{*}(t) - y_{ij}^{*}(t)] \geq 0,\ \text{in } E_0,$$

and

$$\sum_{i=1}^{m}(1 - \tau_{ij}(t))\,[x_{ij}^{*}(t) - y_{ij}^{*}(t)] \leq 0,\ \text{in } E^{*},$$

then

$$\int_{0}^{T}\sum_{i=1}^{m}(1 - \tau_{ij}(t))\,\left[x_{ij}^{*}(t) - y_{ij}^{*}(t)\right] \times \left[r_j(t) - r_j^{*}(t)\right]\,dt$$

$$= \int_{E_0}\sum_{i=1}^{m}(1 - \tau_{ij}(t))\,\left[x_{ij}^{*}(t) - y_{ij}^{*}(t)\right] \times \left[r_j(t) - \underline{r}_j(t)\right]\,dt$$

$$+ \int_{E^{*}}\sum_{i=1}^{m}(1 - \tau_{ij}(t))\,\left[x_{ij}^{*}(t) - y_{ij}^{*}(t)\right] \times \left[r_j(t) - \overline{r}_j(t)\right]\,dt \geq 0,$$

that is (4.55).

Conversely, suppose (4.55) holds. We may rewrite (4.55) as

$$\int_{0}^{T}\sum_{i=1}^{m}(1 - \tau_{ij}(t))\,\left[x_{ij}^{*}(t) - y_{ij}^{*}(t)\right] \times \left[r_j(t) - r_j^{*}(t)\right]\,dt$$

$$= \int_{E_0}\sum_{i=1}^{m}(1 - \tau_{ij}(t))\,\left[x_{ij}^{*}(t) - y_{ij}^{*}(t)\right] \times \left[r_j(t) - \underline{r}_j(t)\right]\,dt$$

$$+ \int_{E_+}\sum_{i=1}^{m}(1 - \tau_{ij}(t))\,\left[x_{ij}^{*}(t) - y_{ij}^{*}(t)\right] \times \left[r_j(t) - r_j^{*}(t)\right]\,dt$$

$$+ \int_{E^{*}}\sum_{i=1}^{m}(1 - \tau_{ij}(t))\,\left[x_{ij}^{*}(t) - y_{ij}^{*}(t)\right] \times \left[r_j(t) - \overline{r}_j(t)\right]\,dt \geq 0.$$

If $\sum_{i=1}^{m}(1 - \tau_{ij}(t))\,\left[x_{ij}^{*}(t) - y_{ij}^{*}(t)\right] > 0$ in E_+ (or in a subset of E_+ with positive measure), choosing

$$r_j(t) = \begin{cases} \underline{r}_j(t) & \text{in } E_0 \\ r_j^{*}(t) - \varepsilon(t) & \text{in } E_+ \\ \overline{r}_j(t), & \text{in } E^{*}, \end{cases}$$

where $0 < \varepsilon(t) < r_j^*(t) - \underline{r}_j(t)$, we get

$$
\int_0^T \sum_{i=1}^m (1 - \tau_{ij}(t)) \, \left[x_{ij}^*(t) - y_{ij}^*(t)\right] \times [r_j(t) - r_j^*(t)] \, dt
$$
$$
= \int_{E_+} \sum_{i=1}^m (1 - \tau_{ij}(t)) \, \left[x_{ij}^*(t) - y_{ij}^*(t)\right] \times [-\varepsilon(t)] \, dt < 0,
$$

which is an absurdity.

On the other hand, if $\sum_{i=1}^m (1 - \tau_{ij}(t)) \, \left[x_{ij}^*(t) - y_{ij}^*(t)\right] < 0$ in E_+ (or in a subset of E_+ with positive measure), choosing

$$
r_j(t) = \begin{cases} \underline{r}_j(t) & \text{in } E_0 \\ r_j^*(t) + \varepsilon(t) & \text{in } E_+ \\ \overline{r}_j(t) & \text{in } E^*, \end{cases}
$$

where $0 < \varepsilon(t) < \overline{r}_j(t) - r_j^*(t)$, we reach

$$
\int_0^T \sum_{i=1}^m (1 - \tau_{ij}(t)) \, \left[x_{ij}^*(t) - y_{ij}^*(t)\right] \times [r_j(t) - r_j^*(t)] \, dt
$$
$$
= \int_{E_+} \sum_{i=1}^m (1 - \tau_{ij}(t)) \, \left[x_{ij}^*(t) - y_{ij}^*(t)\right] \times [\varepsilon(t)] \, dt < 0,
$$

which is also an absurdity. Then we obtain

$$
\sum_{i=1}^m (1 - \tau_{ij}(t)) \, \left[x_{ij}^*(t) - y_{ij}^*(t)\right] = 0 \ \text{ in } E_+.
$$

Moreover, if $\sum_{i=1}^m (1 - \tau_{ij}(t)) \, \left[x_{ij}^*(t) - y_{ij}^*(t)\right] < 0$ in E_0 (or in a subset of E_0 with positive measure), choosing

$$
r_j(t) = \begin{cases} r_j^*(t) & \text{in } E_+ \\ \underline{r}_j(t) + \varepsilon(t) & \text{in } E_0 \\ \overline{r}_j(t) & \text{in } E^*, \end{cases}
$$

where $0 < \varepsilon(t) < r_j^*(t) - \underline{r}_j(t)$, we get

$$\int_0^T \sum_{i=1}^m (1 - \tau_{ij}(t)) \left[x_{ij}^*(t) - y_{ij}^*(t)\right] \times [r_j(t) - r_j^*(t)] \, dt$$
$$= \int_{E_0} \sum_{i=1}^m (1 - \tau_{ij}(t)) \left[x_{ij}^*(t) - y_{ij}^*(t)\right] \times [\varepsilon(t)] \, dt < 0,$$

which is an absurdity. Then $\sum_{i=1}^m (1 - \tau_{ij}(t)) \left[x_{ij}^*(t) - y_{ij}^*(t)\right] \geq 0$ in E_0.

Finally, if $\sum_{i=1}^m (1 - \tau_{ij}(t)) \left[x_{ij}^*(t) - y_{ij}^*(t)\right] > 0$ in E^* (or in a subset of E^* with positive measure), choosing

$$r_j(t) = \begin{cases} r_j^*(t) & \text{in } E_+ \\ \underline{r}_j(t) & \text{in } E_0 \\ \overline{r}_j(t) - \varepsilon(t) & \text{in } E^*, \end{cases}$$

where $0 < \varepsilon(t) < r_j^*(t) - \underline{r}_j(t)$, we get

$$\int_0^T \sum_{i=1}^m (1 - \tau_{ij}(t)) \left[x_{ij}^*(t) - y_{ij}^*(t)\right] \times [r_j(t) - r_j^*(t)] \, dt$$
$$= \int_{E^*} \sum_{i=1}^m (1 - \tau_{ij}(t)) \left[x_{ij}^*(t) - y_{ij}^*(t)\right] \times [-\varepsilon(t)] \, dt < 0,$$

which is an absurdity. Then $\sum_{i=1}^m (1 - \tau_{ij}(t)) \left[x_{ij}^*(t) - y_{ij}^*(t)\right] \leq 0$ in E^*.

Then we may conclude that (4.46) holds. □

We can give the following equivalent variational inequality formulation.

Theorem 4.3.4 *A vector* $(x^*(t), y^*(t), r^*(t)) \in \prod_{i=1}^m P_i \times \mathcal{R}$ *is an evolutionary financial equilibrium if and only if it satisfies the following variational inequality:*

$$\text{Find } (x^*(t), y^*(t), r^*(t)) \in \prod_{i=1}^m P_i \times \mathcal{R} :$$

$$\sum_{i=1}^{m} \int_{0}^{T} \left\{ \sum_{j=1}^{n} \left[-\frac{\partial u_i(t, x_i^*(t), y_i^*(t))}{\partial x_{ij}} - (1 - \tau_{ij}(t)) \, r_j^*(t) \right] \right.$$

$$\times \left[x_{ij}(t) - x_{ij}^*(t) \right]$$

$$+ \sum_{j=1}^{n} \left[-\frac{\partial u_i(t, x_i^*(t), y_i^*(t))}{\partial y_{ij}} + (1 - \tau_{ij}(t)) \, r_j^*(t) \right]$$

$$\times \left[y_{ij}(t) - y_{ij}^*(t) \right]$$

$$\left. + \sum_{j=1}^{n} \left(x_{ij}^*(t) - y_{ij}^*(t) \right) \times (1 - \tau_{ij}(t)) \left[r_j(t) - r_j^*(t) \right] \right\} dt \geq 0,$$

$$\forall (x(t), y(t), r(t)) \in \prod_{i=1}^{m} P_i \times \mathcal{R}. \qquad (4.56)$$

Proof: From Theorems 4.3.1, 4.3.2 and 4.3.3, it immediately follows that if $(x^*(t), y^*(t), r^*(t)) \in \prod_{i=1}^{m} P_i \times \mathcal{R}$ is a financial equilibrium, then it satisfies variational inequalities (4.48), (4.55), and hence variational inequality (4.56), and vice versa. Thus, Theorem 4.3.4 is completely proved.   □

4.3.2   Qualitative Properties

We now address the qualitative properties of the equilibrium pattern through the study of variational inequality (4.56).

Observe that $u_i(t, x_i(t), y_i(t))$ is concave, then $-u_i(t, x_i(t), y_i(t))$ is convex and its gradient is monotone:

$$-\sum_{i=1}^{m} \left[\frac{\partial u_i(t, x_i^1(t), y_i^1(t))}{\partial x_i} - \frac{\partial u_i(t, x_i^2(t), y_i^2(t))}{\partial x_i} \right] \times [x_i^1(t) - x_i^2(t)]$$

$$-\sum_{i=1}^{m} \left[\frac{\partial u_i(t, x_i^1(t), y_i^1(t))}{\partial y_i} - \frac{\partial u_i(t, x_i^2(t), y_i^2(t))}{\partial y_i} \right]$$

$$\times [y_i^1(t) - y_i^2(t)] \geq 0 \qquad (4.57)$$

for any $(x^1(t), y^1(t)), (x^2(t), y^2(t)) \in \prod_{i=1}^{m} P_i$. Observe further that

$$-\sum_{i=1}^{m}\sum_{j=1}^{n}(1 - \tau_{ij}(t))[r_j^1(t) - r_j^2(t)] \left[x_{ij}^1(t) - x_{ij}^2(t)\right]$$

$$+\sum_{i=1}^{m}\sum_{j=1}^{n}(1 - \tau_{ij}(t))[r_j^1(t) - r_j^2(t)] \left[y_{ij}^1(t) - y_{ij}^2(t)\right]$$

$$+\sum_{j=1}^{n}\sum_{i=1}^{m}(1 - \tau_{ij}(t)) \left[x_{ij}^1(t) - x_{ij}^2(t)\right] [r_j^1(t) - r_j^2(t)]$$

$$-\sum_{j=1}^{n}\sum_{i=1}^{m}(1 - \tau_{ij}(t)) \left[y_{ij}^1(t) - y_{ij}^2(t)\right] [r_j^1(t) - r_j^2(t)] = 0 \quad (4.58)$$

for all $(x^1(t), y^1(t), r^1(t)), (x^2(t), y^2(t), r^2(t)) \in \prod_{i=1}^{m} P_i \times \mathcal{R}$. Hence by summing (4.57) and (4.58), it results that

$$-\sum_{i=1}^{m}\left[\frac{\partial U_i(t, x_i^1(t), y_i^1(t), r^1(t))}{\partial x_i} - \frac{\partial U_i(t, x_i^2(t), y_i^2(t), r^2(t))}{\partial x_i}\right]$$

$$\times [x_i^1(t) - x_i^2(t)]$$

$$-\sum_{i=1}^{m}\left[\frac{\partial U_i(t, x_i^1(t), y_i^1(t), r^1(t))}{\partial y_i} - \frac{\partial U_i(t, x_i^2(t), y_i^2(t), r^2(t))}{\partial y_i}\right]$$

$$\times [y_i^1(t) - y_i^2(t)]$$

$$+\sum_{j=1}^{n}\sum_{i=1}^{m}(1 - \tau_{ij}(t)) \left[x_{ij}^1(t) - x_{ij}^2(t)\right] [r_j^1(t) - r_j^2(t)]$$

$$-\sum_{j=1}^{n}\sum_{i=1}^{m}(1 - \tau_{ij}(t)) \left[y_{ij}^1(t) - y_{ij}^2(t)\right] [r_j^1(t) - r_j^2(t)] \geq 0 \quad (4.59)$$

for any $(x^1(t), y^1(t), r^1(t)), (x^2(t), y^2(t), r^2(t)) \in \prod_{i=1}^{m} P_i \times \mathcal{R}$.

Then the function that enters the variational inequality (4.56) is monotone for $(x(t), y(t), r(t)) \in \prod_{i=1}^{m} P_i \times \mathcal{R}$. From the growth condition, it is also hemicontinuous along line segments and, hence, it is lower semicontinuous with respect to the strong and weak topology. By virtue of Corollary 5.1 in [46], since $\prod_{i=1}^{m} P_i \times \mathcal{R}$ is weakly compact, the variational inequality (4.56) admits a solution.

4.4 A Numerical Financial Example

In this section we present a numerical example that is taken from finance. The notable features of the financial example are: the variance–covariance matrices associated with the risk as perceived by the sectors in the economy have elements that can vary over time; the prices of the financial instruments have lower and upper bounds that vary over time; and the financial volumes held by a sector can also vary over time. For background on a variety of financial equilibrium problems that have been formulated and solved as variational inequality problems and, in the dynamic setting, as projected dynamical systems (but finite-dimensional), see the book by Nagurney and Siokos [119]. In [36] a dynamic multi-sector, multi-instrument financial model formulated as evolutionary variational inequalities was proposed for the first time.

Assume an economy with two sectors and two financial instruments, as shown in Figure 4.3, and assume that the variance–covariance matrices of the two sectors are the following:

$$Q^1 = \begin{bmatrix} 1 & 0 & -0.5t & 0 \\ 0 & 1 & 0 & 0 \\ -0.5t & 0 & 1 & 0 \\ 0 & 0 & 0 & 1 \end{bmatrix} \text{ and } Q^2 = \begin{bmatrix} 1 & 0 & 0 & 0 \\ 0 & 1 & -0.5t & 0 \\ 0 & -0.5t & 1 & 0 \\ 0 & 0 & 0 & 1 \end{bmatrix}.$$

Let us choose as feasible set

$$P = \big\{ \big(x_{11}(t), x_{12}(t), x_{21}(t), x_{22}(t), y_{11}(t), y_{12}(t),$$

$$y_{21}(t), y_{22}(t), r_1(t), r_2(t)\big) \in L^2\left([0,1], \mathbb{R}_+^{10}\right) :$$

$$x_{11}(t) + x_{12}(t) = t, \quad y_{11}(t) + y_{12}(t) = t,$$

$$x_{21}(t) + x_{22}(t) = 2, \quad y_{21}(t) + y_{22}(t) = 2,$$

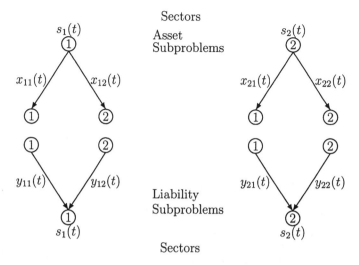

Figure 4.3: Two sectors and two financial instruments network a.e. in $[0, 1]$

$$4 + 2t \le r_1(t) \le 8, \quad 0 \le r_2(t) \le t\}.$$

The variational inequality

$$\sum_{i=1}^{2}\sum_{j=1}^{2}\left[2\left(Q^{i\ T}_{(11)j}(t) \cdot x_i^*(t) + Q^{i\ T}_{(21)j}(t) \cdot y_i^*(t)\right) - r_j^*(t)\right]$$
$$\times \left[x_{ij}(t) - x_{ij}^*(t)\right]$$
$$+ \sum_{i=1}^{2}\sum_{j=1}^{2}\left[2\left(Q^{i\ T}_{(22)j}(t) \cdot y_i^*(t) + Q^{i\ T}_{(12)j}(t) \cdot x_i^*(t)\right) + r_j^*(t)\right]$$
$$\times \left[y_{ij}(t) - y_{ij}^*(t)\right]$$
$$+ \sum_{j=1}^{2}\left[\sum_{i=1}^{2}\left(x_{ij}^*(t) - y_{ij}^*(t)\right)\right] \times \left[r_j(t) - r_j^*(t)\right] \ge 0,$$
$$\forall(x(t), y(t), r(t)) \in P,$$

becomes

$$[2x_{11}^*(t) - ty_{11}^*(t) - r_1^*(t)] \cdot [x_{11}(t) - x_{11}^*(t)]$$

$$+ [2x_{12}^*(t) - r_2^*(t)] \cdot [x_{12}(t) - x_{12}^*(t)]$$

$$+ [2x_{21}^*(t) - r_1^*(t)] \cdot [x_{21}(t) - x_{21}^*(t)]$$

$$+ [2x_{22}^*(t) - ty_{21}^*(t) - r_2^*(t)] \cdot [x_{22}(t) - x_{22}^*(t)]$$

$$+ [2y_{11}^*(t) - tx_{11}^*(t) + r_1^*(t)] \cdot [y_{11}(t) - y_{11}^*(t)]$$

$$+ [2y_{12}^*(t) + r_2^*(t)] \cdot [y_{12}(t) - y_{12}^*(t)]$$

$$+ [2y_{21}^*(t) - tx_{22}^*(t) + r_1^*(t)] \cdot [y_{21}(t) - y_{21}^*(t)]$$

$$+ [2y_{22}^*(t) + r_2^*(t)] \cdot [y_{22}(t) - y_{22}^*(t)]$$

$$+ [x_{11}^*(t) + x_{21}^*(t) - y_{11}^*(t) - y_{21}^*(t)] \cdot [r_1(t) - r_1^*(t)]$$

$$+ [x_{12}^*(t) + x_{22}^*(t) - y_{12}^*(t) - y_{22}^*(t)] \cdot [r_2(t) - r_2^*(t)] \geq 0$$

$$\forall \, (x(t), y(t), r(t)) \in P. \tag{4.60}$$

Now we can derive from the constraints of the convex set $\mathbb{K}$ the values of some variables in terms of the others, namely we derive

$$x_{12}(t) = t - x_{11}(t), \quad x_{22}(t) = 2 - x_{21}(t),$$

$$y_{12}(t) = t - y_{11}(t), \quad y_{22}(t) = 2 - y_{21}(t).$$

Then, setting

$$\tilde{P} = \big\{ \big(x_{11}(t), x_{21}(t), y_{11}(t), y_{21}(t), r_1(t), r_2(t)\big) \in L^2 \left([0,1], \mathbb{R}^6\right) :$$
$$0 \leq x_{11}(t) \leq t, \quad 0 \leq y_{11}(t) \leq t, \quad 0 \leq x_{21}(t) \leq 2, \quad 0 \leq y_{21}(t) \leq 2,$$
$$4 + 2t \leq r_1(t) \leq 8, \quad 0 \leq r_2(t) \leq t \big\},$$

the variational inequality (4.60) can be expressed in the equivalent form:

$$[4x_{11}^*(t) - ty_{11}^*(t) - 2t - r_1^*(t) + r_2^*(t)] \cdot [x_{11}(t) - x_{11}^*(t)]$$

$$+ [4x_{21}^*(t) + ty_{21}^*(t) - 4 - r_1^*(t) + r_2^*(t)] \cdot [x_{21}(t) - x_{21}^*(t)]$$

$$+ [4y_{11}^*(t) - tx_{11}^*(t) - 2t + r_1^*(t) - r_2^*(t)] \cdot [y_{11}(t) - y_{11}^*(t)]$$

$$+ [4y_{21}^*(t) + tx_{21}^*(t) - 2t - 4 + r_1^*(t) - r_2^*(t)] \cdot [y_{21}(t) - y_{21}^*(t)]$$

$$+ [x_{11}^*(t) + x_{21}^*(t) - y_{11}^*(t) - y_{21}^*(t)] \cdot [r_1(t) - r_1^*(t)]$$

$$- [x_{11}^*(t) + x_{21}^*(t) - y_{11}^*(t) - y_{21}^*(t)] \cdot [r_2(t) - r_2^*(t)] \geq 0$$

$$\forall (\tilde{x}(t), \tilde{y}(t), \tilde{r}(t)) \in \tilde{P}.$$

We can solve the variational inequality in a separable way. If we choose $r_1(t) = r_1^*(t)$ and $r_2(t) = r_2^*(t)$, then in the first step, we have to solve the variational inequality in which only the variables x_{ij} and y_{ij} appear. Then, using the direct method, we are led to consider first the system:

$$
\begin{cases}
\Gamma_1 = 0 \\
\Gamma_2 = 0 \\
\Gamma_3 = 0 \\
\Gamma_4 = 0
\end{cases}
\Longleftrightarrow
\begin{array}{l}
4x_{11}^*(t) - ty_{11}^*(t) = 2t + r_1^*(t) - r_2^*(t) \\
4x_{21}^*(t) + ty_{21}^*(t) = 4 + r_1^*(t) - r_2^*(t) \\
4y_{11}^*(t) - tx_{11}^*(t) = 2t - r_1^*(t) + r_2^*(t) \\
4y_{21}^*(t) + tx_{21}^*(t) = 2t + 4 - r_1^*(t) + r_2^*(t),
\end{array}
$$

whose solution is:

$$
\begin{cases}
x_{11}^*(t) = \dfrac{2t^2 + 8t - (t-4)(r_1^*(t) - r_2^*(t))}{16 - t^2} \\[2mm]
y_{11}^*(t) = \dfrac{2t^2 + 8t + (t-4)(r_1^*(t) - r_2^*(t))}{16 - t^2} \\[2mm]
x_{21}^*(t) = \dfrac{-2t^2 - 4t + 16 + (t+4)(r_1^*(t) - r_2^*(t))}{16 - t^2} \\[2mm]
y_{21}^*(t) = \dfrac{4t + 16 + (4-t)(r_1^*(t) - r_2^*(t))}{16 - t^2}.
\end{cases}
$$

But such a solution does not satisfy all the constraints in the definition of $\tilde{P}$. Then, in a second step, we restrict our research to the face obtained by the intersection of $\tilde{P}$ and the conditions $x_{11}^*(t) = t$, $x_{21}^*(t) = 2$, $y_{11}^*(t) = 0$ and $y_{21}^*(t) = 0$. Then such a point is the solution to the variational inequality if the conditions $\Gamma_1 < 0$, $\Gamma_2 < 0$, $\Gamma_3 > 0$ and $\Gamma_4 > 0$ are fulfilled. An easy check shows that they are.

We can pass now to solving the second part of the variational inequality obtained setting in (4.60)

$$
x_{11}(t) = x_{11}^*(t), \quad x_{12}(t) = x_{12}^*(t), \quad x_{21}(t) = x_{21}^*(t), \quad x_{22}(t) = x_{22}^*(t),
$$

$$
y_{11}(t) = y_{11}^*(t), \quad y_{12}(t) = y_{12}^*(t), \quad y_{21}(t) = y_{21}^*(t), \quad y_{22}(t) = y_{22}^*(t).
$$

So, taking into account the solution $x_{11}^*(t) = t$, $x_{21}^*(t) = 2$, $y_{11}^*(t) = 0$ and $y_{21}^*(t) = 0$, we obtain:

$$
(t+2)(r_1(t) - r_1^*(t)) - (t+2)(r_2(t) - r_2^*(t)) \geq 0
$$
$$
\forall\, 4 + 2t \leq r_1(t) \leq 8, \quad 0 \leq r_2(t) \leq t. \tag{4.61}
$$

In order to find the values of $r_1(t)$ and $r_2(t)$, let us choose in the second term of (4.61) $r_2(t) = r_2^*(t)$. Then we get:

$$(t+2)(r_1(t) - r_1^*(t)) \geq 0 \quad \forall 4 + 2t \leq r_1(t) \leq 8$$

and hence

$$r_1^*(t) = 4 + 2t.$$

Analogously, choosing $r_1(t) = r_1^*(t)$ in (4.60), we get:

$$-(t+2)(r_2(t) - r_2^*(t)) \geq 0 \quad \forall 0 \leq r_2(t) \leq t$$

and hence

$$r_2^*(t) = t.$$

Then the solution is:

$$\begin{cases} x_{11}^*(t) = t & x_{12}^*(t) = 0 \\ x_{21}^*(t) = 2 & x_{22}^*(t) = 0 \\ y_{11}^*(t) = 0 & y_{12}^*(t) = t \\ y_{21}^*(t) = 0 & y_{22}^*(t) = 2 \\ r_1^*(t) = 4 + 2t & r_2^*(t) = t. \end{cases}$$

In addition to this procedure, we can also apply the discretization procedure introduced in section 2.5.2 to find the equilibrium solution.

4.5   Sources and Remarks

In the static case the variational inequality formulation of the general financial equilibrium, as well as existence and uniqueness results for the solution, is due to [114] (see also [65], [112], [113], [117] and [121]). In [109], Nagurney develops a financial equilibrium model with utility functions, whereas the policy intervention is studied by Dong in [53]. In [53] and [114] computational procedures are also presented.

The first basic paper for the introduction of time in the general financial model is the book chapter [36]. In the paper [38] a time-dependent utility function is studied, and in [74] the authors are the first to introduce capacity constraints in the formulation with quadratic utility function. Finally, in [41] a policy intervention is considered for a general financial problem expressed in terms of taxes and price controls.

Chapter 5

Projected Dynamical Systems

5.1 Finite-Dimensional PDS

Dupuis and Nagurney in the paper [56] introduced a new class of finite-dimensional dynamical system with a discontinuous right-hand side and provided the foundational theory for the so-called *Projected Dynamical Systems* (PDS). Moreover, they established that the set of stationary points of a projected dynamical system coincides with the set of solutions of a finite-dimensional variational inequality, associated, in a suitable way, to the projected dynamical system. This connection allowed for the investigation of the disequilibrium behavior preceding the attainment of the equilibrium.

We now recall, for the reader's utility, some definitions and results of the finite-dimensional projected dynamical systems theory.

Let $\mathbb{K}$ be a convex set in $\mathbb{R}^n$, $F : \mathbb{K} \to \mathbb{R}^n$ and let us introduce the operator

$$\Pi_{\mathbb{K}} : \mathbb{K} \times \mathbb{R}^n \to \mathbb{R}^n$$

defined by means of the directional derivative in the sense of Gâteaux

$$\Pi_{\mathbb{K}}(x, -F(x)) = \lim_{t \to 0^+} \frac{P_{\mathbb{K}}(x - tF(x)) - x}{t}$$

of the projection operator $P_{\mathbb{K}} : \mathbb{R}^n \to \mathbb{K}$ given by

$$\|P_{\mathbb{K}}(z) - z\| = \inf_{y \in \mathbb{K}} \|y - z\|.$$

In [56], Dupuis and Nagurney considered the differential equation

$$\frac{d\,x(t)}{d\,t} = \Pi_{\mathbb{K}}(x(t), -F(x(t)))$$

and the associated Cauchy problem

$$\begin{cases} \dfrac{d\,x(t)}{d\,t} = \Pi_{\mathbb{K}}(x(t), -F(x(t))) \\ x(0) = x_0 \in \mathbb{K}, \end{cases} \tag{5.1}$$

whose solutions (see also [159]) they called projected dynamical systems (PDS). A similar idea, in different contexts, can be found in the papers [1], [21], [80], and in the book [2], as we shall see in Remark 5.2.2. In [55] and [56] existence theorems of an absolutely continuous solution are shown, provided that F is assumed to be Lipschitz continuous and with linear growth.

The key trait of a projected dynamical system was first found by Dupuis and Nagurney in [56]. In particular, the authors proved the following theorem.

Theorem 5.1.1 *The critical points of equation*

$$\frac{d\,x(t)}{d\,t} = \Pi_{\mathbb{K}}(x(t), -F(x(t))), \tag{5.2}$$

namely, the solutions such that $\dfrac{d\,x(t)}{d\,t} \equiv 0$, *are the same as the solutions to the variational inequality*

$$Find\ x \in \mathbb{K}: \ \langle F(x), y - x \rangle \geq 0, \quad \forall y \in \mathbb{K}. \tag{5.3}$$

Then the finite-dimensional variational inequalities and the essential problems they model have benefited from the theory of projected dynamical systems in terms of analysis and computation (see [16], [108], and the references therein). In the next section we shall be concerned with the infinite-dimensional framework.

5.2 Infinite-Dimensional PDS

Isac and Cojocaru ([83], [84]) initiated the systematic study of projected dynamical systems on infinite-dimensional Hilbert spaces with the fundamental issue of existence of solutions to such problems answered by Cojocaru in [15] and Cojocaru and Jonker in [19]. As noted in [16] (see also [76] and [140]), the theory and application of evolutionary variational inequalities was developing in parallel to that of projected dynamical systems, and the papers mentioned above make explicit for the first time the connection between projected dynamical systems on Hilbert spaces and evolutionary variational inequalities.

Now we provide, following [76] and [140], a self-contained proof of the equivalence between the solutions to an evolutionary variational inequality and the critical points of a projected dynamical system.

We start by recalling the important result contained in the following theorem.

Theorem 5.2.1 *If we denote by $P_{\mathbb{K}} = \mathrm{Proj}\,(\mathbb{K}, \cdot)$ the projection onto $\mathbb{K}$ of an element of H, then:*

$$P_{\mathbb{K}}(x + \lambda h) = x + \lambda P_{T_{\mathbb{K}}(x)}h + o(\lambda)$$

for any x, h, and $\lambda > 0$, where $T_{\mathbb{K}}$ is the support cone to $\mathbb{K}$ at x.

Proof: See [158], Lemma 4.6, p. 300. $\qquad\qquad\qquad\qquad\qquad\square$

From Theorem 5.2.1 the following Corollary immediately derives.

Corollary 5.2.1 *If we define the projection of h at x with respect to $\mathbb{K}$ as the directional derivative in the sense of Gâteaux*

$$\Pi_{\mathbb{K}}(x, h) = \lim_{\lambda \to 0^+} \frac{P_{\mathbb{K}}(x + \lambda h) - x}{\lambda},$$

then

$$\Pi_{\mathbb{K}}(x, h) = P_{T_{\mathbb{K}}(x)}h,$$

namely, $\Pi_{\mathbb{K}}(x, h)$ is the projection of h on the support cone $T_{\mathbb{K}}(x)$.

We can define the set of unit inward normals which will be useful in what follows.

Definition 5.2.1 *The set of unit inward normals to $\mathbb{K}$ at x is defined by*

$$n_{\mathbb{K}}(x) = \{v : \|v\| = 1 \text{ and } \langle v, x - y \rangle \leq 0, \ \forall y \in \mathbb{K}\}.$$

Then, using Proposition A.1, we have the following Proposition.

Proposition 5.2.1 *The set of unit normals to $\mathbb{K}$ at x satisfies:*

$$n_{\mathbb{K}}(x) = \{\partial B(0, 1)\} \cap \left\{ - (T_{\mathbb{K}}(x))^0 \right\},$$

where $\partial B(0, 1) = \{z : \|z\| = 1\}$.

Now, since in infinite dimension the interior as well as the relative algebraic interior of a convex set can be empty, we need to use the concepts of quasi interior (qi) of $\mathbb{K}$, which may be nonempty (see Appendix A, Remark A.2), and quasi boundary (qbdry) (see Definition A.14).

Then the following proposition holds.

Proposition 5.2.2 *$x \in$ qbdry $\mathbb{K}$ if and only if $n_{\mathbb{K}}(x) \neq \emptyset$.*

Proof: Let $x \in$ qbdry $\mathbb{K}$. Then, by virtue of Theorem F.1, there exists a $\xi \neq 0$ such that $\langle \xi, x \rangle \leq \langle \xi, y \rangle$, $\forall y \in \mathbb{K}$, and, hence:

$$\langle \frac{\xi}{\|\xi\|}, x - y \rangle \leq 0 \quad \forall y \in \mathbb{K}.$$

Vice versa, if $n_{\mathbb{K}}(x)$ is nonempty, then there exists a ξ such that $\|\xi\| = 1$ and $\langle \xi, x - y \rangle \leq 0$, $\forall y \in \mathbb{K}$. It means $N_{\mathbb{K}}(x) \neq \{0_{\mathbb{K}}\}$, then $T_{\mathbb{K}}(x) \neq H$, hence $x \notin$ qi $\mathbb{K}$. $\qquad \square$

We present now the fundamental result which gives the geometric interpretation of the operator $\Pi_{\mathbb{K}}$ on infinite-dimensional Hilbert spaces. This fundamental result, proved first by Isac and Cojocaru [84], is presented using a different proof (see also [77] and [140]). The following statements hold.

Theorem 5.2.2

1. *If $x \in$ qi $\mathbb{K}$, then for any $h \in H$ it follows that: $\Pi_{\mathbb{K}}(x, h) = h$;*

2. *If $x \in$ qbdry $\mathbb{K}$, then for any $h \in H \setminus T_{\mathbb{K}}(x)$ there exists $n^*(x) \in n_{\mathbb{K}}(x)$ such that*

$$\beta(x) = -\langle h, n^*(x) \rangle > 0,$$

$$\Pi_{\mathbb{K}}(x, h) = h + \beta(x) n^*(x).$$

Proof: If $x \in$ qi $\mathbb{K}$, then $T_{\mathbb{K}}(x) = H$, by definition of qi $\mathbb{K}$, and it follows that

$$\Pi_{\mathbb{K}}(x, h) = P_{T_{\mathbb{K}}(x)} h = P_H h = h.$$

If $x \in$ qbdry $\mathbb{K}$, then setting $\hat{h} = \Pi_{\mathbb{K}}(x, h)$, we get:

$$\hat{h} = \Pi_{\mathbb{K}}(x, h) = P_{T_{\mathbb{K}}(x)} h,$$

namely:

$$\langle h - \hat{h}, w - \hat{h} \rangle \leq 0, \quad \forall w \in T_{\mathbb{K}}(x).$$

Since $T_{\mathbb{K}}(x)$ is a cone with vertex 0, choosing, in turn, $w = 0$ and $w = 2\hat{h}$, we get:

$$\langle h - \hat{h}, \hat{h} \rangle = 0. \tag{5.4}$$

Moreover, if we set $w = y + \hat{h}$ with $y \in T_{\mathbb{K}}(x)$, we obtain

$$\langle h - \hat{h}, y + \hat{h} - \hat{h} \rangle = \langle h - \hat{h}, y \rangle \leq 0, \quad \forall y \in T_{\mathbb{K}}(x)$$

and, hence, because of Proposition A.1, we get:

$$h - \hat{h} \in (T_{\mathbb{K}}(x))^0 = N_{\mathbb{K}}(x). \tag{5.5}$$

Since $h \neq \hat{h}$, because $h \in H \setminus T_{\mathbb{K}}(x)$ and $\hat{h} \in T_{\mathbb{K}}(x)$ by assumption, then the relation (5.5) implies the existence of some $n^* \in n_{\mathbb{K}}(x)$ and $\beta > 0$ such that

$$\hat{h} - h = \beta n^*.$$

Moreover, taking into account that, by virtue of (5.4) $\langle n^*, \hat{h} \rangle = 0$, we get:

$$\beta = -\langle h, n^* \rangle,$$

and the assertion is proved. □

Remark 5.2.1 From Theorem 5.2.2, it derives that there exists a unique element n_x such that $\Pi_{\mathbb{K}}(x, -F(x)) = -F(x) - n_x$, where $n_x = 0$, if $x \in$ qi $\mathbb{K}$.

We also obtain the following characterization (see also [77]).

Corollary 5.2.2 *Let $x \in \mathbb{K}$. Then for any $h \in H$:*

$$\Pi_{\mathbb{K}}(x, h) = P_{h - N_{\mathbb{K}}(x)}(0) = (h - N_{\mathbb{K}}(x))^{\#}.$$

Proof: If $x \in$ qi $\mathbb{K}$, from Theorem 5.2.2 we derive

$$\Pi_{\mathbb{K}}(x, h) = h.$$

On the other hand, if $x \in$ qi $\mathbb{K}$, by definition, $T_{\mathbb{K}}(x) = H$ and $N_{\mathbb{K}}(x) = (T_{\mathbb{K}}(x))^{-} = H^{-} = \{0\}$ and, hence, we immediately obtain the claim. Let us suppose now that $x \in$ qbdry $\mathbb{K}$. From Theorem 5.2.2 we know that

$$h - \hat{h} \in (T_{\mathbb{K}}(x))^{0} = N_{\mathbb{K}}(x),$$

where $\hat{h} = \Pi_{\mathbb{K}}(x, h)$. Then we get

$$\hat{h} \in h - N_{\mathbb{K}}(x).$$

Since $\hat{h} = \Pi_{\mathbb{K}}(x, h) = P_{T_{\mathbb{K}}(x)}h$, then we have $\hat{h} \in T_{\mathbb{K}}(x)$ and, hence, $\langle z, \hat{h} \rangle \leq 0$, $\forall z \in (T_{\mathbb{K}}(x))^{0} = N_{\mathbb{K}}(x)$. Taking into account (5.4), we get

$$\langle \hat{h}, h - \hat{h} - z \rangle \geq 0, \ \forall z \in N_{\mathbb{K}}(x)$$

and, thus, $\hat{h} = P_{h - N_{\mathbb{K}}(x)}(0)$. $\square$

Now we are able to prove the main result of this section. First, let us give the following definition and specify an existence theorem.

Definition 5.2.2 *A projected dynamical system is given by a mapping $\Phi : \mathbb{R}_{+} \times \mathbb{K} \to \mathbb{K}$ which solves the initial value problem:*

$$\dot{\Phi}(t, x) = \Pi_{\mathbb{K}}(\Phi(t, x), -F(\Phi(t, x))), \quad \Phi(0, x) = x \in \mathbb{K}.$$

In [15] and [19] the following existence theorem has been proved.

Theorem 5.2.3 *Let H be a Hilbert space and let $\mathbb{K} \subset H$ be a nonempty, closed, and convex subset. Let $F : \mathbb{K} \to H$ be a Lipschitz continuous vector field with Lipschitz constant b. Let $x_0 \in \mathbb{K}$ and $L > 0$ such that $\|x_0\| \leq L$. Then the initial value problem (5.1) admits a unique solution in the class of the absolutely continuous functions on the interval $[0, l]$ where $l = \dfrac{L}{\|F(x_0)\| + b\,L}$.*

Then the fundamental result is the following one.

Theorem 5.2.4 *Assume that the hypotheses of Theorem 5.2.3 hold. Then the solutions to the variational inequality*

$$\langle F(x^*), x - x^* \rangle \geq 0, \quad \forall x \in \mathbb{K} \tag{5.6}$$

are the same as the critical points of the projected differential equation (PrDE)

$$\frac{d\,x(t)}{d\,t} = \Pi_{\mathbb{K}}(x(t), -F(x(t))), \tag{5.7}$$

that is, the points $x \in \mathbb{K}$ such that

$$\Pi_{\mathbb{K}}(x(t), -F(x(t))) = 0,$$

and vice versa.

Proof: Let x^* be a solution to the variational inequality (5.6). Using the characterization of the solution by means of the projection, we get

$$x^* = P_{\mathbb{K}}\left(x^* - \lambda F(x^*)\right), \quad \forall \lambda > 0.$$

Hence,

$$\Pi_{\mathbb{K}}(x^*, -F(x^*)) = \lim_{\lambda \to 0^+} \frac{P_{\mathbb{K}}(x^* - \lambda F(x^*)) - x^*}{\lambda} = \lim_{\lambda \to 0^+} \frac{x^* - x^*}{\lambda} = 0.$$

Vice versa, let x^* be a stationary point of the projected dynamical system, namely, x^* is such that

$$0 = \Pi_{\mathbb{K}}(x^*, -F(x^*)) = P_{T_{\mathbb{K}}(x)}(-F(x^*)).$$

First, let us consider the case when $x^* \in$ qbdry $\mathbb{K}$ and $-F(x^*) \notin T_{\mathbb{K}}(x^*)$. By virtue of Theorem 5.2.2, there exist $\beta^* > 0$ and $n^* \in n_{\mathbb{K}}(x^*)$ such that:

$$F(x^*) = \beta^* n^*.$$

Since $n^* \in n_{\mathbb{K}}(x^*)$, we have

$$\langle \beta^* n^*, x^* - y \rangle \leq 0, \quad \forall y \in \mathbb{K}$$

and, therefore,

$$\langle F(x^*), y - x^* \rangle \geq 0, \quad \forall y \in \mathbb{K}.$$

Let us consider now the case when $x^* \in$ qbdry $\mathbb{K}$ and $-F(x^*) \in T_{\mathbb{K}}(x^*)$. In this case we get

$$0 = \Pi_{\mathbb{K}}(x, -F(x^*)) = P_{T_{\mathbb{K}}(x^*)}(-F(x^*)) = -F(x^*)$$

and, hence, the variational inequality (5.6) is satisfied.

Finally, if $x^* \in$ qi $\mathbb{K}$, then $T_{\mathbb{K}}(x^*)$ coincides with H and we get

$$0 = P_H(-F(x^*)) = -F(x^*)$$

as above.   □

Remark 5.2.2 By virtue of Corollary 5.2.2, we derive that

$$\frac{d\,x(t)}{d\,t} = \Pi_{\mathbb{K}}(x, -F(x)) = P_{-F(x)-N_{\mathbb{K}}(x)}(0)$$

$$= \left\{ \hat{v} \in -(F(x) + N_{\mathbb{K}}(x)) : \|\hat{v}\| = \min_{y \in -(F(x)+N_{\mathbb{K}}(x))} \|y\| \right\}.$$

Then, the initial value problem

$$\begin{cases} \dfrac{d\,x(t)}{d\,t} = \Pi_{\mathbb{K}}(x(t), -F(x(t))) \\ x(0) = x_0 \in \mathbb{K} \end{cases} \tag{5.8}$$

consists in finding the 'slow' solution (the solution of minimal norm) to the differential variational inequality

$$\frac{d\,x(t)}{d\,t} \in -(N_{\mathbb{K}}(x(t)) + F(x(t)))$$

under the initial condition

$$x(0) = x_0.$$

Since

$$\Pi_{\mathbb{K}}(x(t), -F(x(t))) = P_{T_{\mathbb{K}}(x(t))}(-F(x(t))),$$

problem (5.8) is equivalent to finding the 'slow' solution to the problem

$$\begin{cases} \dfrac{d\,x(t)}{d\,t} \in P_{T_{\mathbb{K}}(x)}(-F(x(t))) \\ x(0) = x_0 \end{cases} \tag{5.9}$$

where the operator F is single-valued.

Then, as already observed in Section 5.1, the results of [2] Chapter 6, Section 6, and of [1] Theorem 2, can be applied to our projected dynamical system.

Let us observe that choosing the Hilbert space H to be $L^2([0,T], \mathbb{R}^p)$, we find that the solutions to the evolutionary variational inequality:

$$\text{find } u \in \mathbb{K}: \quad \int_0^T \langle F(u(t)), v(t) - u(t)\rangle \, dt \geq 0, \quad \forall v \in \mathbb{K} \tag{5.10}$$

are the same as the critical points of the equation:

$$\frac{d\,u(t,\tau)}{d\,\tau} = \Pi_{\mathbb{K}}(u(t,\tau), -F(u(t,\tau))), \tag{5.11}$$

that is, the points such that

$$\Pi_{\mathbb{K}}(u(t,\tau), -F(u(t,\tau))) \equiv 0 \text{ a.e. in } [0,T],$$

which are obviously stationary with respect to τ. As we shall make clear in the following, t and τ have two different meanings.

In Section 5.3, we show that the problems examined in the previous chapters (that is, time-dependent traffic equilibria, time-dependent spatial equilibrium models in the price formulation and in the quantity formulation, and time-dependent financial network models) can be formulated into a unified structure.

5.3   Common Formulation

We consider the nonempty, convex, closed, bounded subset of the Hilbert space $L^2([0, T], \mathbb{R}^q)$ given by

$$\mathbb{K} = \left\{ u \in L^2([0, T], \mathbb{R}^q) : \lambda(t) \leq u(t) \leq \mu(t) \text{ a.e. in } [0, T]; \right.$$

$$\sum_{i=1}^{q} \xi_{ji} \, u_i(t) = \rho_j(t) \, j = 1, \dots, l, \text{ a.e. in } [0, T],$$

$$\left. \xi_{ji} \in \{-1, 0, 1\} , \quad i \in \{1, \dots, q\} \right\}. \tag{5.12}$$

Let $\lambda, \mu \in L^2([0, T], \mathbb{R}^q)$, $\rho \in L^2([0, T], \mathbb{R}^l)$ be given functions. For chosen values of the scalars ξ_{ji}, of the dimensions q and l, and of the constraints λ and μ, we obtain each of the formulations of the constraint sets in the models cited above (see [16]), as follows:

- for the traffic network problem (see [45], [46] and Chapter 2 in this volume), we let $\xi_{ji} \in \{0, 1\}$, $i \in \{1, \dots, q\}$, $j \in \{1, \dots, l\}$, and $\lambda(t) \geq 0$ for all $t \in [0, T]$;

- for the quantity formulation of spatial price equilibrium (see [37] and Section 3.2 above), we let $q = n + m + nm$, $l = n + m$, $\xi_{ji} \in \{-1, 0, 1\}$, $i \in \{1, \dots, q\}$, $j \in \{1, \dots, l\}$; $\mu(t)$ large and $\lambda(t) = 0$, for any $t \in [0, T]$;

- for the price formulation of spatial price equilibrium (see [35], [43] and Section 3.1 above), we let $q = n + m + mn$, $l = 1$, $\xi_{ji} = 0$, $i \in \{1, \dots, q\}$, $j \in \{1, \dots, l\}$, $\lambda(t) \geq 0$ for all $t \in [0, T]$, and $\rho_j(t) = 0$ for all $t \in [0, T]$ and $j \in \{1, \dots, l\}$,;

- for the financial equilibrium problem (see [36] and Chapter 4 above), we let $q = 2mn + n$, $l = 2m$, $\xi_{ji} \in \{0, 1\}$ for $i \in \{1, \dots, n\}$, $j \in \{1, \dots, l\}$; $\mu(t)$ large and $\lambda(t) = 0$, for any $t \in [0, T]$.

Then, setting

$$\ll \Phi, u \gg = \int_0^T \langle \Phi(t), u(t) \rangle \, dt$$

where $\Phi \in (L^2([0,T], \mathbb{R}^q))^* = L^2([0,T], \mathbb{R}^q)$ and $u \in L^2([0,T], \mathbb{R}^q)$, if F is given such that $F : \mathbb{K} \to L^2([0,T], \mathbb{R}^q)$, we have the following standard form of the evolutionary variational inequality:

$$\text{find } u \in \mathbb{K} : \; \ll F(u), v - u \gg \geq 0, \quad \forall v \in \mathbb{K}. \tag{5.13}$$

In [46] sufficient conditions are given that ensure the existence of a solution to (5.13).

As we noted in Section 5.2, in the equation (5.11) two different time-frames appear. This multiple time structure arises from the synthesis of PDS and EVI.

In Section 5.4 we develop the theory of PDS, providing a uniqueness result under less restrictive assumptions than those existent in the literature.

In Section 5.5 we make precise the relation between the two time-frames.

5.4 General Uniqueness Results

As we have claimed in the previous chapters, (5.13) admits solutions under certain assumptions of hemicontinuity, hemicontinuity along line segments, and pseudomonotonicity (see Theorems D.5 and D.6). Now we shall prove, following the results in [17], that we can relax the strict monotonicity assumption, usually used in order to obtain the uniqueness of the solution. First, let us prove the following proposition for PDS.

Proposition 5.4.1 *Assume F is strictly pseudomonotone and Lipschitz continuous on $\mathbb{K}$ in problem (5.1). Then the PDS has at most one equilibrium point.*

Proof: We prove this by contradiction. Suppose (5.1) has at least two solutions and let us denote them by $u_1 \neq u_2 \in \mathbb{K}$. Then, from Theorem 5.1.1, they are solutions to the variational inequality (5.3) and so we have:

$$\ll F(u_1), y - u_1 \gg \geq 0 \quad \text{and} \quad \ll F(u_2), y - u_2 \gg \geq 0, \quad \forall y \in \mathbb{K}.$$

Since F is strictly pseudomonotone, then we get

$$\ll F(y), y - u_1 \gg > 0 \quad \text{and} \quad \ll F(y), y - u_2 \gg > 0, \quad \forall y \in \mathbb{K},$$

respectively.

Now choosing $y := u_2$ in the first inequality and $y := u_1$ in the second, we obtain

$$\ll F(u_2), u_2 - u_1 \gg, > 0 \quad \text{and} \quad \ll F(u_1), u_1 - u_2 \gg > 0.$$

The last two relations imply that

$$\ll F(u_2) - F(u_1), u_2 - u_1 \gg > 0. \tag{5.14}$$

Since u_1, u_2 are equilibria of the PDS (5.1), we have

$$\Pi_{\mathbb{K}}(u_1, -F(u_1)) = 0 \quad \text{and} \quad \Pi_{\mathbb{K}}(u_2, -F(u_2)) = 0.$$

Equivalently, this means that $-F(u_1) \in N_{\mathbb{K}}(u_1)$ and $-F(u_2) \in N_{\mathbb{K}}(u_2)$.

Since the set-valued mapping $x \mapsto N_{\mathbb{K}}(x)$ is a monotone mapping, that is for any $n_x \in N_{\mathbb{K}}(x)$ and any $n_y \in N_{\mathbb{K}}(y)$, we have that $\langle n_x - n_y, x - y \rangle \geq 0$ (for a proof see [19], Lemma 2.1), then in our case we obtain

$$\ll -F(u_1) + F(u_2), u_1 - u_2 \gg \geq 0,$$

or equivalently,

$$\ll F(u_2) - F(u_1), u_2 - u_1 \gg \leq 0. \tag{5.15}$$

Evidently conditions (5.14) and (5.15) lead to a contradiction. Hence, the PDS (5.1) has at most one equilibrium point whenever F is strictly pseudomonotone. □

Here is a direct and important consequence of the new theory of double-layered dynamics:

Proposition 5.4.2 *Assume either F hemicontinuous with respect to the weak topology or F hemicontinuous along line segments. Further, let F be strictly pseudomonotone and Lipschitz continuous on $\mathbb{K} \subseteq L^2([0, T], \mathbb{R}^q)$. Then the evolutionary variational inequality (5.13) has one solution.*

Proof: The proof is a direct consequence of Theorem 5.2.4 and Proposition 5.4.1. □

Proposition 5.4.2 is considerably easier to use than [145], Theorem 3, even though it is established (so far) only in Hilbert spaces (see Theorem D.10).

5.5 The Relation Between the Two Time-frames

First of all we have to notice that for almost all $\tau \in [0, T]$, arbitrarily fixed, we can identify a closed and convex subset $\mathbb{K}_\tau \in \mathbb{R}^q$, given by

$$\mathbb{K}_\tau := \Big\{ u(\tau) \in \mathbb{R}^q : \ \lambda(\tau) \le u(\tau) \le \mu(\tau); \ \lambda(\tau), \mu(\tau) \text{ given};$$

$$\sum_{i=1}^{q} \xi_{ji} u_i(\tau) = \rho_j(\tau), \ \xi_{ji} \in \{0, 1\}, \ j = 1, \ldots, l, i \in \{1, .., q\} \Big\}. \quad (5.16)$$

Evidently, to each such fixed τ, we have a PDS_τ given by

$$\begin{cases} \dfrac{du(\tau, t)}{dt} = \Pi_{\mathbb{K}_\tau}(u(\tau, t), -F(u(\tau, t))), \\ u(\tau, 0) = u_0^\tau \in \mathbb{K}_\tau. \end{cases} \quad (5.17)$$

We can generalize the definition of locally strongly monotone function with degree α given in [127] in the following way.

Definition 5.5.1 *A map F is called:*

- *locally strongly pseudo-monotone with degree α at $x^* \in \mathbb{K}$ if there exists a subset $S(x^*) \subseteq \mathbb{K}$ and a positive scalar $\eta > 0$ such that:*

$$\ll F(x^*), x - x^* \gg \ge 0 \Longrightarrow$$
$$\ll F(x), x - x^* \gg \ge \eta \|x - x^*\|^\alpha \quad \forall x \in S(x^*); \quad (5.18)$$

- *strongly pseudo-monotone with degree α at $x^* \in \mathbb{K}$ if the above holds for all $x \in \mathbb{K}$;*

- *strongly pseudo-monotone with degree α if the above holds for all $x \in \mathbb{K}$ and all $x^* \in \mathbb{K}$.*

Evidently, if F is strongly pseudo-monotone with degree α, then it is strictly pseudomonotone. Hence, the EVI gives a unique curve of equilibria.

The following result (see also [17]) holds, which specifies at what time the curve of equilibria is reached.

Theorem 5.5.1 *Let F be Lipschitz continuous on $\mathbb{K}$ and strongly pseudo-monotone with degree $\alpha < 2$ on $\mathbb{K}_\tau$, namely there exists $\eta > 0$ such that*

$$\langle u - u^*, F(u^*) \rangle \geq 0 \Longrightarrow \langle u - u^*, F(u) \rangle \geq \eta \|u - u^*\|^\alpha \quad \forall u \in \mathbb{K}_\tau. \ (5.19)$$

For almost all fixed $\tau \in [0, T]$, let $u(\tau, t)$ be the solution to (5.17) starting at the initial point $u_0^\tau \in \mathbb{K}_\tau$. Then there exists a finite $\lambda_\tau > 0$ such that $u(\tau, t)$ is reached by the solution $u^* := u^*(\tau)$ to (5.13), namely $u(\tau, \lambda_\tau) = u^*$.

Proof: Let $u(\tau, t)$ be a solution to (5.17), which starts at some point $u_0^\tau \in \mathbb{K}_\tau$; we remember that it is also $u(\tau, t) \in \mathbb{K}_\tau$. Since F is strongly pseudo-monotone with degree α in $\mathbb{K}_\tau$, we get that assumption (5.19) holds for $u(\tau, t)$, that is:

$$\langle u(\tau, t) - u^*, F(u^*) \rangle \geq 0$$
$$\Longrightarrow \langle u(\tau, t) - u^*, F(u(\tau, t)) \rangle \geq \eta \|u(\tau, t) - u^*\|^\alpha. \quad (5.20)$$

If we let $D(t) := \frac{1}{2}\|u(\tau, t) - u^*\|^2 = \frac{1}{2}\langle u(\tau, t) - u^*, u(\tau, t) - u^* \rangle$, then

$$\dot{D}(t) = \frac{d}{dt}\left(\frac{1}{2}\|u(\tau, t) - u^*\|^2\right)$$

$$= \frac{1}{2}\langle \frac{d\,(u(\tau, t) - u^*)}{dt}, u(\tau, t) - u^* \rangle + \frac{1}{2}\langle u(\tau, t) - u^*, \frac{d\,(u(\tau, t) - u^*)}{dt} \rangle$$

$$= \langle \frac{d\,(u(\tau, t) - u^*)}{dt}, u(\tau, t) - u^* \rangle = \langle -F(u(\tau, t)) - n_{u(\tau, t)}, u(\tau, t) - u^* \rangle$$

$$= \langle -F(u(\tau, t)), u(\tau, t) - u^* \rangle - \langle n_{u(\tau, t)}, u(\tau, t) - u^* \rangle$$

$$\leq -\eta \|u(\tau, t) - u^*\|^\alpha \leq 0, \quad (5.21)$$

since

$$\frac{d\,(u(\tau, t) - u^*)}{dt} = \frac{d\,(u(\tau, t))}{dt} - \frac{d\,u^*}{dt} = \Pi_{\mathbb{K}_\tau}\,(u(\tau, t), -F(u(\tau, t)))$$

$$= -F(u(\tau, t)) - n_{u(\tau, t)},$$

where the last estimate derives from Remark 5.2.1. Therefore, for all t such that $u(\tau, t) \neq u^*$, $D(t)$ is decreasing. Thus, we would now like to show that there exists a time λ_τ such that $u(\tau, \lambda_\tau) = u^*$. Obviously, for

$t > \lambda_\tau$ we have $u(\tau, t) = u^*$. In order to prove the existence of λ_τ, we assume *ad absurdum* that $D(t) > 0$ for all t and we deduce $\|u(\tau, t) - u^*\|^{2-\alpha} > 0$ for any t. Setting $\phi(t) := \|u(\tau, t) - u^*\|$, we get:

$$\frac{d\,\phi(t)}{dt}\phi(t) = \dot{D}(t) \leq -\eta\|u(\tau, t) - u^*\|^\alpha = -\eta\phi(t)^\alpha$$

$$\Longrightarrow \frac{d\,\phi(t)}{dt} \leq -\eta\|u(\tau, t) - u^*\|^{\alpha-1} \tag{5.22}$$

and

$$\frac{d}{dt}\frac{1}{2-\alpha}\|u(\tau, t) - u^*\|^{2-\alpha} = \|u(\tau, t) - u^*\|^{1-\alpha}\frac{d}{dt}\left[\|u(\tau, t) - u^*\|\right]$$

$$= \|u(\tau, t) - u^*\|^{1-\alpha}\frac{d\,\phi(t)}{dt}. \tag{5.23}$$

From estimates (5.22) and (5.23) we obtain:

$$\frac{d}{dt}\left[\frac{1}{2-\alpha}\|u(\tau, t) - u^*\|^{2-\alpha}\right] \leq -\eta \tag{5.24}$$

and integrating (5.24) from 0 to t we have:

$$\|u(\tau, t) - u^*\|^{2-\alpha} \leq \|u_0^\tau - u^*\|^{2-\alpha} - (2 - \alpha)\eta t. \tag{5.25}$$

This is an absurdity because, if we choose $t = \lambda_\tau = \dfrac{\|u_0^\tau - u^*\|^{2-\alpha}}{(2-\alpha)\eta}$, it results in: $D(t) = 0$. Hence, we have proved that for each $u_0^\tau \in \mathbb{K}_\tau$, there exists $\lambda_\tau < \infty$, depending on $\eta, \alpha, \|u_0^\tau - u^*\|$, given by

$$\lambda_\tau := \frac{\|u_0^\tau - u^*\|^{2-\alpha}}{(2-\alpha)\eta},$$

such that whenever $\alpha < 2$, then $D(t) > 0$ when $t < \lambda_\tau$ and $D(t) = 0$ when $t \geq \lambda_\tau$. $\qquad\square$

We are interpreting the evolution time of the EVI, namely t, as 'large-scale dynamics', and the evolution time of the PDS, namely τ, which is a type of adjustment time, as the 'small-scale dynamics'. Theorem 5.5.1 provides a link between the two timescales as follows: for almost any $t \in$

$[0, T]$, we can estimate that the equilibrium on the curve corresponding to t will be reached in the time $\tau := \lambda_t$ if

$$\lambda_t := \frac{\|u_0^t - u^*\|^{2-\alpha}}{(2 - \alpha) \, \eta}.$$

In the next section we present a computational procedure based on the application of the projected dynamical systems theory in order to find the solution to the evolutionary variational inequality (5.10).

5.6 Computational Procedure

We now consider the time-dependent variational inequality (5.10) where $\mathbb{K}$ is given by (5.12). It is worth noting that (5.13) is equivalent to the problem:

find $u \in \mathbb{K}$: $\langle F(u(t)), v(t) - u(t) \rangle \geq 0, \quad \forall v \in \mathbb{K}$, a.e. in $[0, T]$. (5.26)

Let the operator F be strictly monotone (see, for example, [87] and [108]), so that the solution u is unique and assume that the hypotheses of Theorem 3.2 in [5] on the continuity of the solution are fulfilled, namely, for instance, $F(u(t)) = A(t)u(t) + B(t)$ is an affine operator where $A(t)$ is a continuous and positive definite matrix in $[0, T]$ and $B(t)$ is a continuous vector. Hence, it follows that:

$$\langle F(u(t)), v(t) - u(t) \rangle \geq 0, \quad \forall t \in [0, T].$$

Consider now a sequence of partitions π_n of $[0, T]$, such that:

$$\pi_n = \left(t_n^0, t_n^1, \ldots, t_n^{N_n} \right), \quad 0 = t_n^0 < t_n^1 < \ldots < t_n^{N_n} = T$$

and

$$\delta_n = \max \left\{ t_n^j - t_n^{j-1} : \ j = 1, \ldots, N_n \right\}$$

with $\lim_{n \to \infty} \delta_n = 0$. Then, for each value t_n^{j-1}, we consider the variational inequality

$$\langle F \left(u \left(t_n^{j-1} \right) \right), v - u \left(t_n^{j-1} \right) \rangle \geq 0, \quad \forall v \in \mathbb{K} \left(t_n^{j-1} \right) \qquad (5.27)$$

where

$$K\left(t_n^{j-1}\right) = \left\{v \in \mathbb{R}^q : \lambda\left(t_n^{j-1}\right) \leq v \leq \mu\left(t_n^{j-1}\right), \; \sum_{i=1}^{q} \xi_{ji} \, v_i = \rho_j\left(t_n^{j-1}\right)\right\}.$$

We can now compute the unique solution to the finite-dimensional variational inequality (5.27) by means of the critical point of the projected dynamical system

$$\Pi_{\mathbb{K}}\left(u\left(t_n^{j-1}, \tau\right), -F\left(u\left(t_n^{j-1}, \tau\right)\right)\right) = 0$$

and we can construct an interpolation function $u_n(t)$ such that

$$\lim_n \|u_n(t) - u(t)\|_{L^\infty([0,T],\mathbb{R}^q)} = 0.$$

We can overcome the regularization assumption on the solution u, by considering the same discretization procedure proposed in Section 2.5.2, which makes use of the mean value operators in suitable subintervals.

5.7 Numerical Dynamic Traffic Examples

In this section we present numerical examples that are taken from transportation science, and will be solved by means of the direct method and/or the discretization preocedure.

Example 5.7.1

We consider a transportation network consisting of 4 nodes, 5 routes and a single origin–destination pair of nodes (P_1, P_2), as depicted in Figure 5.1. We introduce the following paths connecting the O/D pair:

$$R_1 = (P_1, P_2), \; R_2 = (P_1, P_3) \cup (P_3, P_2), \; R_3 = (P_1, P_4) \cup (P_4, P_3) \cup (P_3, P_2).$$

The feasible set $\mathbb{K}$ is as in (5.12), where we take $p := 2$. We also have that $q := 3$, $l := 1$, $T := 2$, $\rho(t) := 2t$, and $\xi_{ji} := 1$ for $j = 1$ and $i \in \{1, 2\}$:

$$K(t) = \left\{F \in L^2([0, 2], \mathbb{R}^3) : \right.$$

$$0 \leq F_1(t) \leq t, 0 \leq F_2(t) \leq \frac{3}{2}t, 0 \leq F_3(t) \leq 2t \text{ a.e. in } [0, 2];$$

$$\left. F_1(t) + F_2(t) + F_3(t) = 2t \text{ a.e. in } [0, 2]\right\}.$$

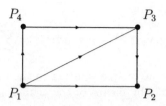

Figure 5.1: Network with a single O/D pair

In this application $F(t)$ denotes the vector of path flows at t. The cost functions on the paths are defined as:

$$C_1(F(t)) = F_1(t), \ C_2(F(t)) = F_2(t) + 1, \ C_3(F(t)) = F_2(t) + F_3(t).$$

We consider a vector field C defined by

$$C : L^2([0,2], \mathbb{R}^3) \to L^2([0,2], \mathbb{R}^3);$$

$$(C_1(F(t)), C_2(F(t)), C_3(F(t))) = (F_1(t), F_2(t) + 1, F_2(t) + F_3(t)).$$

The theory of EVI states that the system has a unique equilibrium, since C is strictly monotone (because of its strong monotonicity), for any arbitrarily fixed point $t \in [0,2]$. Indeed, one can easily see that:

$$\langle C(F(t)) - C(H(t)), F(t) - H(t) \rangle$$

$$= [F_1(t) - H_1(t)]^2 + [F_2(t) - H_2(t)]^2 + [F_3(t) - H_3(t)]^2$$

$$+ [F_2(t) - H_2(t)] \cdot [F_3(t) - H_3(t)]$$

$$= \frac{1}{2}\{ [F_2(t) - H_2(t)]^2 + [F_3(t) - H_3(t)]^2$$

$$+ 2[F_2(t) - H_2(t)] \cdot [F_3(t) - H_3(t)] \} + \frac{1}{2}[F_2(t) - H_2(t)]^2$$

$$+ \frac{1}{2}[F_3(t) - H_3(t)]^2 + [F_1(t) - H_1(t)]^2 \geq \frac{1}{2}\|F(t) - H(t)\|^2.$$

Moreover, the solution is continuous by virtue of Theorem 3.2 in [5]. With the help of PDS theory, we can compute an approximate curve of equilibria, by selecting $t_0 \in \left\{ \dfrac{k}{5} : k \in \{0, \ldots, 10\} \right\}$. Hence, we obtain a sequence of PDS defined by the vector field

$$-C(F_1(t_0), F_2(t_0), F_3(t_0)) = (-F_1(t_0), -F_2(t_0) - 1, -F_2(t_0) - F_3(t_0))$$

on nonempty, closed, convex, 3-dimensional subsets:

$$\mathbb{K}_{t_0} := \left\{ F(t_0) \in \mathbb{R}^3 : 0 \leq F(t_0) \leq t_0, \, 0 \leq F_2(t_0) \leq \frac{3}{2}t_0, \, 0 \leq F_3(t_0) \leq 2t_0; \right.$$

$$\left. F_1(t_0) + F_2(t_0) + F_3(t_0) = 2t_0 \right\}.$$

For each, we can compute the unique equilibrium of the system at the point t_0, that is, the point:

$$(F_1(t_0), F_2(t_0), F_3(t_0)) \in \mathbb{R}^3 \text{ such that}$$

$$-C(F_1(t_0), F_2(t_0), F_3(t_0)) \in N_{\mathbb{K}_{t_0}}(F_1(t_0), F_2(t_0), F_3(t_0)).$$

Proceeding in this manner, we obtain the equilibria consisting of the points in Table 5.1. The interpolation of these points yields the curve of equilibria in Figure 5.2. Studying the same network by means of the

t_0	$H_1(t_0)$	$H_2(t_0)$	$H_3(t_0)$	t_0	$H_1(t_0)$	$H_2(t_0)$	$H_3(t_0)$
0	0	0	0	0.2	0.2	0	0.2
0.4	0.4	0	0.4	0.6	0.6	0	0.6
0.8	0.8	0	0.8	1	1	0	1
1.2	1.199	0.199	1.001	1.4	1.399	0.399	1.001
1.6	1.599	0.599	1.001	1.8	1.799	0.799	1.001
2	1.999	0.999	1.001				

Table 5.1: Equilibrium points for the network in Example 5.7.1

direct method, we have to solve the following evolutionary variational inequality:

$$C_1(H(t)) [F_1(t) - H_1(t)] + C_2(H(t)) [F_2(t) - H_2(t)]$$
$$+ C_3(H(t)) [F_3(t) - H_3(t)] \geq 0 \quad \forall F(t) \in \mathbb{K}(t).$$

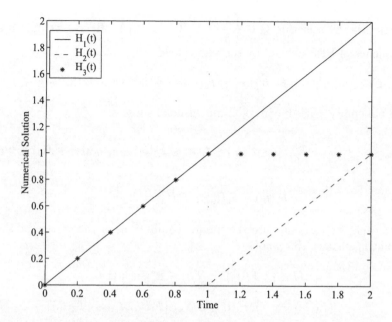

Figure 5.2: Equilibrium flows for Example 5.7.1

Setting $F_3(t) = 2t - F_1(t) - F_2(t)$, the evolutionary variational inequality becomes:

$$[C_1(H(t)) - C_3(H(t))] \cdot [F_1(t) - H_1(t)]$$
$$+ [C_2(H(t)) - C_3(H(t))] \cdot [F_2(t) - H_2(t)] \geq 0 \quad \forall F(t) \in \widetilde{\mathbb{K}}(t),$$

where

$$\widetilde{\mathbb{K}}(t) = \left\{ (F_1(t), F_2(t)) \in L^2([0,2], \mathbb{R}^2) : 0 \leq F_1(t) \leq t, \ 0 \leq F_2(t) \leq \frac{3}{2}t, \right.$$

$$\left. F_1(t) + F_2(t) \leq 2t \text{ a.e. in } [0,2] \right\}.$$

Solving the system

$$\begin{cases} \Gamma_1(H(t)) = C_1(H(t)) - C_3(H(t)) = 0 \\ \Gamma_2(H(t)) = C_2(H(t)) - C_3(H(t)) = 0 \end{cases} \Leftrightarrow \begin{cases} H_1(t) = t \\ H_2(t) = t - 1, \end{cases}$$

we obtain that $(H_1(t), H_2(t)) \in \widetilde{\mathbb{K}}(t)$ if and only if $t \geq 1$. Thus, if $1 \leq t \leq 2$, then the equilibrium solution is

$$\begin{cases} H_1(t) = t \\ H_2(t) = t - 1 \\ H_3(t) = 1. \end{cases}$$

When $0 \leq t < 1$, then we study the problem in the face:

$$\widetilde{\mathbb{K}}^{(2)}(t) = \widetilde{\mathbb{K}}(t) \cap \{F_2(t) = 0\} = \left\{F_1(t) \in L^2([0,2], \mathbb{R}) : \ 0 \leq F_1(t) \leq t\right\},$$

where the evolutionary variational inequality becomes:

$$[2H_1(t) - 2t] \cdot [F_1(t) - H_1(t)] \geq 0, \quad \forall F_1(t) \in \widetilde{\mathbb{K}}^{(2)}(t).$$

The equality $\Gamma_1(t) = 2H_1(t) - 2t = 0$ leads to $H_1(t) = t$ and the necessary and sufficient condition implies: $\Gamma_2(t, 0) = 1 - t > 0$, that is $t < 1$. So, when $0 \leq t < 1$, then the equilibrium solution is

$$\begin{cases} H_1(t) = t \\ H_2(t) = 0 \\ H_3(t) = t. \end{cases}$$

Unifying the previous results yields:

$$\begin{cases} H_1(t) = \quad t \qquad \forall t \in [0, 2] \\ H_2(t) = \begin{cases} 0 & \forall t \in [0, 1[\\ t - 1 & \forall t \in [1, 2] \end{cases} \\ H_3(t) = \begin{cases} t & \forall t \in [0, 1[\\ 1 & \forall t \in [1, 2]. \end{cases} \end{cases}$$

It is remarkable the perfect coincidence of the values of the solutions obtained by using two different methods, one of which is direct and the other is iterative.

Example 5.7.2

We consider now a transportation network consisting of 4 nodes, 6 routes and 2 origin–destination pairs of nodes (P_1, P_2) and (P_1, P_4), as depicted in Figure 5.3. We consider now a transportation network consisting of

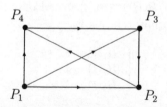

Figure 5.3: Network with 2 O/D pairs

4 nodes, 6 routes and 2 origin–destination pairs of nodes (P_1, P_2) and (P_1, P_4), as depicted in Figure 5.3. We introduce the following paths connecting the first O/D pair:

$$R_1 = (P_1, P_2), \ R_2 = (P_1, P_3) \cup (P_3, P_2), \ R_3 = (P_1, P_4) \cup (P_4, P_3) \cup (P_3, P_2)$$

and the following paths connecting the second O/D pair:

$$R_4 = (P_1, P_2) \cup (P_2, P_4), \ R_5 = (P_1, P_4).$$

The feasible set $\mathbb{K}$ is as in (5.12), where we take $p := 2$. We also have that $q := 5$, $l := 2$, $T := 2$, $\rho_{(P_1,P_2)}(t) := 2t$ and $\rho_{(P_1,P_4)}(t) := 3t$:

$$\mathbb{K}(t) = \Big\{ F \in L^2([0,2], \mathbb{R}^5) :$$

$$0 \leq F_1(t) \leq t, 0 \leq F_2(t) \leq \frac{3}{2}t, 0 \leq F_3(t) \leq 2t,$$

$$0 \leq F_4(t) \leq \frac{3}{2}t, 0 \leq F_5(t) \leq 2t \text{ a.e. in } [0,2];$$

$$F_1(t) + F_2(t) + F_3(t) = 2t, \ F_4(t) + F_5(t) = 3t \text{ a.e. in } [0,2] \Big\}.$$

The cost functions on the paths are defined as:

$$C_1(F(t)) = F_1(t), \ C_2(F(t)) = F_2(t) + 1, \ C_3(F(t)) = F_2(t) + F_3(t),$$

$$C_4(F(t)) = F_1(t) + F_4(t), \ C_5(F(t)) = F_5(t).$$

We consider a vector field C defined by

$$C : L^2([0,2], \mathbb{R}^5) \to L^2([0,2], \mathbb{R}^5);$$

$$(C_1(F(t)), C_2(F(t)), C_3(F(t)), C_4(F(t)), C_5(F(t)))$$

$$= (F_1(t), F_2(t) + 1, F_2(t) + F_3(t), F_1(t) + F_4(t), F_5(t)).$$

Also in this case C is strongly monotone, for any arbitrarily fixed point $t \in [0, 2]$. Indeed, one can easily see that:

$$\langle C(F(t)) - C(H(t)), F(t) - H(t) \rangle = [F_1(t) - H_1(t)]^2 + [F_2(t) - H_2(t)]^2$$

$$+ [F_2(t) + F_3(t) - H_2(t) - H_3(t)] \cdot [F_3(t) - H_3(t)]$$

$$+ [F_1(t) + F_4(t) - H_1(t) - H_4(t)] \cdot [F_4(t) - H_4(t)] + [F_5(t) - H_5(t)]^2$$

$$= \frac{1}{2} \{ [F_1(t) - H_1(t)]^2 + [F_4(t) - H_4(t)]^2 + 2 [F_1(t) - H_1(t)] \cdot [F_4(t) - H_4(t)] \}$$

$$+ \frac{1}{2} \{ [F_2(t) - H_2(t)]^2 + [F_3(t) - H_3(t)]^2 + 2 [F_2(t) - H_2(t)] \cdot [F_3(t) - H_3(t)] \}$$

$$+ \frac{1}{2} [F_1(t) - H_1(t)]^2 + \frac{1}{2} [F_4(t) - H_4(t)]^2 + \frac{1}{2} [F_2(t) - H_2(t)]^2$$

$$+ \frac{1}{2} [F_3(t) - H_3(t)]^2 + [F_5(t) - H_5(t)]^2 \geq \frac{1}{2} \| F(t) - H(t) \|^2.$$

Therefore the system has a unique equilibrium solution which is also continuous in virtue of Theorem 3.2 in [5]. Using the PDS theory, we can compute an approximate curve of equilibria, by selecting:

$$t_0 \in \left\{ \frac{k}{5} : k \in \{0, \ldots, 10\} \right\}.$$

Hence, we obtain a sequence of PDS defined by the vector field:

$$-C(F_1(t_0), F_2(t_0), F_3(t_0), F_4(t_0), F_5(t_0))$$

$$= (-F_1(t_0), -F_2(t_0) - 1, -F_2(t_0) - F_3(t_0), -F_1(t_0) - F_4(t_0), -F_5(t_0))$$

on nonempty, closed, convex, 5-dimensional subsets:

$$\mathbb{K}_{t_0} := \left\{ F(t_0) \in \mathbb{R}^5 : 0 \leq F_1(t_0) \leq t_0, \, 0 \leq F_2(t_0) \leq \frac{3}{2} t_0, \right.$$

$$\left. 0 \leq F_3(t_0) \leq 2t_0, \, 0 \leq F_4(t_0) \leq \frac{3}{2} t_0, \, 0 \leq F_5(t_0) \leq 2t_0; \right.$$

$$F_1(t_0) + F_2(t_0) + F_3(t_0) = 2t_0, \ F_4(t_0) + F_5(t_0) = 3t_0 \Big\}.$$

For each, we can compute the unique equilibrium of the system at the point t_0, that is, the point:

$$(F_1(t_0), F_2(t_0), F_3(t_0), F_4(t_0), F_5(t_0)) \in \mathbb{R}^5 \text{ such that}$$

$$-C(F_1(t_0), F_2(t_0), F_3(t_0), F_4(t_0), F_5(t_0))$$

$$\in N_{\mathbb{K}_{t_0}}(F_1(t_0), F_2(t_0), F_3(t_0), F_4(t_0), F_5(t_0)).$$

Thus, we obtain the equilibria consisting of the points in Table 5.2. Interpolating these points we get the curve of equilibria in Figure 5.4.

t_0	$H_1(t_0)$	$H_2(t_0)$	$H_3(t_0)$	$H_4(t_0)$	$H_5(t_0)$
0	0	0	0	0	0
0.2	0.2	0	0.2	0.2	0.4
0.4	0.4	0	0.4	0.4	0.8
0.6	0.6	0	0.6	0.6	1.2
0.8	0.8	0	0.8	0.8	1.6
1	1	0	1	1	2
1.2	1.199	0.199	1.001	1.2006	2.3994
1.4	1.399	0.399	1.0009	1.4006	2.7994
1.6	1.599	0.599	1.001	1.6006	3.1993
1.8	1.799	0.799	1.0009	1.8006	3.5993
2	1.999	0.999	1.0009	2.0006	3.9994

Table 5.2: Equilibrium points for the network in Example 5.7.2

Studying the same network by means of the direct method, we have to solve the following evolutionary variational inequality:

$$C_1(H(t)) \left[F_1(t) - H_1(t)\right] + C_2(H(t)) \left[F_2(t) - H_2(t)\right]$$

$$+ C_3(H(t)) \left[F_3(t) - H_3(t)\right] + C_4(H(t)) \left[F_4(t) - H_4(t)\right]$$

$$+ C_5(H(t)) \left[F_5(t) - H_5(t)\right] \geq 0 \quad \forall F(t) \in \mathbb{K}(t).$$

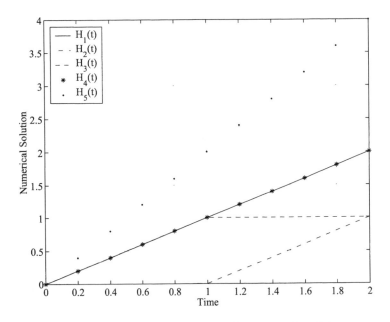

Figure 5.4: Equilibrium flows for Example 5.7.2

Setting $F_3(t) = 2t - F_1(t) - F_2(t)$ and $F_5(t) = 3t - F_4(t)$, the evolutionary variational inequality becomes:

$$[C_1(H(t)) - C_3(H(t))] \cdot [F_1(t) - H_1(t)]$$

$$+ [C_2(H(t)) - C_3(H(t))] \cdot [F_2(t) - H_2(t)]$$

$$+ [C_4(H(t)) - C_5(H(t))] \cdot [F_4(t) - H_4(t)] \geq 0 \quad \forall F(t) \in \widetilde{\mathbb{K}}(t),$$

where

$$\widetilde{\mathbb{K}}(t) = \Big\{ (F_1(t), F_2(t), F_4(t)) \in L^2([0,2], \mathbb{R}^3) :$$

$$0 \leq F_1(t) \leq t, \ 0 \leq F_2(t) \leq \frac{3}{2}t, 0 \leq F_4(t) \leq \frac{3}{2}t,$$

$$F_1(t) + F_2(t) \leq 2t, \text{ a.e. in } [0,2] \Big\}.$$

Solving the system

$$\begin{cases} \Gamma_1(H(t)) = C_1(H(t)) - C_3(H(t)) = 0 \\ \Gamma_2(H(t)) = C_2(H(t)) - C_3(H(t)) = 0 \\ \Gamma_2(H(t)) = C_4(H(t)) - C_5(H(t)) = 0 \end{cases} \Leftrightarrow \begin{cases} H_1(t) = t \\ H_2(t) = t - 1 \\ H_4(t) = t \end{cases}$$

we obtain that $(H_1(t), H_2(t), H_4(t)) \in \widetilde{\mathbb{K}}(t)$ if and only if $t \geq 1$. Thus, if $1 \leq t \leq 2$, then the equilibrium solution is

$$\begin{cases} H_1(t) = t, \quad H_2(t) = t - 1, \quad H_3(t) = 1, \\ H_4(t) = t, \quad H_5(t) = 2t. \end{cases}$$

When $0 \leq t < 1$, then we study the problem in the face:

$$\widetilde{\mathbb{K}}^{(2)}(t) = \widetilde{\mathbb{K}}(t) \cap \{F_2(t) = 0\}$$

$$= \left\{ (F_1(t), F_4(t)) \in L^2([0, 2], \mathbb{R}^2) : \ 0 \leq F_1(t) \leq t, \ 0 \leq F_4(t) \leq \frac{3}{2}t \right\},$$

where the evolutionary variational inequality becomes:

$$[2H_1(t) - 2t] \cdot [F_1(t) - H_1(t)] + [H_1(t) + 2H_4(t) - 3t] \cdot [F_4(t) - H_4(t)] \geq 0,$$

$$\forall F(t) \in \widetilde{\mathbb{K}}^{(2)}(t).$$

From the system

$$\begin{cases} \Gamma_1(H(t)) = 0 \\ \Gamma_2(H(t)) = 0 \end{cases} \Leftrightarrow \begin{cases} H_1(t) = t \\ H_4(t) = t, \end{cases}$$

we derive that $(H_1(t), H_4(t)) = (t, t) \in \mathbb{K}^{(2)}(t)$ and the necessary and sufficient condition implies: $\Gamma_2(t, t) = -t + 1 > 0$, that is $t < 1$. So, when $0 \leq t < 1$, the equilibrium solution is

$$\begin{cases} H_1(t) = t \\ H_2(t) = 0 \\ H_3(t) = t \\ H_4(t) = t \\ H_5(t) = 2t. \end{cases}$$

Unifying the previous results yields:

$$
\left\{
\begin{array}{lll}
H_1(t) = & t & \forall t \in [0, 2] \\
H_2(t) = & \left\{ \begin{array}{l} 0 \\ t \doteq 1 \end{array} \right. & \begin{array}{l} \forall t \in [0, 1[\\ \forall t \in [1, 2] \end{array} \\
H_3(t) = & \left\{ \begin{array}{l} t \\ 1 \end{array} \right. & \begin{array}{l} \forall t \in [0, 1[\\ \forall t \in [1, 2]. \end{array} \\
H_4(t) = & t & \forall t \in [0, 2] \\
H_5(t) = & 2t & \forall t \in [0, 2].
\end{array}
\right.
$$

Example 5.7.3

We consider now the same transportation network as in Example 5.7.2, but with different cost functions, which are defined as follows:

$$
\begin{aligned}
C_1(F(t)) &= F_1(t), \\
C_2(F(t)) &= F_2(t) + F_3(t), \\
C_3(F(t)) &= F_2(t) + F_3(t) + F_5(t), \\
C_4(F(t)) &= F_1(t) + F_4(t), \\
C_5(F(t)) &= F_3(t) + F_5(t).
\end{aligned}
$$

In this example we only use the discretization procedure and we can compute an approximate curve of equilibria, by selecting:

$$
t_0 \in \left\{ \frac{k}{5} : k \in \{0, \ldots, 10\} \right\}.
$$

Hence, we obtain a sequence of PDS defined by the vector field:

$$
-C(F_1(t_0), F_2(t_0), F_3(t_0), F_4(t_0), F_5(t_0))
$$

$$
= (-F_1(t_0), -F_2(t_0) - F_3(t_0), -F_2(t_0) - F_3(t_0) - F_5(t_0),
$$

$$
-F_1(t_0) - F_4(t_0), -F_3(t_0) - F_5(t_0))
$$

on nonempty, closed, convex, 5-dimensional subsets:

$$
\mathbb{K}_{t_0} := \left\{ F(t_0) \in \mathbb{R}^5 : 0 \le F(t_0) \le t_0, \, 0 \le F_2(t_0) \le \frac{3}{2}t_0, \right.
$$

$$
0 \le F_3(t_0) \le 2t_0, \, 0 \le F_4(t_0) \le \frac{3}{2}t_0, \, 0 \le F_5(t_0) \le 2t;
$$

$$F_1(t_0) + F_2(t_0) + F_3(t_0) = 2t_0, \ F_4(t_0) + F_5(t_0) = 3t_0 \Big\}.$$

For each, we can compute the unique equilibrium of the system at the point t_0, that is, the point:

$$(F_1(t_0), F_2(t_0), F_3(t_0), F_4(t_0), F_5(t_0)) \in \mathbb{R}^5 \text{ such that}$$

$$-C(F_1(t_0), F_2(t_0), F_3(t_0), F_4(t_0), F_5(t_0)) \in$$

$$N_{\mathbb{K}_{t_0}}(F_1(t_0), F_2(t_0), F_3(t_0), F_4(t_0), F_5(t_0)).$$

Thus, we obtain the equilibria consisting of the points in Table 5.3. The

t_0	$H_1(t_0)$	$H_2(t_0)$	$H_3(t_0)$	$H_4(t_0)$	$H_5(t_0)$
0	0	0	0	0	0
0.2	0.2	0.2	0	0.2007	0.3993
0.4	0.4	0.4	0	0.4007	0.7993
0.6	0.6	0.6	0	0.6007	1.1993
0.8	0.8	0.8	0	0.8006	1.5993
1	1	1	0	1.0007	1.9993
1.2	1.2	1.2	0	1.2007	2.3993
1.4	1.4	1.4	0	1.4007	2.7993
1.6	1.6	1.6	0	1.6007	3.1993
1.8	1.8	1.8	0	1.8007	3.5993
2	2	2	0	2.0007	3.9993

Table 5.3: Equilibrium points for the network in Example 5.7.3

interpolation of these points yields the curve of equilibria in Figure 5.5.

5.8   Sources and Remarks

In the early 1990s, Dupuis and Nagurney (see [56]) introduced a class of dynamics given by solutions to a differential equation with a discontinuous right-hand side, namely

$$\frac{d\,x(t)}{d\,t} = \Pi_{\mathbb{K}}(x(t), -F(x(t))). \tag{5.28}$$

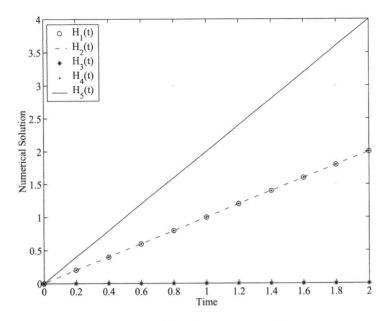

Figure 5.5: Equilibrium flows for Example 5.7.3

Theorem 5.1 in Dupuis and Ishii (see [55]) proves the existence of local solutions (on an interval $[0, l] \subset \mathbb{R}$) for the initial value problem

$$\begin{cases} \dfrac{d\,x(t)}{d\,t} = \Pi_{\mathbb{K}}(x(t), -F(x(t))), \\ x(0) \in \mathbb{K}. \end{cases}$$

Dupuis and Nagurney (see [56]) came back to the class of differential equations (5.28), extended the existence of solutions to the real axis, and introduced the notion of projected dynamical systems defined by these solutions, together with several examples, and applications of such dynamics (see also [82], [115], [116], [122], [124], [125], [128], and [129]).

Although the papers above were the first to introduce PDS, a similar idea appears in the literature earlier in the papers by Henry (see [80]), Cornet (see [21]), Attouch and Damlamian (see [1]) and in the book by Aubin and Cellina (see [2]), where (5.28) is a particular case of the differential inclusion

$$\frac{d\,x(t)}{d\,t} \in \Pi_{\mathbb{K}}(x(t), -F(x(t)). \tag{5.29}$$

In [81] Hipfel shows another existence result for the solutions to equation (5.28), for the particular case of $\mathbb{K} := \mathbb{R}^n_+$, but with no relation to projected dynamics.

Isac and Cojocaru (see [83]) studied the PDS on infinite-dimensional Hilbert spaces and Cojocaru (see [15] and also Cojocaru and Jonker [19]) established existence results of solutions.

The essential trait of a projected dynamical system in the finite-dimensional case was first noted in Dupuis and Nagurney [56]. The authors showed that the critical points of equation (5.28) are the same as the solutions to a variational inequality problem.

In [15], Cojocaru showed that the same result holds on a Hilbert space of any dimension, for any closed and convex subset $\mathbb{K}$ and a Lipschitz field F.

In [77] and [140] the authors propose a study of the projected dynamical systems theory and a computational procedure based on the discretization method.

In [16] the connection between projected dynamical systems and evolutionary variational inequalities is deeply studied and in [18] the same authors present a survey with applications to traffic network problems. In [17] the interdependence between the two timeframes used in this new theory is made explicit.

Appendix A

Definitions and Properties

A.1 Functions and Related Properties

Let E be a real topological vector space and let S be a subset of E. Moreover, let E' be the dual space of E.

Definition A.1 *A functional $f : S \to \mathbb{R} \cup \{\pm\infty\}$ is said to be:*

- *upper semicontinuous (in brief u. s. c.) if for each x' we have*

$$\limsup_{x \to x'} f(x) \leq f(x');$$

- *lower semicontinuous (in brief l. s. c.) if $-f(x)$ is upper semi-continuous.*

Let us denote by $\langle \cdot, \cdot \rangle$ the canonical bi-linear form on $E' \times E$.

Definition A.2 *A function $f : S \to E'$ is said to be:*

- *monotone on S if*

$$\langle f(x_1) - f(x_2), x_1 - x_2 \rangle \geq 0 \quad \forall x_1, x_2 \in S;$$

- *strictly monotone on S if*

$$\langle f(x_1) - f(x_2), x_1 - x_2 \rangle > 0 \quad \forall x_1 \neq x_2;$$

201

- *strongly monotone on S if for some $\alpha > 0$*

$$\langle f(x_1) - f(x_2), x_1 - x_2 \rangle \geq \alpha \|x_1 - x_2\|^2 \quad \forall x_1, x_2 \in S;$$

- *quasi-monotone on S if $\forall x, y \in S$*

$$\langle y - x, f(x) \rangle \geq 0 \text{ implies } \langle y - x, f(y) \rangle \geq 0;$$

- *pseudomonotone on S if $\forall x, y \in S$*

$$\langle y - x, f(x) \rangle \geq 0 \text{ implies } \langle y - x, f(y) \rangle \geq 0;$$

- *strictly pseudomonotone on S if $\forall x, y \in S$, $x \neq y$*

$$\langle y - x, f(x) \rangle \geq 0 \text{ implies } \langle y - x, f(y) \rangle > 0;$$

- *strongly pseudomonotone with degree α on S if $\exists \eta > 0 : \forall\, x, y \in S$, $x \neq y$*

$$\langle y - x, f(x) \rangle \geq 0 \text{ implies } \langle y - x, f(y) \rangle \geq \eta \|y - x\|^\alpha.$$

Definition A.3 *Let E be a real topological vector space and let $\mathbb{K} \subset E$ a convex set. A function $f : \mathbb{K} \to E'$ is said to be:*

- *hemicontinuous if $\forall y \in \mathbb{K}$, the function*

$$\mathbb{K} \ni \xi \to \langle f(\xi), y - \xi \rangle$$

is upper semicontinuous on $\mathbb{K}$;

- *hemicontinuous along line segments if $\forall x, y \in \mathbb{K}$, the function*

$$\xi \to \langle f(\xi), y - x \rangle$$

is upper semicontinuous on the line segment $[x, y]$.

Another important concept for the optimization theory is the definition of convex functionals. We recall the definitions of convex set and function.

Definition A.4 *A set $\mathbb{K} \subseteq \mathbb{R}^n$ is said to be convex if and only if it is the empty set or if and only if*

$$(1 - \alpha)x_1 + \alpha\, x_2 \in \mathbb{K}, \quad \forall \alpha \in [0, 1], \ \forall x_1, x_2 \in \mathbb{K}.$$

Definition A.5 *Let $\mathbb{K} \subseteq \mathbb{R}^n$ be convex. A function $f : \mathbb{K} \to \mathbb{R}$ is said to be convex if and only if*

$$(1 - \alpha)f(x_1) + \alpha f(x_2) \geq f\left[(1 - \alpha)x_1 + \alpha\, x_2\right],$$
$$\forall \alpha \in [0, 1], \ \forall x_1, x_2 \in \mathbb{K}. \tag{A.1}$$

If

$$(1 - \alpha)f(x_1) + \alpha f(x_2) = f\left[(1 - \alpha)x_1 + \alpha\, x_2\right], \quad \forall \alpha \in\,]0, 1[, \ \forall x_1 \neq x_2,$$

then f is called strictly convex.

Definition A.6 *If*

$$(1 - \alpha)f(x_1) + \alpha f(x_2) = f\left((1 - \alpha)x_1 + \alpha\, x_2\right), \quad \forall \alpha \in [0, 1], \ \forall x_1 \neq x_2$$

$$\implies (1 - \alpha)f(x_1) + \alpha f(x_2) = f\left((1 - \alpha)x_1 + \alpha\, x_2\right), \quad \forall \alpha \in \mathbb{R},$$

then f is called quasi strictly convex.

As a consequence, a function f is called (quasi) (strictly) concave if and only if $-f$ is (quasi) (strictly) convex; a vector function is (quasi) (strictly) convex (concave) if and only if each component is (quasi) (strictly) convex (concave).

A.2 Multifunctions and Related Properties

Let X, Y be two Hausdorff topological vector spaces and let $\mathbb{K}$ be a subset of X. Moreover, let X' denote the dual space of X.

Definition A.7 *A multifunction $F : \mathbb{K} \to 2^Y$ is said to be:*

- *upper semicontinuous in $x' \in \mathbb{K}$ if for any open subset Ω of Y such that $F(x') \subseteq \Omega$, there exists a neighborhood V of x' such that $\forall x \in V : F(x) \subseteq \Omega$;*

- *lower semicontinuous in $x' \in X$ if for any open set Ω of Y such that $F(x') \cap \Omega \neq \emptyset$, there exists a neighborhood V of x' such that $\forall x \in V \ F(x) \cap \Omega \neq \emptyset$;*

- *continuous if it is both upper and lower semicontinuous;*

- *closed if its graph*

$$G = \{(x, y) : x \in \mathbb{K}, y \in F(x)\}$$

is a closed subset of $X \times Y$.

Remark A.1 It is easy to show that if X and Y are real topological linear locally convex Hausdorff spaces,

1. F is closed if and only if for any sequence $\{x_n\}$, $x_n \to x$ and any $\{y_n\}$, $y_n \in F(x_n)$, $y_n \to y$, then it results $y \in F(x)$;

2. F is l. s. c. in $x \in \mathbb{K}$ if and only if for any $y \in F(x)$ and any $\{x_n\}$, $x_n \to x$, there exists a sequence $\{y_n\}$ such that $y_n \in F(x_n)$ and $y_n \to y$.

Definition A.8 *Let (X, d) and (Y, δ) be two metric spaces. A multifunction $F : X \to 2^Y$ is said to be a Lipschitz multifunction if there exists a positive number L (which is called the Lipschitz constant) such that, for every pair of points $a, b \in X$, we have:*

$$\delta_H(F(a), F(b)) \leq L \, d(a, b),$$

where δ_H is defined as follows: if $A, B \subseteq Y$, then $\delta^*(A, B) = \sup_{y \in A} \delta(y, B)$ and $\delta_H(A, B) = \max(\delta^*(A, B), \delta^*(B, A))$.

Upper semicontinuous multifunctions are closed and the contrary holds if the image $f(\mathbb{K})$ is compact.

A.3   Cones and Related Properties

Let us start by introducing the concept of a cone.

Definition A.9 *Let X be a real linear space and $C \subseteq X$ nonempty.*

- *C is said to be a cone if $x \in C$, $\lambda \geq 0 \Longrightarrow \lambda x \in C$;*

- *a cone C is called pointed if $x \in C$, $-x \in C \Longrightarrow x = 0_X$.*

Definition A.10 *Let X be a real linear space and $S \subseteq X$ nonempty. The set*

$$\text{cone } (S) = \{\lambda s : \lambda \geq 0, \ s \in S\}$$

is called the cone generated by S.

Let H be a real Hilbert space, whose inner product we denote by $\langle \cdot, \cdot \rangle$.

Definition A.11 *For a subset $M \subset H$ the polar M^0 is defined by*

$$M^0 = \{\xi \in H : \langle \xi, x \rangle \leq 1, \ \ \forall x \in M\}.$$

For a cone C, Definition A.11 simplifies into

$$C^0 = C^- = \{\xi \in H : \langle \xi, x \rangle \leq 0, \ \forall x \in C\}.$$

Definition A.12 *Let $\mathbb{K}$ be a nonempty, closed, convex subset of H. For all $x \in \mathbb{K}$ we define the support cone (or Bouligand tangent cone, or contingent cone) to $\mathbb{K}$ at x as the set*

$$T_{\mathbb{K}}(x) = \overline{\bigcup_{\lambda > 0} \lambda (\mathbb{K} - x)}.$$

Definition A.13 *We define the normal cone to $\mathbb{K}$ at x as the set*

$$N_{\mathbb{K}}(x) = \{\xi \in H : \ \langle \xi, z - x \rangle \leq 0, \ \forall z \in \mathbb{K}\}.$$

Proposition A.1 *We then have the following result:*

$$(T_{\mathbb{K}}(x))^0 = N_{\mathbb{K}}(x) = (T_{\mathbb{K}}(x))^-.$$

Proof: It is clear (see [2], Proposition 2, p. 220) that

$$(T_{\mathbb{K}}(x))^0 \subseteq N_{\mathbb{K}}(x) = \{\xi \in H : \langle \xi, z - x \rangle \le 0, \ \forall z \in \mathbb{K}\},$$

because $z - x \in T_{\mathbb{K}}(x)$, $\forall z \in \mathbb{K}$. Vice versa, $N_{\mathbb{K}}(x) \subseteq (T_{\mathbb{K}}(x))^0$, because if $y = \lim_n \lambda_n(z_n - x)$, $z_n \in \mathbb{K}$, $\lambda_n \ge 0 \ \forall n \in \mathbb{N}$, for each $\xi \in N_{\mathbb{K}}(x)$:

$$\langle \xi, \lambda_n(z_n - x) \rangle \le 0, \ \forall n \in \mathbb{N}$$

and hence,

$$\langle \xi, y \rangle \le 0, \ \forall y \in T_{\mathbb{K}}(x),$$

and the assertion is proved. $\qquad\qquad\qquad\qquad\qquad\qquad\qquad\square$

Remark A.2 The set $T_{\mathbb{K}}(x)$ is clearly a closed convex cone with vertex 0 and it is the smallest cone C whose translate $x + C$ has vertex x and contains $\mathbb{K}$. $T_{\mathbb{K}}(x)$ is very useful to introduce the essential concept of quasi interior and quasi relative interior. Such a necessity comes from the fact that the usual ordering cones and the convex sets which appear in the infinite-dimensional theory of variational inequalities have empty interior. The difficulties arising from these limitations can be overcome by introducing the new concepts of *quasi interior* (qi) and *quasi relative interior* (qri) (see also [11] and [40]).

Definition A.14 *Let $\mathbb{K}$ be a nonempty subset of a Hilbert space H. We call:*

- *quasi interior of $\mathbb{K}$ the set* qi $\mathbb{K}$ *of those $x \in \mathbb{K}$ for which $T_{\mathbb{K}}(x) = H$;*

- *quasi relative interior of $\mathbb{K}$ the set* qri $\mathbb{K}$ *of those $x \in \mathbb{K}$ for which $T_{\mathbb{K}}(x)$ is a subspace of H;*

- *quasi boundary of $\mathbb{K}$ (denoted by* qbdry $\mathbb{K}$*) the set $\mathbb{K} \setminus$ qi $\mathbb{K}$.*

Often we can identify qi $\mathbb{K}$ and qri $\mathbb{K}$ with an appropriate choice of the space H.

In [158], Zarantonello defines $x \in \mathbb{K}$ as an *inner point* of $\mathbb{K}$ if $T_{\mathbb{K}}(x)$ is only a subspace.

Proposition A.2 *Let* $\mathbb{K}$ *be a convex subset of* H *and* $\bar{x} \in \mathbb{K}$. *Then* $\bar{x} \in$ qri $\mathbb{K}$ *if and only if* $N_{\mathbb{K}}(\bar{x})$ *is a linear subspace of* H.

Proof: See Proposition 2.8 in [8]. $\qquad\qquad\qquad\square$

Proposition A.3 *Let* $\mathbb{K}$ *be a convex subset of* H *and* $\bar{x} \in \mathbb{K}$. *Then* $\bar{x} \in$ qi $\mathbb{K}$ *if and only if* $N_{\mathbb{K}}(\bar{x}) = \{\theta_H\}$.

Proof: See Proposition 2.8 in [8]. $\qquad\qquad\qquad\square$

Appendix B

Weak Convergence

Definition B.1 *Let $(X, \| \cdot \|)$ be a normed space. A sequence $\{x_n\}_{n \in \mathbb{N}}$ of elements of X is called weakly convergent to some $\bar{x} \in X$ if for all continuous linear functionals l on X we have that $\langle l, x_n \rangle$ is strongly convergent to $\langle l, \bar{x} \rangle$. In this case $\bar{x}$ is called a weak limit of the sequence $\{x_n\}_{n \in \mathbb{N}}$.*

In a finite dimensional normed space a sequence is weakly convergent if and only if it is convergent. In an arbitrary normed space every convergent sequence is also weakly convergent; the converse statement does not hold in general.

Proposition B.1

1. *If $\{x_n\}_{n \in \mathbb{N}}$ is weakly convergent to some $\bar{x} \in X$, then $\|x_n\|$ is bounded and $\|\bar{x}\| \leq \liminf \|x_n\|$.*

2. *If $\{x_n\}_{n \in \mathbb{N}}$ is weakly convergent to some $\bar{x} \in X$ and $\{f_n\}_{n \in \mathbb{N}}$ is strongly convergent to some $\bar{f} \in X'$, then $\langle f_n, x_n \rangle \rightarrow \langle \bar{f}, \bar{x} \rangle$.*

Proposition B.2 *If X is a finite-dimensional space, then weak and strong topology coincide. In particular, a sequence $\{x_n\}_{n \in \mathbb{N}} \subseteq X$ is weakly convergent if and only if it is strongly convergent.*

Every weakly closed set is also a strongly closed set. In infinite dimension the converse is not true, but for the convex sets the two notions coincide.

Theorem B.1 *Let C be a convex subset of X. Then C is weakly closed if and only if C is strongly closed.*

Corollary B.1 *Let $\varphi : X \to]-\infty, +\infty]$ be a convex and strongly lower semicontinuous function. Then φ is weakly lower semicontinuous. In particular, if $\{x_n\}_{n\in\mathbb{N}}$ is weakly convergent to $\bar{x}$, then*

$$\varphi(\bar{x}) \leq \liminf \varphi(x_n).$$

Theorem B.2 ([10]) *Let X be a reflexive Banach space and let $\mathbb{K} \subset E$ be a convex, closed, and bounded subset of X. Then $\mathbb{K}$ is weakly compact.*

We introduce now some definitions and properties on the weak* topology.

Let X be a Banach space, let X' be its dual space provided with the norm $\|f\| = \sup_{\substack{x \in X \\ \|x\| \leq 1}} |\langle f, x \rangle|$ and let X'' be its bi-dual provided with the norm $\|\xi\| = \sup_{\substack{f \in X' \\ \|f\| \leq 1}} |\langle \xi, f \rangle|$.

We have a canonical injection $J : X \to X''$ defined in the following way: we fix $x \in X$, the function $f \to \langle f, x \rangle$ from X' to $\mathbb{R}$ is a linear and continuous form on X', namely it is an element of X'' denoted by Jx. Then, we have:

$$\langle Jx, f \rangle = \langle f, x \rangle \quad \forall x \in X, \ \forall f \in X'.$$

It is easy to prove that J is linear and $\|Jx\|_{X''} = \|x\|_X \ \forall x \in X$.

Definition B.2 *The weak* topology is the less fine topology which makes continuous all the applications $(\varphi x)_{x\in X'}$.*

Proposition B.3 *The weak* topology is separated.*

Proposition B.4 *Let $\{f_n\}_{n\in\mathbb{N}} \subseteq X'$. Then, it results that:*

1. *$\{f_n\}_{n\in\mathbb{N}}$ is weakly* convergent to f if and only if $\langle f_n, x \rangle$ is strongly convergent to $\langle f, x \rangle$ $\forall x \in X$.*

2. If $\{f_n\}_{n\in\mathbb{N}}$ is strongly convergent to f, then $\{f_n\}_{n\in\mathbb{N}}$ is weakly convergent to f and if $\{f_n\}_{n\in\mathbb{N}}$ is weakly convergent to f, then $\{f_n\}_{n\in\mathbb{N}}$ is weakly* convergent to f.

3. If $\{f_n\}_{n\in\mathbb{N}}$ is weakly* convergent to f, then $\|f_n\|$ is bounded and $\|f\| \le \liminf \|f_n\|$.

4. If $\{f_n\}_{n\in\mathbb{N}}$ is weakly* convergent to f and $\{x_n\}_{n\in\mathbb{N}}$ is strongly convergent to $\bar{x}$ in X, then $\langle f_n, x_n \rangle$ is strongly convergent to $\langle f, \bar{x} \rangle$.

Proposition B.5 *Let* $\varphi : X' \to \mathbb{R}$ *be a linear and continuous function with respect to the weak* topology. Then there exists* $x \in X$ *such that*

$$\varphi(f) = \langle f, x \rangle \quad \forall f \in X'.$$

Definition B.3 *Let* E *be a Banach space and let* J *be the canonical immersion of* X *into* X''. X *is said to be reflexive if* $J(X) = X''$.

When X is a reflexive space, then we can identify X and X''.

Theorem B.3 (Kakutani) *Let* X *be a Banach space. Then* X *is reflexive if and only if* $B_X = \{x \in X : \|x\| \le 1\}$ *is weakly* compact.*

Corollary B.2 *Let* X *be a reflexive Banach space and let* $\mathbb{K}$ *be a convex, closed, and bounded subset of* X. *Then* $\mathbb{K}$ *is weakly* compact.*

Corollary B.3 *Let* X *be a reflexive Banach space,* A *a nonempty, closed, and convex subset of* X, *and* $\varphi : A \to]-\infty, +\infty]$ *a convex, lower semicontinuous function such that*

$$\varphi \not\equiv +\infty \quad and \quad \lim_{\substack{x\in A \\ \|x\|\to\infty}} \varphi(x) = +\infty.$$

Then, there exists $x_0 \in A$ *such that* $\varphi(x_0) = \min_A \varphi$.

Appendix C

Generalized Derivatives

C.1 Directional Derivatives

We recall some concepts of a generalized derivative and we present some properties, following [85].

Definition C.1 *Let $(X, \| \cdot \|)$ and $(Y, \| \cdot \|)$ be two real normed spaces, let S be a nonempty subset of X and let $f : S \to Y$ be a given mapping. If for two elements $\overline{x} \in S$ and $h \in X$ the limit*

$$f'(\overline{x})(h) := \lim_{\lambda \to 0^+} \frac{f(\overline{x} + \lambda h) - f(\overline{x})}{\lambda}$$

exists, then $f'(\overline{x})(h)$ is called the directional derivative of f at $\overline{x}$ in the direction h. If this limit exists for all $h \in X$, then f is called directionally differentiable at $\overline{x}$.

The following theorem claims that every convex functional is directionally differentiable.

Theorem C.1 *Let X be a real linear space and let $f : X \to \mathbb{R}$ be a convex functional. Then at every $\overline{x} \in X$ and in every direction $h \in X$ the directional derivative $f'(\overline{x})(h)$ exists.*

Definition C.2 *Let X be a real linear space. A functional $f : X \to \mathbb{R}$ is called sublinear, if*

1. $f(\alpha x) = \alpha f(x)$ for all $x \in X$ and for all $\alpha \geq 0$ (positive homogeneity);

2. $f(x + y) \leq f(x) + f(y)$ for all $x, y \in X$ (sub-additivity).

The next theorem shows that the directional derivative of a convex functional is sublinear with respect to the direction.

Theorem C.2 Let X be a real linear space and let $f : X \to \mathbb{R}$ be a convex functional. Then for every $\overline{x} \in X$ the directional derivative $f'(\overline{x})(\cdot)$ is a sublinear functional.

Theorem C.3 Let S be a nonempty subset of a real linear space and let $f : S \to \mathbb{R}$ be a given functional.

(a) Let $\overline{x} \in S$ be a minimal point of f on S. If the functional f has a directional derivative at $\overline{x}$ in every direction $x - \overline{x}$ with arbitrary $x \in S$, then

$$f'(\overline{x})(x - \overline{x}) \geq 0 \quad \forall x \in S. \tag{C.1}$$

(b) Let the set S be convex and let the functional f be convex. If the functional f has a directional derivative at some $\overline{x} \in S$ in every direction $x - \overline{x}$ with arbitrary $x \in S$ and the inequality (C.1) is satisfied, then $\overline{x}$ is a minimal point of f on S.

C.2   Gâteaux and Fréchet Derivatives

Definition C.3 Let $(X, \|\cdot\|_X)$ and $(Y, \|\cdot\|_Y)$ be real normed spaces; let S be an open and nonempty subset of X and let $f : S \to Y$ be a given mapping. If for some $\overline{x} \in S$ and for every $h \in X$ there exists a linear and continuous functional denoted by $f'(\overline{x}) : X \to Y$ such that there exists

$$\lim_{\lambda \to 0} \frac{f(\overline{x} + \lambda h) - f(\overline{x})}{\lambda} = f'(\overline{x})(h),$$

then $f'(\overline{x})$ is called the Gâteaux derivative of f at $\overline{x}$ and f is called Gâteaux differentiable at $\overline{x}$.

Let us present now a stronger concept of a derivative.

Definition C.4 *Let $(X, \|\cdot\|_X)$ and $(Y, \|\cdot\|_Y)$ be real normed spaces; let S be an open and nonempty subset of X and let $f : S \to Y$ be a given mapping. Moreover, let $\overline{x} \in S$ be a given element. If there exists a linear and continuous mapping $f'(\overline{x}) : X \to Y$ with the property*

$$\lim_{\|h\|_X \to 0} \frac{\|f(\overline{x} + h) - f(\overline{x}) - f'(\overline{x})(h)\|_Y}{\|h\|_X} = 0,$$

then $f'(\overline{x})$ is called the Fréchet derivative of f at $\overline{x}$ and f is called Fréchet differentiable at $\overline{x}$.

Such a definition is equivalent to:

$$f(\overline{x} + h) = f(\overline{x}) + f'(\overline{x})(h) + o(\|h\|_X), \tag{C.2}$$

where $o(\|h\|_X)$ has the following property:

$$\lim_{\|h\|_X \to 0} \frac{o(\|h\|_X)}{\|h\|_X} = \lim_{\|h\|_X \to 0} \frac{f(\overline{x} + h) - f(\overline{x}) - f'(\overline{x})(h)}{\|h\|_X} = 0_Y.$$

Let us recall now some important properties of Fréchet derivatives.

Theorem C.4 *Let $(X, \|\cdot\|_X)$ and $(Y, \|\cdot\|_Y)$ be real normed spaces; let S be an open and nonempty subset of X and let $f : S \to Y$ be a given mapping. If there exists the Fréchet derivative of f at $\overline{x} \in S$, then there exists the Gâteaux derivative of f at $\overline{x}$ as well and both are equal.*

Corollary C.1 *Let $(X, \|\cdot\|_X)$ and $(Y, \|\cdot\|_Y)$ be real normed spaces; let S be an open and nonempty subset of X and let $f : S \to Y$ be a given mapping. If f is Fréchet differentiable at $\overline{x} \in S$, then the Fréchet derivative is uniquely determined.*

The following theorem states that Fréchet differentiability implies continuity as well.

Theorem C.5 *Let $(X, \|\cdot\|_X)$ and $(Y, \|\cdot\|_Y)$ be real normed spaces; let S be an open and nonempty subset of X and let $f : S \to Y$ be a given mapping. If f is Fréchet differentiable at some $\overline{x} \in S$, then f is continuous at $\overline{x}$.*

Theorem C.6 *Let S be a nonempty, open, and convex subset of a real normed space $(X, \| \cdot \|)$ and let $f : S \to \mathbb{R}$ be a given mapping which is Fréchet differentiable at every $x \in S$. Then the function f is convex if and only if*

$$f(y) \geq f(x) + f'(x)(y - x) \quad \forall x, y \in S. \tag{C.3}$$

Theorem C.7 *Let S be a nonempty, open, and convex subset of a real normed space $(X, \| \cdot \|)$ and let $f : S \to \mathbb{R}$ be a given mapping which is Fréchet differentiable at every $x \in S$. Then the function f is convex if and only if $f'(x)$ is monotone.*

Now we formulate a necessary optimality condition for Gâteaux differentiable functionals.

Theorem C.8 *Let $(X, \| \cdot \|)$ be a real normed space and let $f : X \to \mathbb{R}$ be a given functional. If $\bar{x} \in X$ is a minimal point of f on X and f is Gâteaux differentiable at $\bar{x}$, then it follows*

$$f'(\bar{x})(h) = 0 \quad \forall h \in X.$$

C.3   Subdifferential

Now we present an additional concept of a derivative which is formulated especially for convex functionals (see [85]).

Definition C.5 *Let $(X, \| \cdot \|)$ be a real normed space and let $f : X \to \mathbb{R}$ be a convex functional. For an arbitrary $\bar{x} \in X$ the set $\partial f(\bar{x})$ of all continuous linear functionals l on X such that*

$$f(x) \geq f(\bar{x}) + l(x - \bar{x}) \quad \forall x \in X$$

is called the subdifferential of f at $\bar{x}$. A continuous linear functional $l \in \partial f(\bar{x})$ is called a subgradient of f at $\bar{x}$.

The following lemma gives an equivalent formulation of the subdifferential.

Lemma C.1 *Let $(X, \|\cdot\|)$ be a real normed space and let $f : X \to \mathbb{R}$ be a convex functional. Then we have for an arbitrary $\bar{x} \in X$*

$$\partial f(\bar{x}) = \{l \in X' : f'(\bar{x})(h) \geq l(h) \ \forall h \in X\}$$

(where $f'(\bar{x})(h)$ denotes the directional derivative of f at $\bar{x}$ in the direction h).

The following theorem provides the assumption under which a convex functional has a nonempty subdifferential.

Theorem C.9 *Let $(X, \|\cdot\|)$ be a real normed space and let $f : X \to \mathbb{R}$ be a continuous convex functional. Then the subdifferential $\partial f(\bar{x})$ is nonempty for every $\bar{x} \in X$.*

With the aid of subgradients we can immediately present a necessary and sufficient optimality condition.

Theorem C.10 *Let $(X, \|\cdot\|)$ be a real normed space and let $f : X \to \mathbb{R}$ be a convex functional. A point $\bar{x} \in X$ is a minimal point of f on X if and only if $0_{X'} \in \partial f(\bar{x})$.*

The next theorem establishes the connection between the directional derivative and the subdifferential of a convex functional.

Theorem C.11 *Let $(X, \|\cdot\|)$ be a real normed space and let $f : X \to \mathbb{R}$ be a convex functional. Then for every $\bar{x}, h \in X$ the directional derivative of f at $\bar{x}$ in the direction h is given by*

$$f'(\bar{x})(h) = \max\{l(h) : l \in \partial f(\bar{x})\}.$$

As a result of the previous theorem the following necessary and sufficient optimality condition can be given.

Corollary C.2 *Let $(X, \|\cdot\|)$ be a real normed space, $S \subset X$ nonempty and let $f : X \to \mathbb{R}$ be a continuous convex functional.*

(a) If $\bar{x} \in S$ is a minimal point of f on S and S is star-shaped with respect to $\bar{x}$, then

$$\max\{l(x - \bar{x}) : l \in \partial f(\bar{x})\} \geq 0 \quad \forall x \in S. \tag{C.4}$$

(b) If for some $\bar{x} \in S$ the inequality (C.4) is satisfied, then $\bar{x}$ is a minimal point of f on S.

Appendix D

Variational Inequalities

D.1 Finite Dimension

Definition D.1 *Let* $\mathbb{K} \subseteq \mathbb{R}^n$ *be a nonempty, convex, and closed set and let* $F : \mathbb{K} \to \mathbb{R}^n$. *The finite-dimensional variational inequality is the problem to find* $x^* \in \mathbb{K}$ *such that*

$$\langle F(x^*), x - x^* \rangle \geq 0 \quad \forall x \in \mathbb{K}. \tag{D.1}$$

The following theorems are classical existence results due to Stampacchia.

Theorem D.1 ([79]) *Let* $\mathbb{K} \subseteq \mathbb{R}^n$ *be nonempty, convex, and compact and let* $F : \mathbb{K} \to \mathbb{R}^n$ *be a continuous operator, then (D.1) admits at least one solution.*

Theorem D.2 ([92]) *If* F *is strictly monotone, then the solution of (D.1), if it exists, is unique.*

If the set $\mathbb{K}$ is unbounded, then we need to add the coercivity condition of the function F to get existence results.

Theorem D.3 ([87]) *If*

$$\lim_{\|x\| \to \infty} \frac{\langle F(x) - F(x'), x - x' \rangle}{\|x - x'\|} = \infty \tag{D.2}$$

for $x \in \mathbb{K}$ *and some* $x' \in \mathbb{K}$, *then (D.1) admits a solution.*

D.2   Infinite Dimension

Let X be a reflexive Banach space and let $\mathbb{K} \subset X$ a closed convex set (see also [67] and [68]). Denote by $\mathbb{B}_R$ the closed ball with centre in O and radius R and consider the closed and convex set $\mathbb{K}_r = \mathbb{K} \cap \mathbb{B}_R$.

Theorem D.4 ([151]) *If $F : \mathbb{K} \to X'$ is a monotone function, and hemicontinuous along line segments, then (D.1) admits a solution if and only if there exists a constant R such that at least one solution to the variational inequality*

$$x_R^* \in \mathbb{K}_R \quad \langle F(x_R^*), x - x_R^* \rangle \geq 0, \quad \forall x \in \mathbb{K}_R \qquad (D.3)$$

satisfies the condition

$$\|x_R^*\| < R. \qquad (D.4)$$

If the set $\mathbb{K}$ is unbounded, then the following conditions for the existence of solutions are provided:

1. if there exist $x_0^* \in \mathbb{K}$ and $R > \|x_0^*\|$ such that $\langle F(x), x_0^* - x \rangle < 0$, $\forall x \in \mathbb{K}$, $\|x\| = R$, then (D.4) is satisfied;

2. if there exists x_0^* such that F satisfies the coercivity condition (D.2), then (D.3) holds;

3. if the following weak coercivity condition holds

$$\lim_{\|x\| \to \infty} \frac{\langle F(x), x \rangle}{\|x\|} = +\infty, \quad \forall x \in \mathbb{K},$$

then (D.4) is verified.

Theorem D.5 ([46]) *Let X be a real vector topological space and let $\mathbb{K} \subseteq X$ be a nonempty and convex set. Let $F : \mathbb{K} \to X'$ be a given function such that*

1. *there exist two sets $A \subseteq \mathbb{K}$ nonempty and compact, and $B \subseteq \mathbb{K}$ compact and convex such that $\forall x \in \mathbb{K} \setminus A$ there exists $y \in B$ with $\langle F(x), y - x \rangle < 0$;*

and furthermore

2. *F is pseudomonotone and hemicontinuous along line segments.*

Then there exists $\bar{x} \in A$ such that $\langle F(\bar{x}), y - \bar{x} \rangle \geq 0 \quad \forall y \in \mathbb{K}$.

Theorem D.6 ([46]) *Let X be a real vector topological space and let $\mathbb{K} \subseteq X$ be a nonempty and convex set. Let $F : \mathbb{K} \to X'$ be a given function such that*

1. *there exist two sets $A \subseteq \mathbb{K}$ nonempty and compact, and $B \subseteq \mathbb{K}$ compact and convex such that, $\forall x \in \mathbb{K} \setminus A$ there exists $y \in B$ with $\langle F(x), y - x \rangle < 0$;*

and furthermore

2. *F is hemicontinuous.*

Then there exists $\bar{x} \in A$ such that $\langle F(\bar{x}), y - \bar{x} \rangle \geq 0 \quad \forall y \in \mathbb{K}$.

In order to obtain the next result, we need to recall the definition of an inner point.

Definition D.2 *Let B be a real Banach space. A point $x_0 \in B$ is called an inner point of a nonempty set $D \subseteq B$ if for all $u \in B' \setminus \{0\}$*

$$\langle x, u \rangle \leq \langle x_0, u \rangle \quad \forall x \in D \text{ implies } \langle x, u \rangle = \langle x_0, u \rangle \quad \forall x \in D.$$

By using the quasi-monotonicity assumption, we derive the following theorem.

Theorem D.7 ([145]) *Let B be a reflexive Banach space. Consider a nonempty, closed, and convex set $\mathbb{K} \subseteq B$ having an inner point and such that it is either bounded or there exists $\rho > 0$ such that $\forall x \in \mathbb{K}$ with $\|x\| \geq \rho$ there exists $y \in \mathbb{K}$ satisfying the following conditions*

$$\| y \| < \rho \text{ and } \langle x - y, F(x) \rangle \geq 0.$$

Let $F : \mathbb{K} \to B'$ be hemicontinuous along line segments and quasi-monotone. Then the variational inequality

$$\bar{x} \in \mathbb{K} \quad \langle x - \bar{x}, F(\bar{x}) \rangle \geq 0, \quad \forall x \in \mathbb{K}$$

admits a solution.

With a weakened coercivity assumption, we get the following theorem.

Theorem D.8 (See [142]) *Let X be a Hausdorff real topological vector space and $\mathbb{K} \subset X$ be a closed and convex subset with nonempty relative interior (that is the interior of $\mathbb{K}$ in its affine hull) and $\Phi : \mathbb{K} \to X'$ a weakly* continuous function. Moreover, let $\mathbb{K}_1$ and $\mathbb{K}_2$ be two nonempty and compact subsets of X with $\mathbb{K}_2 \subseteq \mathbb{K}_1$ and $\mathbb{K}_2$ having finite dimension, such that $\forall x \in X \setminus \mathbb{K}_1$, we have:*

$$\sup_{y \in \mathbb{K}_2} \langle \Phi(x), x - y \rangle > 0.$$

Then the variational inequality

$$\langle \Phi(x), y - x \rangle \geq 0 \quad \forall y \in \mathbb{K}$$

admits solutions in $\mathbb{K}$.

Finally, we are interested in existence theorems for minimal points.

Theorem D.9 *Let $(X, \|\cdot\|)$ be a real normed space, let S be a nonempty and weakly sequentially compact subset of X and let $f : S \to \mathbb{R}$ be a weakly lower semicontinuous functional, then there is at least one $\bar{x} \in S$ such that*

$$f(\bar{x}) \leq f(x) \text{ for all } x \in S.$$

In addition to Corollary B.1, now we are able to give more general assumptions under which every continuous functional is also weakly lower semicontinuous.

Lemma D.1 *Let $(X, \|\cdot\|)$ be a real normed space, let S be a nonempty, convex, and closed subset of X and let $f : S \to \mathbb{R}$ be a continuous and quasi-convex functional, then f is weakly lower semicontinuous.*

Now we need to recall some important definitions to get the next result.

Definition D.3 *Let B be a reflexive Banach space and let $\mathbb{K} \subseteq B$ be a nonempty, closed, and convex cone which induces the partial order*

$$x \leq y \quad \text{for } x, y \in B \quad \text{if } y - x \in \mathbb{K}.$$

Then B is called a vector lattice with respect to $\leq$ if for all x, $y \in B$, there exists a unique element, called infimum and denoted by $x \wedge y$, such that

$$x \wedge y \leq x, \ x \wedge y \leq y \quad \text{and} \quad z \leq x, \ z \leq y \Longrightarrow z \leq x \wedge y.$$

Definition D.4 Let B be a reflexive Banach space and let $\mathbb{K} \subseteq B$ be a nonempty, closed, and convex cone which induces the partial order

$$x \leq y \quad \text{for } x, y \in B \quad \text{if } y - x \in \mathbb{K}.$$

A map $T : \mathbb{K} \to B'$ is called a Z-map if

$$\langle z, T(x) - T(y) \rangle \leq 0 \ \text{whenever} \ (x - y) \wedge z = 0.$$

Definition D.5 The map T is called positive at infinity if $\forall x \in \mathbb{K}$ there exists $\rho(x) > 0$ such that

$$\langle y - x, T(y) \rangle > 0 \quad \forall y \in \mathbb{K}, \ \|y\| \geq \rho(x).$$

Theorem D.10 ([145]) Let B be a real reflexive Banach space and $\mathbb{K} \subseteq B$ a nonempty, closed, convex cone such that B is a vector lattice. Consider a hemicontinuous, strictly pseudomonotone Z-map $T : \mathbb{K} \to B'$ which is positive at infinity. Let $u \in \mathbb{K}'$ be strictly positive. Then there exists a unique $\bar{x} \in \mathcal{F} = \{x \in B : x \in \mathbb{K}, T(x) \in \mathbb{K}'\}$ which is a solution to the variational inequality:

$$\bar{x} \in \mathbb{K} : \langle x - \bar{x}, T(\bar{x}) \rangle \geq 0 \quad \forall x \in \mathbb{K}.$$

Appendix E

Quasi-Variational Inequalities

E.1 Finite Dimension

Definition E.1 *Let X be a nonempty subset of $\mathbb{R}^m$ and let $F : X \to \mathbb{R}^m$ and $K : X \to 2^X$ be a function and a multifunction, respectively. The quasi-variational inequality is the problem to find $x^* \in K(x^*)$ such that*

$$\langle F(x^*), x - x^* \rangle \geq 0, \quad \forall x \in K(x^*). \tag{E.1}$$

Theorem E.1 (See [78]) *If X is a compact and convex set, F, K are continuous and, $\forall x^* \in X$, $K(x^*)$ is a nonempty, closed, and convex subset of $\mathbb{R}^m_+$, then (E.1) admits a solution.*

Theorem E.2 ([51]) *If X is a compact and convex set, K is continuous, $\forall x^* \in X$ the set $K(x^*)$ is a nonempty, closed, and convex subset of $\mathbb{R}^m_+$ and F is such that $\{x^* \in X : F(x^*)x \leq 0\}$ is closed $\forall x \in X - X$, then (E.1) admits a solution.*

Theorem E.3 ([48]) *If X is a compact and convex set, K is continuous, $\forall x^* \in X$ the set $K(x^*)$ is a nonempty, closed, and convex subset of $\mathbb{R}^m_+$ and $F : X \to 2^{\mathbb{R}^m_+}$ is a multifunction (possibly discontinuous) such that:*

$$\forall x \in X - X \text{ the set } G_x = \left\{ x^* \in X : \inf_{z \in F(x^*)} z\,x \leq 0 \right\} \text{ is closed,}$$

then there exist $x^* \in K(x^*) \cap X$ and $z \in F(x^*)$ such that $z(x - x^*) \geq 0$, $\forall x \in K(x^*) \cap X$.

E.2   Infinite Dimension

The quasi-variational inequality (E.1) (see also [14]) can be extended to an infinite dimensional setting by replacing $\mathbb{R}^m$ with a real topological vector space Y and assuming $F : X \rightarrow Y'$, where Y' is the topological dual space of Y. Hence, we have the following existence theorems for quasi-variational inequalities in infinite dimension.

Theorem E.4 ([154]) *If Y is a topological linear locally convex Hausdorff space, $X \subset Y$ is a convex, compact, and nonempty set, $F : X \rightarrow 2^{Y'}$ is an u. s. c. multivalued mapping with $F(x)$, $x \in X$, convex, compact, and nonempty and $K : X \rightarrow 2^X$ is a closed l. s. c. multivalued mapping with $K(x)$, $x \in X$, convex, compact, and nonempty and $\varphi : X \rightarrow \mathbb{R}$ is a convex l. s. c. function, then there exists $x^* \in F$ such that:*

1. $x^* \in K(x^*)$,

2. *there exists $u^* \in F(x^*)$ for which*

$$\langle x - x^*, u^* \rangle + \varphi(x) - \varphi(x^*) \geq 0, \quad \forall x \in K(x^*).$$

Theorem E.5 ([155]) *Let X be a convex subset in a locally convex Hausdorff topological vector space Y. Let us assume that:*

(i) *$K : X \rightarrow 2^X$ is a closed l. s. c. correspondence with nonempty, closed, and convex values;*

(ii) *$F : X \rightarrow Y'$ is a monotone, continuous along line segments and bounded single-valued map;*

(iii) *there exist a nonempty, compact, convex set $Z \subset X$ and a nonempty subset $B \subset Z$ such that:*

(iiia) *$K(B) \subset Z$;*

(iiib) *$K(x) \cap Z \neq \emptyset$ for all $x \in Z$;*

(iiic) *for each $x \in Z \backslash B$ there exists $\hat{x} \in K(x) \cap Z$ with $\langle F(x), \hat{x} - x \rangle < 0$.*

Then there exists x^* such that:

$$x^* \in K(x^*) \quad \langle F(x^*), x - x^* \rangle \geq 0, \quad x \in K(x^*).$$

Appendix F

Infinite Dimensional Duality

The separation theorems play a very important role in the duality theory. In the infinite-dimensional case the following simple separation theorem, in which the concepts of quasi interior and quasi relative interior are involved, is fundamental.

Theorem F.1 *If $\bar{x} \in$ qbdry $\mathbb{K}$, then there exists $g \neq 0_{\mathbb{K}}$ such that $g(x) \leq g(\bar{x}) \ \forall x \in \mathbb{K}$.*

Proof: If $\bar{x} \in$ qbdry $\mathbb{K}$, then $\bar{x} \notin$ qi $\mathbb{K}$ and hence $T_{\mathbb{K}}(\bar{x}) \neq H$ and $N_{\mathbb{K}}(\bar{x}) \neq \{0_{\mathbb{K}}\}$. As a consequence, let $g \in N_{\mathbb{K}}(\bar{x})$. It follows $\langle g, x - \bar{x} \rangle \leq 0$ $\forall x \in \mathbb{K}$ and the assertion is achieved. $\qquad\square$

Obviously, Theorem F.1 holds even if we use the notion of qri $\mathbb{K}$ instead of that of qi $\mathbb{K}$ (see [40]).

First of all, we recall the following definition.

Definition F.1 *Let S be a nonempty subset of a real linear space X and let Y be a real linear space partially ordered by a convex cone C. A function $f : S \to Y$ is called convex-like if the set $f(S) + C$ is convex.*

Now we make the following assumptions which we denote by (Hp.1):

- let X be a real linear topological space;

- let S be a nonempty subset of X;

- let $(Y\|\cdot\|)$ be a Hilbert space partially ordered by a convex cone C;

- let $f : S \to \mathbb{R}$ and $g : S \to Y$ be two functions such that the function $(f,g) : S \to \mathbb{R} \times Y$ is convex-like with respect to the cone $\mathbb{R}_+ \times C$ of $\mathbb{R} \times Y$;

- let qri $[g(S) + C] \neq \emptyset$;

- let the set $T = \{x \in S : g(x) \in -C\}$ be nonempty;

- let qri $C \neq \emptyset$ and cl $(C - C) = Y$.

Let us consider the minimum problem

$$\min_{x \in T} f(x) \tag{F.1}$$

and its dual problem

$$\max_{u \in C'} \inf_{x \in S} [f(x) + u(g(x))], \tag{F.2}$$

where C' is the dual cone of C. Actually, in our case, since Y is a Hilbert space, we can assume $C = C'$.

In [40] the following theorem is proved where the condition of nonempty quasi interior is replaced by the one of nonempty quasi relative interior, which is verified in the applications till now examined.

Theorem F.2 *Let the assumptions (Hp.1) be satisfied and let $\hat{x} \in S$ exist such that $g(\hat{x}) \in -$ qri C. If problem (F.1) is solvable, then problem (F.2) is also solvable and the extremal values of the two problems are equal.*

From the above theorem the following interesting characterization in terms of saddle points holds.

Theorem F.3 *If $\bar{x} \in S$ is a solution to problem (F.1), then there exists $\bar{u} \in C'$ such that $(\bar{x}, \bar{u}) \in S \times C'$ is a saddle point of the Lagrangean functional*

$$\mathcal{L}(x, u) = f(x) + u(g(x)) \quad \forall x \in S \text{ and } u \in C',$$

namely

$$\mathcal{L}(\bar{x}, u) \leq \mathcal{L}(\bar{x}, \bar{u}) \leq \mathcal{L}(x, \bar{u}) \quad \forall x \in S, \forall u \in C'.$$

We remark that Theorem F.3 holds since we are working under the assumption qri $C \neq \emptyset$, which is verified in the applications, whereas theorems of this type known in the literature do not work for the applications, because they require int $C \neq \emptyset$, which usually is not fulfilled.

In the previous problem we have considered only constraints of the type $g(x) \in -C$. We now consider a minimum problem with the presence also of constraints of the kind $h(x) = 0$.

First of all, we make the following assumptions which we denote by (Hp.2):

- let $(X, \| \cdot \|_X)$ and $(Z, \| \cdot \|)_Z$ be real Banach spaces;

- let $(Y, \| \cdot \|_Y)$ be a partially ordered real normed space with ordering cone C;

- let $\hat{S}$ be a convex subset of X;

- let $f : X \to \mathbb{R}$ be a given functional;

- let $g : X \to Y$, $h : X \to Z$ be given mappings;

- let the constraint set $S = \left\{ x \in \hat{S} : g(x) \in -C, \ h(x) = 0_Z \right\}$ be nonempty.

Under these assumptions, we consider the optimization problem

$$\min_{x \in S} f(x).$$

The following theorem presents the generalized Lagrangean multiplier rule.

Theorem F.4 ([85]) *Let the assumptions (Hp.2) be satisfied and let $\bar{x}$ be a minimal point of f in S. Let the functional f and the mapping g be Fréchet differentiable at $\bar{x}$. Let the mapping h be Fréchet differentiable in a neighborhood of $\bar{x}$, let $h'(\cdot)$ be continuous at $\bar{x}$. Let the set*

$$\begin{pmatrix} g'(\bar{x}) \\ h'(\bar{x}) \end{pmatrix} \text{cone } (\hat{S} - \{\bar{x}\}) + \text{cone } \begin{pmatrix} C + \{g(\bar{x})\} \\ \{0_Z\} \end{pmatrix}$$

be closed. Then there are a real number $\mu > 0$ and continuous linear functionals $l_1 \in C'$ and $l_2 \in Z'$ with $(\mu, l_1, l_2) \neq (0, 0_{Y'}, 0_{Z'})$ such that

$$[\mu\, f'(\bar{x}) + l_1(g'(\bar{x})) + l_2(h'(\bar{x}))]\,(x - \bar{x}) \geq 0 \quad \forall x \in \hat{S} \qquad (F.3)$$

and

$$l_1(g(\bar{x})) = 0. \qquad (F.4)$$

The following condition

$$\left(\begin{array}{c} g'(\bar{x}) \\ h'(\bar{x}) \end{array} \right) \text{cone } (\hat{S} - \{\bar{x}\}) + \text{cone } \left(\begin{array}{c} C + \{g(\bar{x})\} \\ \{0_Z\} \end{array} \right) = Y \times Z \qquad (F.5)$$

is known as the *Kurcyusz-Robinson-Zowe condition.*

Under the assumptions (Hp.2) it is possible to consider the Lagrangean functional

$$L = f + l_1(g) + l_2(h) \qquad (F.6)$$

and, as a consequence, (F.3) can be rewritten as follows:

$$L'(\bar{x})(x - \bar{x}) \geq 0 \quad \forall x \in \hat{S},$$

where $L'(\bar{x})$ denotes the Fréchet derivative of the Lagrangean functional at $\bar{x}$, namely:

$$L'(\bar{x}) = f'(\bar{x}) + l_1(g'(\bar{x})) + l_2(h'(\bar{x})).$$

Then the following result holds.

Theorem F.5 *In addition to the assumptions of Theorem F.4 let us assume that f, g, h are convex, then $\bar{x} \in S$ is a minimal point of the problem $\min\limits_{x \in S} f(x)$ if and only if there exist $\bar{l}_1 \in C'$, and $\bar{l}_2 \in Z'$ such that the triplet $(\bar{x}, \bar{l}_1, \bar{l}_2)$ is a saddle point of the Lagrangean functional (F.6), namely*

$$L(\bar{x}, l_1, l_2) \leq L(\bar{x}, \bar{l}_1, \bar{l}_2) \leq L(x, \bar{l}_1, \bar{l}_2) \quad \forall x \in \hat{S}, \; \forall l_1 \in C', \; \forall l_2 \in Z'$$

and, moreover, it results that

$$l_1(g(\bar{x})) = 0.$$

Proof: Let us start assuming that $f(\bar{x}) = \min\limits_{x \in S} f(x)$. Then

$$L'(\bar{x})(x - \bar{x}) \geq 0, \quad \forall x \in \hat{S}. \tag{F.7}$$

Since $L(x, \bar{l}_1, \bar{l}_2)$ is a convex function, condition (F.7) is sufficient to ensure that $\bar{x}$ is a minimal point of the problem $\min\limits_{x \in \hat{S}} L(x, \bar{l}_1, \bar{l}_2)$, namely:

$$L(x, \bar{l}_1, \bar{l}_2) \geq L(\bar{x}, \bar{l}_1, \bar{l}_2), \quad \forall x \in \hat{S}.$$

We have to prove now that

$$L(\bar{x}, l_1, l_2) \leq L(\bar{x}, \bar{l}_1, \bar{l}_2), \quad \forall l_1 \in C' \text{ and } \forall l_2 \in Z',$$

which means:

$$l_1(g(\bar{x})) \leq 0 \quad \forall l_1 \in C'.$$

We recall that $l_1(y) \geq 0 \, \forall y \in C'$; moreover, $g(\bar{x}) \in -C$ means $-g(\bar{x}) \in C$, hence $l_1(-g(\bar{x})) \geq 0 \, \forall l_1 \in C'$ and, because of the linearity of l_1, we get $-l_1(g(\bar{x})) \geq 0 \, \forall l_1 \in C'$, or, equivalently: $l_1(g(\bar{x})) \leq 0 \, \forall l_1 \in C'$.

Conversely, let us assume that $(\bar{x}, \bar{l}_1, \bar{l}_2)$ is a saddle point of the Lagrangean functional (F.6):

$$L(\bar{x}, l_1, l_2) \leq L(\bar{x}, \bar{l}_1, \bar{l}_2) \leq L(x, \bar{l}_1, \bar{l}_2) \quad \forall x \in \hat{S}, \, \forall l_1 \in C', \, \forall l_2 \in Z'.$$

The right-hand side is equivalent to:

$$f(\bar{x}) + \bar{l}_1(g(\bar{x})) + \bar{l}_2(h(\bar{x})) \leq f(x) + \bar{l}_1(g(x)) + \bar{l}_2(h(x)) \quad \forall x \in \hat{S},$$

that is:

$$f(\bar{x}) \leq f(x) + \bar{l}_1(g(\bar{x})) + \bar{l}_2(h(\bar{x})) \quad \forall x \in \hat{S}. \tag{F.8}$$

If we choose $x \in S$, then $-g(x) \in C$ and $h(x) = 0$, so $\bar{l}_1(g(x)) = 0$ and $\bar{l}_2(h(x)) = 0$. Moreover, $\bar{l}_1(g(\bar{x})) = 0$ by assumption and $\bar{l}_2(h(\bar{x})) = 0$, hence (F.8) becomes

$$f(\bar{x}) \leq f(x) \quad \forall x \in S. \qquad \square$$

As an application of Theorem F.5 we get the following theorem.

Theorem F.6 $u \in \mathbb{K}$ *is a solution to the variational inequality*

$$Find \ u \in \mathbb{K} \ such \ that$$

$$\ll F(u), v - u \gg = \int_0^T \langle F(t, u(t)), v(t) - u(t) \rangle \, dt \geq 0 \ \forall v \in \mathbb{K}, \quad (F.9)$$

where

$$\mathbb{K} = \left\{ u \in L^2([0, T], \mathbb{R}^q) : \lambda(t) \leq u(t) \leq \mu(t) \ a.e. \ in \ [0, T]; \right.$$

$$\sum_{i=1}^q \xi_{ji} u_i(t) = \rho_j(t) \ a.e. \ in \ [0, T],$$

$$\left. \xi_{ji} \in \{0, 1\}, \ i \in \{1, \ldots, q\}, \ j \in \{1, \ldots, l\} \right\}$$

if and only if there exist $\bar{l}_1, \bar{l}_2 \in C$ and $\overline{m} \in L^2([0, T], \mathbb{R}^l)$ such that $(u, \bar{l}_1, \bar{l}_2, \overline{m})$ is a saddle point of the Lagrangean functional

$$\mathcal{L}(v, l_1, l_2, m) = \Psi(v) - \int_\Omega \langle l_1(t), v(t) - \lambda(t) \rangle \, dt$$

$$+ \int_\Omega \langle l_2(t), v(t) - \mu(t) \rangle \, dt + \int_\Omega \langle m(t), \Phi v(t) - \rho(t) \rangle \, dt$$

$$\forall v \in L^2([0, T], \mathbb{R}^q), \quad \forall l_1, l_2 \in C, \ \forall m \in L^2([0, T], \mathbb{R}^l),$$

where $\psi(v) = \ll F(u), v - u \gg$, namely

$$\mathcal{L}(u, l_1, l_2, m) \leq \mathcal{L}(u, \bar{l}_1, \bar{l}_2, \overline{m}) \leq \mathcal{L}(v, \bar{l}_1, \bar{l}_2, \overline{m})$$

$$\forall v \in L^2([0, T], \mathbb{R}^q), \quad \forall l_1, l_2 \in C \ and \ \forall m \in L^2([0, T], \mathbb{R}^l)$$

and in addition

$$\int_0^T \langle \bar{l}_1(t), u(t) - \lambda(t) \rangle \, dt = 0, \quad \int_0^T \langle \bar{l}_2(t), u(t) - \mu(t) \rangle \, dt = 0.$$

Bibliography

[1] H. Attouch and A. Damlamian, *Problèmes d'Évolution dans les Espaces de Hilbert et Applications*, Journal de Mathématiques Pures et Appliquées, **54**, 1975, 53–74.

[2] J.P. Aubin and A. Cellina, **Differential Inclusions**, Springer-Verlag, Berlin, Germany, 1984.

[3] A. Auslender, **Optimisation: Méthodes Numériques**, Masson, Paris, France, 1976.

[4] C. Baiocchi and A. Capelo, **Variational and Quasivariational Inequalities: Applications to Free Boundary Problems**, John Wiley and Sons, New York, 1984.

[5] A. Barbagallo, *Regularity Results for Time-dependent Variational and Quasi-variational Inequalities and Computational Procedures*, M3AS: Mathematical Models and Methods in Applied Sciences, 2006.

[6] M.J. Beckmann, C.B. McGuire and C.B. Winstein, **Studies in the Economics of Transportation**, Yale University Press, New Haven, Connecticut, 1956.

[7] M.C.J. Bliemer and P.H.L. Bovy, *Quasi-Variational Inequality Formulation of the Multiclass Dynamic Traffic Assignment Problem*, Transportation Research, **37**, 2003, 501–519.

[8] J.M. Borwein and A.S. Lewis, *Partially Finite Convex Programming, Part I: Quasi Relative Interiors and Duality Theory*, Mathematical Programming, **57**, 1992, 15–48.

[9] H. Brezis, *Inequations d'Évolution Abstraites*, Comptes Rendus de l'Académie des Sciences Paris, Ser. A-B 264, 1967, 732–735.

[10] H. Brezis, **Analyse Fonctionnelle: Théorie et Applications**, Masson, Paris, 1983.

[11] F. Cammaroto and B. Di Bella, *Separation Theorem Based on the Quasirelative Interior and Application to Duality Theory*, Journal of Optimization Theory and Applications, **125**, no. 1, 2005, 223–229.

[12] C. Carstensen and J. Gwinner, *A Theory of Discretization for Nonlinear Evolution Inequalities Applied to Parabolic Signorini Problems*, Annali di Matematica Pura e Applicata, **177**, 1999, 363–394.

[13] M. Castellani and G. Mastroeni, *On the Duality Theory for Finite Dimensional Variational Inequalities*, in **Variational Inequalities and Network Equilibrium Problems**, F. Giannessi and A. Maugeri (eds), Plenum Publishing, New York, 1995, 21–31.

[14] D. Chan and J.S. Pang, *The Generalized Quasi-Variational Inequality Problem*, Mathematics of Operations Research, **7**, no. 2, 1982, 211–224.

[15] M.G. Cojocaru, *Projected Dynamical Systems on Hilbert Spaces*, PhD Thesis, Queen's University, Canada, 2002.

[16] M.G. Cojocaru, P. Daniele and A. Nagurney, *Projected Dynamical Systems and Evolutionary (Time-Dependent) Variational Inequalities Via Hilbert Spaces with Applications*, Journal of Optimization Theory and Applications, **27**, no. 3, 2005, 1–15.

[17] M.G. Cojocaru, P. Daniele and A. Nagurney, *Double-Layered Dynamics: A Unified Theory of Projected Dynamical Systems and Evolutionary Variational Inequalities*, European Journal of Operational Research, forthcoming.

[18] M.G. Cojocaru, P. Daniele and A. Nagurney, *Projected Dynamical Systems, Evolutionary Variational Inequalities, Applications, and a Computational Procedure*, in **Pareto Optimality, Game Theory**

and Equilibria, A. Migdalas, P. Pardalos and L. Pitsoulis (eds), Nonconvex Optimization and its Applications Series (NOIA), Springer, Berlin, Germany, 2005.

[19] M.G. Cojocaru and L.B. Jonker, *Existence of Solutions to Projected Differential Equations in Hilbert Spaces*, Proceedings of the American Mathematical Society, **132**, 2004, 183–193.

[20] J.B. Conway, **A Course in Functional Analysis**, 2nd Edition, Springer, New York, 1990.

[21] B. Cornet, *Existence of Slow Solutions for a Class of Differential Inclusions*, Journal of Mathematical Analysis and Applications, **96**, 1983, 130–147.

[22] A.A. Cournot, **Researches into the Mathematical Principles of the Theory of Wealth**, 1838, English translation, Macmillan, London, England, 1897.

[23] P. Cubiotti, *Generalized Quasi-Variational Inequalities Without Continuities*, Journal of Optimization Theory and Applications, **92**, no. 3, 1997, 477–495.

[24] P. Cubiotti and N.D. Yen, *A Result Related to Ricceri's Conjecture on Generalized Quasi-Variational Inequalities*, Archivum Mathematicum, **69**, 1997, 507–514.

[25] S. Dafermos, *Traffic Equilibrium and Variational Inequalities*, Transportation Science, **14**, 1980, 42–54.

[26] S. Dafermos, *Exchange Price Equilibrium and Variational Inequalities*, Mathematical Programming, **46**, 1990, 391–402.

[27] S. Dafermos and A. Nagurney, *Sensitivity Analysis for the General Spatial Economic Equilibrium Problem*, Operations Research, **32**, 1984, 1069–1086.

[28] S.C. Dafermos and F.T. Sparrow, *The Traffic Assignment Problem for a General Network*, Journal of Research of the National Bureau of Standards, **73B**, 1969, 91–118.

[29] P. Daniele, *Dual Variational Inequality and Applications to Asymmetric Traffic Equilibrium Problem with Capacity Constraints*, Le Matematiche, **49**, Fasc. II, 1994, 211–222.

[30] P. Daniele, *Duality Theory for Variational Inequalities*, Communications in Applied Analysis, **1**, no. 2, 1997, 257–167.

[31] P. Daniele, *A Remark on a Dynamic Model of a Quasi-Variational Inequality*, Rendiconti del Circolo Matematico di Palermo, Serie II, Suppl. **48**, 1997, 91–100.

[32] P. Daniele, *Lagrangean Function for Dynamic Variational Inequalities*, Rendiconti del Circolo Matematico di Palermo, Serie II, Suppl. **58**, 1999, 101–119.

[33] P. Daniele, *Variational Inequalities, Equivalent Optimization Problems and Associated Lagrangean Function*, in **Proceedings of the 9th International Colloquium on Differential Equations**, D. Bainov (ed), VSP, Utrecht, The Netherlands, 1999, 107–112.

[34] P. Daniele, *Variational Inequalities for Static Equilibrium Market: Lagrangean Function and Duality*, in **Equilibrium Problems: Nonsmooth Optimization and Variational Inequality Models**, F. Giannessi, A. Maugeri and P. Pardalos (eds), Kluwer Academic Publishers, Dordrecht, The Netherlands, 2001, 43–58.

[35] P. Daniele, *Evolutionary Variational Inequalities and Economic Models for Demand–Supply Markets*, M3AS: Mathematical Models and Methods in Applied Sciences, **4**, no. 13, 2003, 471–489.

[36] P. Daniele, *Variational Inequalities for Evolutionary Financial Equilibrium*, in **Innovations in Financial and Economic Networks**, A. Nagurney (ed), Edward Elgar Publishing, Cheltenham, England, 2003, 84–109.

[37] P. Daniele, *Time-Dependent Spatial Price Equilibrium Problem: Existence and Stability Results for the Quantity Formulation Model*, Journal of Global Optimization, **28**, 2004, 283–295.

[38] P. Daniele, *Variational Inequalities for General Evolutionary Financial Equilibrium*, in **Variational Analysis and Applications**, F. Giannessi and A. Maugeri (eds), Springer, New York, 2005, 279–299.

[39] P. Daniele, F. Giannessi and A. Maugeri (eds), **Equilibrium Problems and Variational Models**, Kluwer Academic Publishers, Boston, Massachusetts, 2002.

[40] P. Daniele, S. Giuffrè, G. Idone and A. Maugeri, *Infinite Dimensional Duality and Applications*, forthcoming.

[41] P. Daniele, S. Giuffrè and S. Pià, *Competitive Financial Equilibrium Problems with Policy Interventions*, Journal of Industrial and Management Optimization, **1**, no. 1, 2005, 39–52.

[42] P. Daniele and A. Maugeri, *Vector Variational Inequalities and Modelling of a Continuum Traffic Equilibrium Problem*, in **Vector Variational Inequalities and Vector Equilibria**, F. Giannessi (ed), Kluwer Academic Publishers, The Netherlands, 2000, 97–111.

[43] P. Daniele and A. Maugeri, *On Dynamical Equilibrium Problems and Variational Inequalities*, **Equilibrium Problems: Non-smooth Optimization and Variational Inequality Models**, F. Giannessi, A. Maugeri and P. Pardalos (eds), Kluwer Academic Publishers, The Netherlands, 2001, 59–69.

[44] P. Daniele and A. Maugeri, *The Economic Model for Demand–Supply Problems*, in **Equilibrium Problems and Variational Models**, P. Daniele, F. Giannessi and A. Maugeri (eds), Kluwer Academic Publishers, Boston, Massachusetts, 2002, 61–78.

[45] P. Daniele, A. Maugeri and W. Oettli, *Variational Inequalities and Time-Dependent Traffic Equilibria*, Comptes Rendus de l'Académie des Sciences Paris, **326**, Serie I, 1998, 1059–1062.

[46] P. Daniele, A. Maugeri and W. Oettli, *Time-Dependent Traffic Equilibria*, Journal of Optimization Theory and Applications, **103**, 1999, 543–555.

[47] E. De Giorgi, *Teoremi di Semicontinuità nel Calcolo delle Variazioni*, Istituto Nazionale di Alta Matematica, 1968.

[48] M. De Luca, *Generalized Quasi-Variational Inequality and Traffic Equilibrium Problems*, in **Variational Inequalities and Network Equilibrium Problems**, F. Giannessi and A. Maugeri (eds), Plenum Publishing, New York, 1995, 45–55.

[49] M. De Luca, *Existence of Solutions for a Time-Dependent Quasi-Variational Inequality*, Rendiconti del Circolo Matematico di Palermo, Serie II, Suppl. **48**, 1997, 101–106.

[50] M. De Luca and A. Maugeri, *Quasi-Variational Inequalities and Applications to the Traffic Equilibrium Problem; Discussion of a Paradox*, Journal of Computational and Applied Mathematics, **28**, 1989, 163–171.

[51] M. De Luca and A. Maugeri *Discontinuous Quasi-Variational Inequalities and Applications to Equilibrium Problems*, **Nonsmooth Optimization: Methods and Applications**, F. Giannessi (ed), Gordon and Breach Science Publishers, London, 1992, 70–74.

[52] M.B. Donato, M. Milasi and C. Vitanza, *Sensitivity Analysis for Time Dependent Spatial Price Equilibrium Problem*, Mathematics and Computers in Simulation, **71**, 2006, 229–239.

[53] J. Dong, *Formulation and Computation of General Financial Equilibria in the Presence of Taxes and Price Controls*, School of Management, University of Massachusetts, Amherst, Massachusetts, 1992.

[54] J. Dong, D. Zhang and A. Nagurney, *A Projected Dynamical Systems Model of General Financial Equilibrium with Stability Analysis*, Mathematical and Computer Modelling, **24**, 1996, 35–44.

[55] P. Dupuis and H. Ishii, *On Lipschitz Continuity of the Solution Mapping to the Skorokhod Problem, with Applications*, Stochastics and Stochastics Reports, **35**, 1990, 31–62.

[56] P. Dupuis and A. Nagurney, *Dynamical Systems and Variational Inequalities*, Annals of Operations Research, **44**, 1993, 9–42.

[57] S. Enke, *Equilibrium among Spatially Separated Markets: Solution by Electronic Analogue*, Econometrica, **10**, 1951, 40–47.

[58] P. Ferrari, *Equilibrium in Asymmetric Multimodal Transport Networks with Capacity Constraints*, Le Matematiche, **49**, 1994, 223–241.

[59] P. Ferrari, *Equilibrium in Transport Networks with Capacity Constraints*, in **Variational Inequalities and Network Equilibrium Problems**, F. Giannessi and A. Maugeri (eds), Plenum Publishing, New York, 1995, 85–100.

[60] G. Fichera, *Problemi Elastostatici con Vincoli Unilaterali: il Problema di Signorini con Ambigue Condizioni al Contorno*, Memorie dell'Accademia Nazionale dei Lincei, 1964, 91–140.

[61] T.L. Friesz, D. Bernstein, T.E. Smith, R.L. Tobin and B.W. Wie, *A Variational Inequality Formulation of the Dynamic Network User Equilibrium Problem*, Operations Research, **41**, 1993, 179–191.

[62] S. Fucik and A. Kufner, **Nonlinear Differential Equations**, Elsevier Scientific Publishing Company, New York, 1980.

[63] M. Fukushima and T. Itoh, *A Dual Approach to Asymmetric Traffic Equilibrium Problems*, Mathematica Japonica, **32**, 1987, 701–721.

[64] D. Gabay and H. Moulin, *On the Uniqueness and Stability of Nash Equilibria in Noncooperative Games*, in **Applied Stochastic Control of Econometrics and Management Science**, A. Bensoussan, P. Kleindorfer and C. S. Tapiero (eds), North-Holland, Amsterdam, The Netherlands, 1980, 115–158.

[65] J. Geunes and P.M. Pardalos, *Network Optimization in Supply Chain Management and Financial Engineering: An Annotated Bibliography*, Networks, **42**, 2003, 66–84.

[66] F. Giannessi, **Metodi Matematici della Programmazione: Problemi Lineari e non Lineari**, Pitagora Editrice, Bologna, 1982.

[67] F. Giannessi, *Theorems of the Alternative for Multifunctions with Applications to Optimization: General Results*, Journal of Optimization Theory and Applications, **55**, 1987, 233–256.

[68] F. Giannessi, *A Remark on Infinite-Dimensional Variational Inequalities*, Le Matematiche, **49**, 1994, 243–247.

[69] F. Giannessi, *Separation of Sets and Gap Functions for Quasi-Variational Inequalities*, in **Variational Inequalities and Network Equilibrium Problems**, F. Giannessi and A. Maugeri (eds), Plenum Publishing, New York, 1995, 101–121.

[70] F. Giannessi (ed), **Vector Variational Inequalities and Vector Equilibria**, **38**, Kluwer Academic Publishers, Dordrecht, The Netherlands, 2000.

[71] F. Giannessi and A. Maugeri (eds), **Variational Inequalities and Network Equilibrium Problems**, Plenum Publishing, New York, 1995.

[72] F. Giannessi and A. Maugeri (eds), **Variational Analysis and Applications**, Springer, New York, 2005.

[73] F. Giannessi, A. Maugeri and P.M. Pardalos (eds), **Equilibrium Problems: Nonsmooth Optimization and Variational Inequality Models**, Kluwer Academic Publishers, Dordrecht, The Netherlands, 2001.

[74] S. Giuffrè and S. Pià, *Variational Inequalities for Time-Dependent Financial Equilibrium with Price Constraints*, in **Variational Analysis and Applications**, F. Giannessi and A. Maugeri (eds), Springer, New York, 2005, 477–496.

[75] G. Gurkan, A.Y. Ozge and S. Robinson, *Sample-Path Solution of Variational Inequalities with Application to Option Pricing*, in **Proceedings of the 1996 Winter Simulation Conference**, D.J.

Morrice, D.T. Brunner and J.M. Swain (eds), Coronado, California, 1996, 337–344.

[76] J. Gwinner, *Stability of Monotone Variational Inequalities with Various Applications*, in **Variational Inequalities and Network Equilibrium Problems**, F. Giannessi and A. Maugeri (eds), Plenum Press, New York, 1995, 123–142.

[77] J. Gwinner, *Time Dependent Variational Inequalities – Some Recent Trends*, in **Equilibrium Problems and Variational Models**, P. Daniele, F. Giannessi and A. Maugeri (eds), Kluwer Academic Publishers, Dordrecht, The Netherlands, 2003, 225–264.

[78] P.T. Harker and J.S. Pang, *Finite-Dimensional Variational Inequality and Nonlinear Complementarity Problems: a Survey of Theory, Algorithms and Applications*, Mathematical Programming, **48**, 1990, 161–220.

[79] P. Hartmann and G. Stampacchia, *On Some Nonlinear Elliptic Differential Functional Equations*, Acta Matematica, **115**, 1966, 271–310.

[80] C. Henry, *An Existence Theorem for a Class of Differential Equations with Multivalued Right Hand Sides*, Journal of Mathematical Analysis and Applications, **41**, 1973, 179–186.

[81] D. Hipfel, *The Nonlinear Differential Complementarity Problem*, PhD Thesis, Rensselaer Polytechnic Institute, Troy, New York, 1993.

[82] G. Isac, V.A. Bulasky and V.V. Kalashnikov, **Complementarity, Equilibrium, Efficiency and Economics**, Kluwer Academic Publishers, Dordrecht, The Netherlands, 2002.

[83] G. Isac and M.G. Cojocaru, *Variational Inequalities, Complementarity Problems and Pseudo-Monotonicity: Dynamical Aspects*, **Seminar on Fixed Point Theory Cluj-Napoca** (Proceedings of the International Conference on Nonlinear Operators, Differential Equations and Applications, September 2002, Romania), Babes-Bolyai University of Cluj-Napoca, III, 2002, 41–62.

[84] G. Isac and M.G. Cojocaru, *The Projection Operator in a Hilbert Space and its Directional Derivative: Consequences for the Theory of Projected Dynamical Systems*, Journal of Function Spaces and Applications, **2**, 2004, 71–95.

[85] J. Jahn, **Introduction to the Theory of Nonlinear Optimization**, Springer, Berlin, 1996.

[86] P. Jaillet, D. Lamberton and B. Lapeyre, *Variational Inequalities and the Pricing of American Options*, Acta Applicanda Mathematicae, **21**, 1990, 253–289.

[87] D. Kinderlehrer and G. Stampacchia, **An Introduction to Variational Inequalities and Their Applications**, Academic Press, New York, 1980.

[88] R. Landes, *On a Necessary Condition in the Calculus of Variations*, Rendiconti del Circolo Matematico di Palermo, **61**, 1992, 369–387.

[89] T. Larsson and M. Patriksson, *Equilibrium Characterizations of Solutions to Side Constrained Asymmetric Traffic Assignment Models*, Le Matematiche, **49**, 1994, 249–280.

[90] T. Larsson and M. Patriksson, *On Side Constrained Models of Traffic Equilibria*, in **Variational Inequalities and Network Equilibrium Problems**, F. Giannessi and A. Maugeri (eds), Plenum Publishing, New York, 1995, 169–178.

[91] J.L. Lions and G. Stampacchia, *Variational Inequalities*, Communications on Pure and Applied Mathematics, **22**, 1967, 493–519.

[92] O. Mancino and G. Stampacchia, *Convex Programming and Variational Inequalities*, Journal of Optimization Theory and Applications, **9**, 1972, 3–23.

[93] H.M. Markowitz, *Portfolio Selection*, Journal of Finance, **7**, 1952, 77–91.

[94] H.M. Markowitz, **Portfolio Selection: Efficient Diversification of Investments**, Wiley & Sons, New York, 1959.

[95] A. Maugeri, *Convex Programming, Variational Inequalities and Applications to the Traffic Equilibrium Problem*, Applied Mathematics and Optimization, **16**, 1987, 169–185.

[96] A. Maugeri, *Disequazioni Variazionali e Quasi-variazionali e Applicazioni a Problemi di Ottimizzazione su Reti*, Bollettino della Unione Matematica Italiana (7), **4-B**, 1990, 327–343.

[97] A. Maugeri, *Optimization Problems with Side Constraints and Generalized Equilibrium Principles*, Le Matematiche, **49**, 1994, 305–312.

[98] A. Maugeri, *Variational and Quasi-Variational Inequalities in Network Flow Models: Recent Developments in Theory and Algorithms*, in **Variational Inequalities and Network Equilibrium Problems**, F. Giannessi and A. Maugeri (eds), Plenum Publishing, New York, 1995, 195–211.

[99] A. Maugeri, *Monotone and Nonmonotone Variational Inequalities*, Rendiconti del Circolo Matematico di Palermo, Serie II, Suppl. **48**, 1997, 179–184.

[100] A. Maugeri, *Dynamic Models and Generalized Equilibrium Problems*, in **New Trends in Mathematical Programming**, F. Giannessi, S. Komlósi and T. Rapcsák (eds), Kluwer Academic Publishers, Dordrecht, The Netherlands, 1998, 191–202.

[101] A. Maugeri and E. Galligani (eds), **Rendiconti del Circolo Matematico di Palermo**, Serie II, Suppl. **58**, 1999.

[102] A. Maugeri, W. Oettli and D. Schläger, *A Flexible Form of Wardrop's Principle for Traffic Equilibria with Side Constraints*, Rendiconti del Circolo Matematico di Palermo, Serie II, Suppl. **48**, 1997, 185–193.

[103] A. Maugeri and C. Vitanza, *Time-Dependent Equilibrium Problems*, in **Pareto Optimality, Game Theory and Equilibria**, A. Migdalas, P. Pardalos and L. Pitsoulis (eds), Nonconvex Optimization and its Applications Series (NOIA), Kluwer Academic Publishers, forthcoming.

[104] R.P. McLean, *Approximation Theory for Stochastic Variational Inequality and Ky Fan Inequalities in Finite Dimensions*, Annals of Operations Research, **44**, 1993, 43–61.

[105] M. Milasi and C. Vitanza, *Variational Inequality and Evolutionary Market Disequilibria: the Case of Quantity Formulation*, in **Variational Analysis and Applications**, F. Giannessi and A. Maugeri (eds), Springer, New York, 2005, 681–696.

[106] U. Mosco, *Convergence of Convex Sets and of Solutions of Variational Inequalities*, Advances in Mathematics, **3**, 1969, 510–585.

[107] U. Mosco, *Dual Variational Inequalities*, Journal of Mathematical Analysis and Applications, **40**, 1972, 202–206.

[108] A. Nagurney, **Network Economics – a Variational Inequality Approach**, Kluwer Academic Publishers, Dordrecht, The Netherlands, 1993.

[109] A. Nagurney, *Variational Inequalities in the Analysis and Computation of Multi-Sector, Multi-Instrument Financial Equilibria*, Journal of Economic Dynamics and Control, **18**, 1994, 161–184.

[110] A. Nagurney, *Finance and Variational Inequalities*, Quantitative Finance, **1**, 2001, 309–317.

[111] A. Nagurney (ed), **Innovations in Financial and Economic Networks**, Edward Elgar Publishing, Cheltenham, England, 2003.

[112] A. Nagurney and J. Cruz, *Dynamics of International Financial Networks with Risk Management*, Quantitative Finance, **156**, 2004, 194–212.

[113] A. Nagurney and K. Dhanda, *Noncompliant Oligopolistic Firms and Marketable Pollution Permits: Statics and Dynamics*, Annals of Operations Research, **95**, 2000, 285–312.

[114] A. Nagurney, J. Dong and M. Hughes, *Formulation and Computation of General Financial Equilibrium*, Optimization, **26**, 1992, 339–354.

[115] A. Nagurney, J. Dong and D. Zhang, *A Projected Dynamical Systems Model of General Financial Equilibrium with Stability Analysis*, Mathematical and Computer Modelling, **24**, 1996, 35–44.

[116] A. Nagurney, P. Dupuis and D. Zhang, *A Dynamical Systems Approach for Network Oligopolies and Variational Inequalities*, Annals of Regional Science, **28**, 1994, 263–283.

[117] A. Nagurney and K. Ke, *Financial Networks with Intermediation*, Quantitative Finance, **1**, 2001, 309–317.

[118] A. Nagurney, J. Pan and L. Zhao, *Human Migration Networks*, European Journal of Operational Research, **59**, 1992, 262–274.

[119] A. Nagurney and S. Siokos, **Financial Networks: Statics and Dynamics**, Springer-Verlag, Heidelberg, Germany, 1997.

[120] A. Nagurney and S. Siokos, *Variational Inequalities for International General Financial Equilibrium Modelling and Computation*, Mathematical and Computer Modelling, **25**, 1997, 31–49.

[121] A. Nagurney and S. Siokos, *Dynamic Multi–Sector, Multi–Instrument Financial Networks with Futures: Modeling and Computation*, Networks, **33**, 1999, 93–108.

[122] A. Nagurney, T. Takayama and D. Zhang, *Massively Parallel Computation of Spatial Price Equilibrium Problems as Dynamical Systems*, Journal of Economic Dynamics and Control, **19**, 1995, 3–37.

[123] A. Nagurney, T. Takayama and D. Zhang, *Projected Dynamical Systems Modeling and Computation of Spatial Price Network Equilibria*, Networks, **26**, 1995, 69–85.

[124] A. Nagurney and D. Zhang, *On the Stability of Projected Dynamical Systems*, Journal of Optimization Theory and Applications, **85**, 1995, 97–124.

[125] A. Nagurney and D. Zhang, *Stability of Spatial Price Equilibrium Modeled as a Projected Dynamical System*, Journal of Economic Dynamics and Control, **20**, 1996, 43–63.

[126] A. Nagurney and D. Zhang, *On the Local and Global Stability of a Travel Route Choice Adjustment Process*, Transportation Research B, **30**, 1996, 245–262.

[127] A. Nagurney and D. Zhang, **Projected Dynamical Systems and Variational Inequalities with Applications**, Kluwer Academic Publishers, Boston, Massachusetts, 1996.

[128] A. Nagurney and D. Zhang, *Formulation, Stability, and Computation of Traffic Network Equilibria as Projected Dynamical Systems*, Journal of Optimization Theory and Applications, **93**, 1997, 417–444.

[129] A. Nagurney and D. Zhang, *Projected Dynamical Systems in the Formulation, Stability Analysis and Computation of Fixed Demand Traffic Network Equilibria*, Transportation Science, **31**, 1997, 147–158.

[130] A. Nagurney and L. Zhao, *Disequilibrium and Variational Inequalities*, Journal of Computational and Applied Mathematics, **33**, 1990, 181–198.

[131] A. Nagurney and L. Zhao, *A Network Equilibrium Formulation of Market Disequilibrium and Variational Inequalities*, Networks, **21**, 1991, 109–132.

[132] W. Oettli, *An Iterative Method, Having Linear Rate of Convergence, for Solving a Pair of Dual Linear Programs*, Mathematical Programming, **3**, 1972, 302–311.

[133] W. Oettli and D. Schläger, *Generalized Vectorial Equilibria and Generalized Monotonicity*, in **Functional Analysis with Current Applications**, M. Brokate and A.H. Siddiqi (eds), Longman, Harlow, England, 1998, 145–154.

[134] M. Patriksson, **The Traffic Assignment Problem – Models and Methods**, VSP BV, Utrecht, The Netherlands, 1994.

[135] A.C. Pigou, **The Economics of Welfare**, Macmillan, London, 1920.

[136] B.T. Polyak, *A General Method for Solving Extremum Problems*, Doklady Akademii Nauk SSR, **174**, 1967, 33–36.

[137] F. Raciti, *Equilibrium in Time-Dependent Traffic Networks with Delay*, in **Equilibrium Problems: Nonsmooth Optimization and Variational Inequality Models**, F. Giannessi, A. Maugeri and P.M. Pardalos (eds), Kluwer Academic Publishers, The Netherlands, 2001, 247–253.

[138] F. Raciti, *On the Calculation of Equilibrium in Time Dependent Traffic Networks*, in **Equilibrium Problems and Variational Models**, P. Daniele, F. Giannessi and A. Maugeri (eds), Kluwer Academic Publishers, Boston, Massachusetts, 2003, 369–377.

[139] F. Raciti, *Equilibria Trajectories as Stationary Solutions of Infinite Dimensional Projected Dynamical Systems*, Applied Mathematics Letters, **17**, 2004, 153–158.

[140] F. Raciti, *Bicriterion Weight Varying Spatial Price Networks*, Journal of Optimization Theory and Applications, **122**, 2004, 387–403.

[141] B. Ran and D.E. Boyce, **Modeling Dynamic Transportation Networks: an Intelligent System Oriented Approach**, Second Edition, Springer-Verlag, Berlin, Germany, 1996.

[142] B. Ricceri, *Basic Existence Theorems for Generalized Variational and Quasi-Variational Inequalities*, in **Variational Inequalities and Network Equilibrium Problems**, F. Giannessi and A. Maugeri (eds), Plenum Press, New York, 1995, 251–255.

[143] P. A. Samuelson, *Spatial price equilibrium and linear programming*, American Economic Review, **42**, 1952, 283–303.

[144] H.H. Schaefer, **Topological Vector Spaces**, Springer, New York, 1971.

[145] S. Schaible, *Generalized Monotonicity – Concepts and Uses*, in **Variational Inequalities and Network Equilibrium Problems**, F. Giannessi and A. Maugeri (eds), Plenum Press, New York, 1995, 289–299.

[146] L. Scrimali, *Quasi-Variational Inequalities in Transportation Networks*, Mathematical Models and Methods in Applied Sciences, **14**, no. 10, 2004, 1541–1560.

[147] L. Scrimali, *Quasi-Variational Inequalities Applied to Retarded Equilibria in Time-Dependent Traffic Problems*, in **Variational Analysis and Applications**, F. Giannessi and A. Maugeri (eds), Springer, New York, 2005, 1007–1023.

[148] M.H. Shih and K.K. Tan, *Generalized Quasi-Variational Inequalities in Locally Convex Topological Vector Spaces*, Journal of Mathematical Analysis and Applications, **108**, 1985, 333–343.

[149] M.J. Smith, *The Existence, Uniqueness and Stability of Traffic Equilibrium*, Transportation Research, **138**, 1979, 295–304.

[150] M.J. Smith, *A New Dynamic Traffic Model and the Existence and Calculation of Dynamic User Equilibria on Congested Capacity-constrained Road Networks*, Transportation Research, **27B**, 1993, 49–63.

[151] G. Stampacchia, *Variational Inequalities*, in **Theory and Applications of Monotone Operators**, A. Ghizzetti (ed), Edizioni 'Oderisi', 1969, 101–192.

[152] J. Steinbach, *On a Variational Inequality Containing a Memory Term with an Application in Electro-Chemical Machining*, Journal of Convex Analysis, **5**, no. 1, 1998, 63–80.

[153] T. Takayama and G.G. Judge, **Spatial and Temporal Price and Allocation Models**, North-Holland, Amsterdam, The Netherlands, 1971.

[154] N.X. Tan, *Quasi-Variational Inequality in Topological Linear Locally Convex Hausdorff Spaces*, Mathematische Nachrichten, **122**, 1985, 231–245.

[155] G. Tian and J. Zhou, *Quasi-Variational Inequalities with Non-Compact Sets*, Journal of Mathematical Analysis and Applications, **160**, 1991, 583–595.

[156] A. Tourin and T. Zariphopoulou, *Numerical Schemes for Investment Models with Singular Transactions*, Computational Economics, **7**, 1994, 287–307.

[157] J.G. Wardrop, *Some Theoretical Aspects of Road Traffic Research*, Proceedings of the Institute of Civil Engineers, Part II, 1952, 325–378.

[158] E.H. Zarantonello, *Projections on Convex Sets in Hilbert Space and Spectral Theory*, Contributions to Nonlinear Functional Analysis, **27**, Mathematical Research Center, University of Wisconsin, Academic Press, 1971, 237–424.

[159] D. Zhang and A. Nagurney, *On the Stability of Projected Dynamical Systems*, Journal of Optimization Theory and Applications, **85**, 1995, 97–124.

Index